DATE DUE

JAN 1 1 2010			
OCT 1 7 2011			
MAY 2 3 2014			
GAYLORD			PRINTED IN U.S.A.

N 7 2005

TRANSMITTING THE PAST

TRANSMITTING THE PAST

Historical and Cultural Perspectives on Broadcasting

Edited by
J. EMMETT WINN
and
SUSAN L. BRINSON

THE UNIVERSITY OF ALABAMA PRESS
Tuscaloosa

∞

The paper on which this book is printed meets the minimum requirements of American
National Standard for Information Science–Permanence of Paper for Printed Library Materials, ANSI Z39.48–1984.

Library of Congress Cataloging-in-Publication Data

Transmitting the past : historical and cultural perspectives on broadcasting / edited by
J. Emmett Winn and Susan L. Brinson.
p. cm.
Includes bibliographical references and index.
ISBN 0-8173-1453-9 (cloth : alk. paper) — ISBN 0-8173-5175-2 (pbk. : alk. paper)
1. Radio broadcasting—United States—History. 2. Television broadcasting—United
States—History. 3. Radio broadcasting—Social aspects—United States. 4. Television
broadcasting—Social aspects—United States. I. Winn, J. Emmett (John Emmett), 1959–
II. Brinson, Susan L., 1958–
PN1990.6.U5T73 2005
384.54'0973—dc22
2004019077

For Our Students

Contents

TRANSMITTING THE PAST

From Marconi to *Cop Rock*

An Introduction to Broadcasting History

SUSAN L. BRINSON

Television screens stare at us from every corner. Regardless of where we might find ourselves, the likelihood is great that a television set will be turned on to provide us electronic company. Retail stores, bars and restaurants, waiting areas of every variety, offices, and nearly every room of our homes are populated by the ever-present screen. Environments that lack the cool glow of a TV picture often provide radio entertainment lest our ears become too accustomed to silence. Broadcast messages are so pervasive that we pay little attention to them except when we desire gratification. Television and radio are ubiquitous, yet characterizing them as such understates and oversimplifies their significance to life in the United States. Since 1920, broadcasting has been one of the defining features of modern American sociocultural, political, and economic life. In the post–World War I economic boom of the 1920s, Americans spent millions of dollars buying radio sets and incorporating radio programming into their daily lives; by 1926 there were more than 4.5 million radios in people's homes.[1] Music, religion, sports, education, and politics were delivered "through the ether" directly into the living rooms, kitchens, and bedrooms of American homes. Regardless of age, education, or even nationality, nearly everyone consumed radio messages. From 1920 to today, the vast potential of radio and television to woo votes, educate the masses, save souls, and make billions of dollars has contributed to the extraordinary growth of the media. It is now virtually impossible to escape television or radio broadcasts or their omnipresent messages. Indeed, there are few Americans who *want* to avoid them, as the explosion of portable media devices continually invites consumers to "plug in" to the newest handheld, earphone-equipped, multimedia gadget.

The anthology of essays before you focuses on historical aspects of radio and television by analyzing the centrality of broadcasting to American life. However, the compilation of these essays is intended to provide two explanations for the reader, both historical and historiographical. As history lessons, each essay concentrates on a particular moment in broadcasting history, assessing the complex interweaving of a broadcasting phenomenon and the context in which it developed and played itself out. Beyond observation and description, each essay represents a type of research that may be understood in binary opposition as "objective" versus "subjective" historical interpretation. This introduction establishes the contexts of the essays by briefly explaining their position within the larger field of historical research and providing a brief overview of broadcasting history.

THE VIEW FROM THE ACADEMY: OBJECTIVE VERSUS SUBJECTIVE HISTORY

The intellectual foundation for Western objective historical research was constructed in the scientific philosophies of the eighteenth-century Enlightenment and solidified for decades thereafter. Legions of historians trained their considerable analytical and interpretive skills on understanding the past. Their approach to historical research was strictly objective, utilizing the scientific method for the collection and interpretation of historical facts. Historian Peter Novick explained that "historians . . . purge[d] themselves of external loyalties: the historian's primary allegiance [was] to 'the objective historical truth.'"[2] Thus, historians trained in this approach became meticulous collectors of historical data, able to scrutinize archival documents and organize countless facts into a narrative that communicated the "truth" about an event, person, or idea without belying the historian's own personal values. They were "like scientists [who turned] themselves into neutral and passionless investigators in order to reconstruct the past exactly like it happened."[3] It was a solid, well-built foundation. Thousands of historians trained in objective research wrote the history of the United States that for decades became known as The History of the United States, taught from elementary classrooms on up to graduate seminars. Thus, politicians and their wars, scientists and their discoveries, entrepreneurs and their economic accomplishments became the heroes of American history, underscored by the fact that their significance was objectively indisputable.

While objectivity remained the strong foundation of historical research well into the twentieth century, cracks in the infrastructure began to appear as early as the interwar period between 1918 and 1941 that resulted in "the general breakdown of ideological and interpretive consensus within the profession."[4] The vast sociopolitical shifts in the post–World War II era further weakened the grip of objectivity as a methodological value. The postwar democratization of American citizens, motivated by a variety of experiences including the G.I. Bill, the civil rights movement, and the women's movement, resulted in a similar democratization of the academy of historians. The revolutionary spirit of 1960s American political and social life found expression in the academy. Politically liberal historians and their students took a fresh look at American history. Methodologically, they challenged the notion of a historian's ability to objectively assess the meaning of historical artifacts. In other words, there were "the records of the past and there [was] the interpretation of those records. The gap between them [was] the source of concern."[5] Historians trained in scientific methods did not see (or did not wish to see) the gap, but the new historians recognized the significance of the researcher's own values and attitudes in the interpretation of historical records; thus the gap was an inherently significant aspect of historical research. Moreover, in addition to the interpretation of historical facts, the historian's personal philosophy influenced the selection of subject matter to be researched, and an untapped source of subjects that were once perceived to be inappropriate for historical research was discovered. People and institutions that were once judged politically and economically weak or culturally suspect became the topics of virtual explosions of historical analyses. Black history, women's history, labor history, immigrant history, and a host of other social histories once deemed unimportant and irrelevant were revealed. At the core of this theoretical shift was the axiomatic belief that historians should "explore the connections between the inequalities of social relationships and power in shaping human behavior, ideas, and artifacts."[6]

The development of social history is one aspect of a broader philosophical shift that found expression in nearly all areas of social scientific and humanities disciplines, a research perspective now known as "cultural studies." While it is quite difficult to provide a single definition of cultural studies, there are at least two significant aspects of the approach. First, cultural studies asserts the centrality of understanding a phenomenon from its cultural perspective, within its historical and cultural contexts, a concept that applies to both the researcher and the researched. Cultural studies researchers embrace the notion that they interpret historical events from both their personal and cultural perspectives. They fundamentally agree that "people think within the parameters of their mental universe; they cannot catapult out of that universe in order to form independent judgments about it."[7] Moreover, situating the historical person or event within its context is the central responsibility of the historian; that which is under study may be fully understood only within the contexts of its time and place. As historian E. P. Thompson asserted, "'[T]he discipline of history is . . . the discipline of context; each fact can be given meaning only within an ensemble of other meanings.'"[8] Second, cultural studies represents an important political shift within academic circles, as it argues that subjects heretofore considered inappropriate for serious scholarly inquiry are in fact legitimate areas of research. As Robert Berkhofer explains, the application of cultural studies to historical inquiries suggested "new subject matter, additional actors, and in general a history more inclusive of multicultural viewpoints."[9]

Radio and television lurked among the "inconsequential" subjects of study, dismissed by the cultural elite as simply the opiate of the masses and cultural pollution. Although broadcasting was an integral aspect of American political, industrial, and sociocultural life, its history received no noteworthy attention by the historical academy. Even within historical work on other media, broadcasting was ignored. The history of the print media is widespread, no doubt due to the importance of newspapers to American political life. The history of film is similarly well documented, due in no small measure to the increasing perception of some motion pictures as an art form. Until the mid-1960s, however, the history of radio and television remained largely unresearched and unwritten, the result of a cultural aristocracy that perpetuated "the scholarly and aesthetic boundaries dividing elite from popular cultures."[10] Erik Barnouw's three-volume *History of American Broadcasting*,[11] published between 1966 and 1970, is considered the first serious analysis of the development of broadcasting and is the foundation for subsequent historical analyses. A masterpiece of superior writing and storytelling, Barnouw's books nonetheless represent historical analyses that focus on explaining who, what, when, and where, with considerable emphasis on the great white men of broadcasting. Despite its conformity to traditional modes of historicism, Barnouw's work was the important first step in uncovering the development of radio and television in the United States.

Prodded by Barnouw, scholars across the country undertook investigations into broadcasting history, following the habitual paths of uncovering the roles of great white men in broadcasting, and the governmental and corporate influences in radio and television. In 1974 communication scholar James Carey urged fellow historians to accomplish more than the simple recitation of facts. Carey advocated a paradigm shift among broadcast historians, arguing that "we must penetrate beyond mere appearance to the structure of imagination that gives [histories] their significance."[12] In other words, Carey argued that historians must progress beyond simply providing detailed descriptions of who, what, when, and where and must connect those facts to their historical and cultural contexts. As one historian later explained, historical events "make sense only when placed in their proper social and cultural contexts. . . . [They] must all be situated in their contexts."[13] It was a call to action that was answered by many broadcasting historians.

The larger context of the development of cultural studies coupled with James Carey's guidance resulted in an important shift in broadcasting history. Although broadcasting history was once considered an unimportant area of historical inquiry, today broadcast historians mine the rich veins of the historical development of the media. The past fifteen years in particular have witnessed a sharp increase in cultural studies approaches to broadcasting history. At least seven academic journals consistently publish broadcasting history (*Journal of Broadcasting and Electronic Media, Journalism and Mass Communication Quarterly, Journal of Communication, Journal of Radio Studies, Journalism History, Journalism Quarterly,* and *Historical Journal of Film, Radio, and Television*). Each year more books are published that concentrate on particular historical issues.

Thus, the essays included in this anthology teach two historical lessons. All of them represent some of the best historical research on broadcasting in the United States currently under way and clearly demonstrate the significance of broadcasting to America's past. They also function as examples of the opposing historiographical viewpoints. The essays contained in the first section of the book predominantly represent traditional objective history, while those in the second half exemplify cultural studies research. All make significant contributions to our understanding of broadcasting history.

BROADCASTING HISTORY: A BRIEF OVERVIEW

This section provides a brief overview of broadcasting history in order to establish a general framework for understanding the essays contained in this volume. The interconnections among technology, industry, government, and the public resonate throughout the history of radio and television.

1899–1920

The twenty-one-year period between 1899 and 1920 witnessed the creation and development of the basic aspects of broadcasting that still define the industry today. The most significant development was the invention of the technology that enabled the "wireless" transmission of messages over the airwaves, so called because it eliminated the need for telegraph wires. Historical recognition for inventing wireless is controversial, but most American historians credit Italian-born Guglielmo Marconi with the invention. In 1899 Marconi traveled to the United States and formed the country's first wireless company, American Marconi, successfully establishing both a corporate hold on the new industry and a public image as a "great inventor" similar to that of Thomas Edison and Alexander Graham Bell. Marconi's significance as the great inventor of wireless technology is the foundation of Michael Brown's essay on the scientist. The technological development of wireless continued rapidly throughout the 1900s and 1910s. Although wireless was used primarily as a form of point-to-point communication using Morse code, early experimentation in voice transmissions also occurred (notably, the independent work of Reginald Fessenden on the East Coast and Charles "Doc" Herrold on the West Coast). Considerable experimentation by engineers such as Lee de Forest and Howard Armstrong vastly increased the distances over which wireless signals were clearly transmitted and received.

The technological development of wireless resulted in the growth of public, corporate, and governmental interest in the technology. Corporate involvement in wireless increased during this period as American Marconi grew exponentially as the only reputable and reliable supplier of receivers and transmitters, General Electric and Westinghouse made gradual steps into the wireless manufacturing industry, and commercial and naval shipping rapidly became dependent upon wireless for communication. While the public at large was only vaguely aware of the technology, a growing legion of amateur wireless operators developed around the country, only to find themselves in a fight over access to its use with corporate and military interests. The U.S. government stepped into the fray as early as 1910 and, more significantly, with the passage of the Radio Act of 1912, when it established federal administrative authority over the technology. By 1920 the precedent of federal government regulation was established, and American Marconi was forced out of business but was replaced by four corporations (RCA, General Electric, Westinghouse, and AT&T) that would fundamentally shape the broadcasting industry. The American public was reduced from the role of active amateurs to passive consumers.

1920–1930

Prior to 1920 the technology that allowed the transmission of messages through the airwaves was used principally as a form of point-to-point communication using Morse code. In 1920 wireless was radically transformed into broadcasting, in which the technology became mass communication. In late 1920 Dr. Frank Conrad, an engineer for Westinghouse, started the first commercially licensed broadcasting station, KDKA, in Pittsburgh. From that inauspicious beginning, radio broadcasting developed into a phenomenon that captured the imagination of the American people.

Four key events occurred concurrently that allowed the astonishing development of radio. First, average Americans bought radio sets in vast numbers and integrated radio programming into their daily lives. Second, the four corporations, which by 1920 formed an oligopoly through cross-licensing agreements, were caught briefly unprepared for the startling development of wireless as a mass medium but quickly retooled their plants to mass-produce receivers (radios) and transmitters. Third, the U.S. Department of Commerce (the federal arm that administered wireless) was inundated with requests for broadcasting licenses and soon found itself without adequate legal authority to effectively regulate the emerging and chaotic broadcasting industry. This oversight was eventually remedied with passage of the Radio Act of 1927, which, among many other things, created the Federal Radio Commission to regulate broadcasting. Finally, the questionable quality of many radio programs was significantly improved by the end of the 1920s as the result of the creation of three national radio networks (NBC Red, NBC Blue, and CBS) that provided a variety of high-quality programs to their affiliates. Thus, in the short ten years between 1920 and 1930, wireless became radio broadcasting. Once active as wireless amateurs, the general public was effectively limited to the role of mass audience and potential consumer. Major corporations were now solidly in control of broadcasting as a big business, as industry giant RCA dominated research, development, and manufacturing, while the radio networks, most notably NBC and CBS, provided the lion's share of programming throughout the United States. Local radio stations increasingly turned to the national networks for programming. It had been a whirlwind courtship and marriage. The 1920s were a tumultuously giddy decade for radio. The rapid expansion of the popularity and profitability of the new mass medium seemed to make everyone happy —audiences, industries, and government alike.

Three of the essays included in this volume focus on the development of broadcasting during this decade. The rise of corporate influence in the 1920s and the concurrent de-emphasis on individual contributions to the industry is fundamental to Michael Brown's work, in which he analyzes 1920s newspaper accounts of Marconi's alleged belief in radio messages from Mars, concluding that the accounts were an attempt to reconstruct Marconi's centrality to the development of wireless technology. Sam Brumbeloe and J. Emmett Winn provide a case study of a larger issue facing the developing industry during the 1920s, which was emphasis on the commercial opportunities of broadcasting at the expense of educational programs. Their analysis of Auburn University's station WAPI serves as a microcosm of the broader shifts in programming during the decade and sheds light on the struggles to define radio's role in everyday life. Finally, Fritz Messere analyzes the federal government's response to the technological crises facing the booming radio industry in the 1920s, paying particular attention to the intersection of competing demands of what radio should be. All three essays are excellent histories. Brown's work analyzes how the powerful attempted to redefine Marconi as powerless and inconsequential; Brumbeloe and Winn focus attention on the significance of a small radio station in a small southern town and, in so doing, effectively legitimate the contributions of average people in the development of broadcasting. While pursuing more conventional subject matter, Messere nevertheless effectively situates the complex struggle for hegemony between corporate and political interests in the context of 1920s United States.

1930–1940

The excitement of the 1920s was replaced with the sobering reality of the economically and psychologically depressed 1930s. The American audience tenaciously maintained its grip on its radios when all else around them was either literally or figuratively repossessed. Escapist programming provided by the networks gave audiences a sense of welcome respite from the reality of 1930s American life and also vastly increased the profitability of NBC and CBS. By the end of the 1930s nearly three-quarters of all radio stations in the country were affiliated with one of the national networks. Indeed, the radio broadcasting industry, composed of the national networks and the manufacturers (particularly RCA), held considerably more influence over the development of the industry than did the Federal Communications Commission (formed in 1934 to expand the federal government's administrative authority over all forms of electronic communication). The technology of broadcasting also developed as Howard Armstrong perfected FM transmissions and as Philo T. Farnsworth and Vladymir Zworykin independently experimented with television. By the end of the 1930s, radio was a significant aspect of the American economy and central to the daily lives of American citizens.

1940–1950

The decade of the 1940s may easily be bifurcated into two periods, the first five years devoted to the significance of radio, and the second five years dedicated to the explosive growth of television as a mass medium. Between 1940 and 1945 radio remained the primary source of entertainment to Americans and, as a result of broadcast journalistic coverage of World War II, also became an important source of news. Radio programming was the central undertaking of the broadcast networks, which provided thousands of hours of programming to American audiences. Indeed, by the early 1940s the programming cog of the industry ran like a well-oiled machine pumping out stories for mass consumption. As Michele Hilmes explains in her essay, during these years women became "program toppers" for the first time, achieving a level of stardom and power till that point unknown. Hilmes's essay is an excellent example of cultural studies research that concentrates on women's history and reveals the considerable contributions women made to the development of radio, a subject long ignored by traditional historians.

Although immensely popular, radio was rapidly replaced by television in the hearts and minds of many Americans and the broadcasting industry in the immediate postwar years. Similar to the development of radio in the 1920s, four conditions were necessary for the expansion of television in the late 1940s, three of which occurred. First, buoyed by the postwar economy, Americans started buying the television sets that were, second, mass-produced by the manufacturers. Third, four national networks (ABC, NBC, CBS, and DuMont) developed very limited schedules of television programming, an undertaking that was problematic for NBC, as Chad Dell explains in his essay. Dell's essay is significant because it takes a fresh look at NBC's corporate history, particularly the network's struggles to define itself as a television network.

The fourth key ingredient necessary for the development of a nationwide television system was the existence of local television stations, which the networks needed to deliver their programming to local audiences. Unfortunately, there were very few local stations. For all of their attempts at planning, the FCC had not reserved enough frequency space to accommodate all the television stations that broadcasters wanted, and by 1948 only fifty TV stations were on the air (with another fifty in various stages of federally approved construction). The development of television, then, began to stall in 1948 when the FCC stopped licensing TV stations until several significant technological issues could be resolved. Despite the temporary freeze, the popularity of television celebrities such as Milton Berle and Sid Caesar maintained Americans' interests in the new medium, and they eagerly awaited the day when they, too, could watch TV.

1950–1960

The growth of television in the 1950s was matched by the decline of radio. While still a significant source of entertainment, the radio industry was forced to redefine itself from the ground up. Instead of serving as the conduits of national network programming, radio stations refocused their attention on local markets, developing programming intended to attract local listeners by trying out different formats and disc jockeys. The industry also attempted to broaden its broadcasting reach through technological innovations such as the increase in the number of car radios. Matthew Killmeier situates the popularity of car radios in the 1950s to the concurrent development of both television and middle-class suburbia in his essay "Space and the Speed of Sound: Mobile Media, 1950s Broadcasting, and Suburbia," and he provides an excellent cultural analysis of the interconnections between a rapidly expanding middle class and an entertainment industry redefining itself. More importantly, station owners and managers turned to local advertisers as the principal source of income and profit. The rapid changes in radio in the 1950s and the FCC's virtually single-minded attention to television resulted in the payola/plugola scandal in 1958, in which popular disc jockeys were accused of taking illegal payments to promote songs and local businesses. It was a scandal the radio industry could ill afford.

Television faced its own growing pains. Audiences continued to rapidly expand (by 1960, 90 percent of Americans owned at least one TV set), particularly after the FCC lifted the "freeze" in 1952 and television stations started going on the air throughout the country. The television networks quickly cultivated affiliates, with NBC and CBS dominating the industry (ABC gathered affiliates more slowly, although it received a boost when DuMont quit operations in 1955). One of the most notable aspects of broadcasting in the 1950s is the dizzying incorporation of television into average people's lives. Whether it was Lucy's antics, violent Westerns, the stellar productions of the anthology dramas, or Murrow's and Friendly's journalistic investigations, American audiences ravenously consumed television programs. By the late 1950s, after the anthology dramas were canceled and the public learned of the rigged quiz shows and the complicity of media darling Charles Van Doren, the glory days of early television ended. Unlike virtually all other aspects of the 1960s, television and radio spent the decade healing their damaged reputations with conformity.

1960–1970

The 1960s witnessed the firm establishment of radio as a local medium and TV as a national medium. Radio experienced growth for the first time since the 1940s, with an increase in the number of FM stations going on the air and with the growing practice of program formatting that targeted narrowly defined demographic groups within the local market. As the profitability of market segmentation increased, so too did the number of FM stations on the air.

By the 1960s television was established as the primary form of entertainment for Americans, but the quality of programming was questionable. Indeed, in early 1960 the new FCC chair, Newton Minow, uttered his now famous description of television programming as a "vast wasteland" and warned broadcasters to provide better, more educational shows. They did not respond as he intended. Instead of providing more educational fare, the three networks flooded their schedules with the likes of *The Beverly Hillbillies, Gomer Pyle: USMC,* and *Bewitched.* While one could make a convincing argument that the country certainly needed escapist programming during the 1960s, there was very little connection between the realities of American life in the 1960s (sociocultural and political protests to the extreme) and the television world. With the exception of nightly news programs, which provided glimpses into the American chaos of the 1960s, television programming was indeed a "vast wasteland" of conformity and complacency, refusing to acknowledge the struggles for civil rights, women's rights, and the antiwar movement.

1970–1980

We were a much different country in 1970 than we were in 1960. At least four assassinations, a war, the civil and women's rights movements, riots, and a host of other challenges to our typical way of life left us deeply shaken as a country. Television programmers responded to our new realities by attempting to provide more accurate representations of who we were in all of our manifestations. The homogeneity of the 1950s and 1960s television worlds gave way to a new "realistic" television world populated by Archie Bunker in *All in the Family,* Mary Richards in *The Mary Tyler Moore Show,* the Evans family in *Good Times* and the Jeffersons in *The Jeffersons,* the anti-authority surgeons in *M*A*S*H,* and the multicultural casts of *Barney Miller* and *Taxi.* After 1974, Watergate, and the first resignation of an American president, television programmers supplemented "realism" with pure escapism. Programs that looked to another time period with wistful nostalgia became popular, as though the Depression in which *The Waltons* lived was a better time and place and the postwar, anti-Red hysteria of the 1950s in *Happy Days* and *Laverne and Shirley* was preferable to the 1970s. Escapism was also served up in the form of more cheesecake (*Three's Company,*

Charlie's Angels) and beefcake (*Starsky and Hutch, CHiPs, The Six Million Dollar Man*) than previously seen on TV.

For all practical purposes, ABC, CBS, and NBC were the only game in town. The great majority of U.S. television stations were affiliated with one of the "Big Three," and the American audience had virtually nowhere else to turn for entertainment or information. In one of its last activist efforts, the FCC passed the Prime Time Access Rule (PTAR) in 1970, which was intended to significantly curtail network domination. Network influence over virtually all phases of television was minimally influenced by the PTAR. The real threat to industry domination didn't come from government regulation but instead from the industry itself. The most significant development in television in the 1970s was the sudden growth of cable television. In place now for over twenty years, cable grew significantly during the 1970s after HBO was launched in 1972. Unedited and uncut feature-length Hollywood movies were an irresistible draw for TV viewers accustomed to the networks' editing films to accommodate commercials and to eliminate profanity, sexuality, nudity, and violence. From their position on the top of the heap, the broadcast networks paid little attention to the growth of cable programming and continued doing business with advertisers and consumers as if nothing new was happening.

1980–Present

The period 1980 to the present is more difficult to characterize, because we don't yet have adequate historical distance. Some trends are clear, however. Born out of the liberalism of the 1960s and the cynicism and hedonism of the 1970s were the conservative 1980s, guided by the conservative presidencies of Ronald Reagan and George H. W. Bush. This conservatism found expression in both television programming and the structure of the radio and television industries. Since the early 1980s the FCC has slowly exorcized itself from active regulation of the broadcasting and cable industry, with the exception of indecent content. Once carefully regulated by the FCC, the sale and purchase of radio and television stations is now a frequent occurrence, treated no differently than the transfer of other businesses. In fact, one of the most significant trends of the past twenty years is the growth of media conglomerates that own or control a wide variety of media outlets, including television (individual stations, broadcast and cable networks, and cable distribution systems), radio, film, Internet, and print publishing. The success of these conglomerates depends in large part on their ability to effectively target specific demographic markets, a practice initiated and refined by radio broadcasters after 1950.

Indeed, the market segmentation to which radio was firmly devoted became a fact in television programming in the early 1980s. A wide variety of cable networks were launched in the early 1980s, most notably CNN, MTV, CNN Headline News, and ESPN, all of which devote all of their programming and advertising efforts toward capturing specific demographic niche groups. Their strategies were enormously successful, much to the chagrin of the broadcast networks, which continued to target large, heterogeneous audiences. The networks eventually understood that they would have to adopt similar programming strategies to stop the audience hemorrhage. Some of the networks' earliest attempts to attract and maintain one of the most important demographic groups—young adults 18–35—were found in the "edgy" dramas of Stephen Bochco, particularly *Hill Street Blues, L.A. Law,* and *NYPD Blue.* Bochco's attempt to mix police drama with MTV-style music in *Cop Rock* is the subject of George Plasketes's essay in this volume. Situation comedies with much more adult content also served the networks in their competition for younger viewers. One of the most blatantly sexual was *Cheers.* As Heather Hundley asserts in her essay, *Cheers* communicated mixed messages regarding male and female sexuality during the age of AIDS. Finally, some television programmers believed the way to lure viewers back to broadcast television was to colorize "classic" movies and television shows, which is the subject of Douglas Ferguson's "The Importance of Colorization of Motion Pictures and Syndicated Television Programs to Broadcasting, 1985–1990." Despite programmers' hopes, colorized movies and television programs did not lure audiences back to traditional broadcast television.

CONCLUSION

From its infancy in the early 1920s to its current maturity, radio and television broadcasting have consistently been vital sources of entertainment and information. From Edward R. Murrow's broadcasts of the London Blitz in the summer of 1940, to the cultural phenomenon of *Roots* in 1977, to the tragic and visually mesmerizing events of September 11, 2001, radio and television are integral to who we are as Americans. Understanding the complex relationships among radio, television, and American culture is the goal of the essays contained in this volume, as well as the continuing work of historians of all methodological stripes.

NOTES

1. Bureau of the Census, U.S. Department of Commerce, "Radio and Television Stations, Sets Produced, and Households With Sets," *Historical Statistics of the United States, Colonial Times to 1970,* pt. 2 (Washington, DC: U.S. Government Printing Office, 1975), 796.

2. Peter Novick, *That Noble Dream: The "Objectivity" Question and the American Historical Profession* (Cambridge, UK: Cambridge UP, 1988), 2.

3. Joyce Appleby, Lynn Hunt, and Margaret Jacob, *Telling the Truth about History* (New York: W. W. Norton, 1994), 241.

4. Novick, *That Noble Dream,* 207.

5. Appleby, Hunt, and Jacob, *Telling the Truth,* 248.

6. Robert F. Berkhofer Jr., *Beyond the Great Story: History as Text and Discourse* (Cambridge, MA: Harvard UP, 1995), 5

7. Appleby, Hunt, and Jacob, *Telling the Truth,* 218.

8. As quoted in Michael Kammen, *Selvages and Biases: The Fabric of History in American Culture* (Ithaca, NY: Cornell UP, 1987), 38.

9. Berkhofer, *Beyond the Great Story,* 8.

10. Ibid., 6.

11. Eric Barnouw, *A Tower in Babel: A History of Broadcasting in the United States,* vol. 1, *to 1933* (New York: Oxford UP, 1966); *The Golden Web: A History of Broadcasting in the United States,* vol. 2, *1933 to 1953* (New York: Oxford UP, 1968); and *The Image Empire* (New York: Oxford UP, 1970).

12. James W. Carey, "The Problem of Journalism History," *Journalism History* 1 (1974): 4.

13. Berkhofer, *Beyond the Great Story,* 31.

1 / Radio Mars

The Transformation of Marconi's Popular Image, 1919–1922

MICHAEL BROWN

The transformation of radio from wireless telegraphy to broadcasting dramatically changed the way the technology was perceived and used. After World War I a significant number of amateur radio operators emerged from the armed services, and the United States lifted its ban on the use of amateur radio equipment. The U.S. Navy released the radio patents it controlled through World War I, and American research began with a renewed sense of competition and vigor. What followed was a popular revolution as Americans started listening to the work of these amateurs, who were using the latest technology to broadcast a variety of messages. Between 1919 and 1922 the role of radio was transformed from a means of communicating at sea to a way of reaching millions of American homes. By 1922 there were thousands of licensed amateur broadcasters and nearly a quarter of a million Americans with receivers.[1] Waldemar Kaempffert summarized the transformation: "No one dreamed of broadcasting's possibilities. . . . It was regarded as a serious limitation that radio communication was not secret. . . . What was once a drawback is now a technical virtue. Broadcasting, a new way of reaching thousands and even millions at the same time, is the outcome."[2]

Guglielmo Marconi was the public figure most closely associated with the use of radio prior to 1919. Current scholarly accounts of Marconi describe him as an innovator and entrepreneur rather than a premier scientist. His most significant contribution to the development of wireless communication was his ability to apply theoretical principles of radio to develop a practical instrument.[3] For popular audiences Marconi was the most visible and successful scientist associated with wireless technology. His early successful demonstrations of the technology created the impression that Marconi was the inventor of wireless communication.[4] By 1919 Marconi's future as a central character in the popular world of American radio was uncertain, since broadcasting was a use of wireless technology that was unfamiliar and unrelated to his work.

The year 1919 was significant for Marconi. Many patents Marconi controlled prior to World War I became available to other researchers. More important, he sold the American Marconi Company as a result of pressure within the United States to prohibit foreign ownership of American corporations, including radio. American Marconi was purchased by General Electric, reorganized into the Radio Corporation of America (RCA), and instantly became a significant force in radio. These changes effectively removed Marconi from the main economic, scientific, and institutional development of radio in the United States and had a profound effect on how radio would be developed and controlled; yet there was virtually no press coverage of the changes.[5] The scientist who had come to personify the technology during the early years of radio was no longer a relevant player, and popular audiences were not told. Scholars have extensively studied the change of power that occurred when RCA emerged. Studies have focused on the scientists, government agencies, economic conditions, and institutions that influenced the rise of broadcasting between 1919 and 1922; however, no studies have examined how Marconi's popular image changed. This essay demonstrates how popular culture, in the absence of an official voice marking the end of Marconi's reign as an icon for radio, reshaped his popular image within the emerging institution of broadcasting.

In order to more completely understand the transformation that occurred when Marconi relinquished control of American radio, we need to examine how his popular image changed to reflect this new order. Most scholars now accept that stories told in the popular press are an important part of our culture because they contribute to our sense of identity, unity, and collective belonging.[6] In radio's formative years, the press helped shape public perceptions of radio and define patterns of ideas and beliefs.[7] Some of the best research concerning radio history has relied on the popular press in order to understand how radio was integrated into American culture. An important part of Marconi's success was his popular appeal. He skillfully used the popular press to create and maintain an image of power and control within radio culture. The *New York Times* signaled a change in Marconi's popular image when on January 20, 1919, the front page declared, "Radio to Stars, Marconi's Hope: Gets Strange Signals Now." The accompanying article reprinted a portion of a London interview with Marconi in which he speculated about the future possibilities of radio. The article marked the beginning of Marconi's involvement in a popular discussion about intelligent life on Mars. From 1919 to 1922 the popular press reported that Marconi was receiving messages from Mars. The *New York Times* and *Scientific American,* both known for their serious treatment of science, were among the many magazines and newspapers that provided coverage and commentary. The years from 1919 to 1922 were the critical years during which American broadcasting developed. An examination of press reports about Marconi's mysterious messages from Mars reveals how his popular image transformed during this period.

The idea that discussions about radio messages from Mars might have scholarly value and provide insight into the transformation of wireless telegraphy into radio broadcasting seems a little odd at best. Susan Douglas briefly mentions the coverage of Martian radio signals as an example of the sensational enthusiasm expressed for the future of radio. She also notes that communicating with Mars would not have been taken seriously by some sectors of American society, particularly the emerging modern scientific community.[8] However, there is evidence that a significant number of Americans believed that contact with Mars was quite possible, and the issue was frequently discussed in the popular press.[9] In addition, when the popular press writes about contemporary science, the distinction between fact and fiction is not always clear.[10] In spite of what might be identified today as a frivolous topic, the press discussions about Marconi and Mars from 1919 to 1922 gave popular audiences a new image of Marconi.

Examining seemingly unrelated elements of a culture, such as Marconi and messages from Mars, as a way to identify and articulate a common thread of significance is not new to historical research. Cultural historian Jacques Barzun said, "From any part of it [culture] the searching eye will discover connections with another part seemingly remote."[11] The "new historicism" that emerged from literary criticism in the late 1980s has proven to be a successful approach for examining historical texts in order to identify their connections.[12] New historicism assumes that historical texts are radically intertextual, meaning that all texts have strong and definite connections to primary forces that shape our culture. By understanding the context in which texts are created—in this case, popular discussions about Marconi and Mars—their significance begins to make sense.[13] This approach to historical research suggests that the discussions of radio messages from Mars are relevant and revealing as far as our understanding of the transformation of American radio from wireless telegraphy to broadcasting.

New historicism assumes that a significant part of the context involves power struggles. Therefore, all texts are political. Evidence can be found within every text concerning power struggles that are central to the culture of the times.[14] The assumptions that come with new historicism suggest that Marconi's image in popular discussions about radio messages from Mars was firmly anchored in the power struggles occurring within radio in the 1920s. In this particular case, the struggle was between forces working to prevent Marconi from serving a significant role in American radio and Marconi's attempts to maintain his scientific credibility. In this interpretive context, the discussions of radio signals from Mars provide a unique opportunity to examine Marconi's place in American radio at a time when America's collective consciousness about radio was being redefined by broadcasting. This essay examines the popular discussions of Marconi's radio messages from Mars and interprets how the discussions redefined Marconi's popular image.

MARCONI PERSONIFIES WIRELESS TELEGRAPHY

Marconi's popular image was created and shaped by the press. Modern radio technology was quite mysterious and difficult for naive audiences to understand, so the press used scientist-heroes to personify, simplify, and humanize the technology.[15] Marconi's demonstrations of wireless technology provided excellent opportunities for the popular press to report the development of wireless telegraphy and to associate a scientist with the technology. In 1897 the *New York World* identified Marconi as a "boy wizard."[16] The *New York Times* suggested his apparatus would "astonish the world" and reported that Marconi's work caused a "great stir" among scientists.[17] His invention was judged "the most important matter now before the civilized world."[18] And in the March 1897 edition of *McClure's* magazine, Marconi expressed a belief in an unlimited future for wireless telegraphy.[19] His wireless experiments had successfully solved insurmountable technical obstacles, and he enjoyed using the press as part of his public demonstrations of the power of wireless communication. Radio historian Hugh Aitken claims that Marconi took particular pleasure in conquering the distance limitations that other scientists placed on wireless communication.[20] One of his earliest experiments relayed yacht race results to a newspaper in Dublin from a boat a few miles off the coast of Ireland. Not only did he successfully relay immediate results, he did so over a distance judged impossible by most scientists. Marconi transmitted the first successful wireless signal across the English Channel in 1899. The message was sent from Paris by Cleveland Moffett of *McClure's* magazine to S. S. McClure in London and "astounded the world."[21] When Marconi successfully sent the first transatlantic signal, the *New York Times* announced "the most wonderful scientific development of recent times."[22] By the turn of the century, Marconi had demonstrated his mastery of wireless telegraphy, and the claims made that he was the inventor of radio received substantial support in the popular press.

Scientific American defined an inventor as the person who "develops the idea . . . to the complete, practicable apparatus, capable of taking its place among the serviceable appliances of our modern life,"[23] and concluded that Marconi met this criteria and should receive "his full meed of credit."[24] In 1903 a resolution was put before the United States Congress to thank Marconi for the benefits brought by wireless telegraphy. By 1909 Marconi was operating the world's most successful and lucrative network of ship-to-shore wireless stations and transmitting "marconigrams" across the globe.[25] In 1909 his scientific status was affirmed when he received the Nobel Prize in physics. By the close of World War I, he was at the peak of his success as an inventor, scientist, businessman, and statesman. For popular audiences he represented radio's success. In 1919 Marconi purchased a yacht retired from World War I by the British, named it the *Elettra,* and turned it into a floating laboratory in order to continue his work. During his experiments on the *Elettra* he received strange signals of an undetermined origin. The press reported that these signals were thought by some to have come from Mars.

CONTACT WITH MARS

The idea of communicating with Mars has a long history in the American popular press. In the mid-1890s, when Marconi was conducting his first wireless experiments, one of America's most notorious astronomical legends was unfolding. In 1895 Percival Lowell, director of the Lowell Observatory in Flagstaff, Arizona, announced that intelligent engineers were digging canals on Mars. In an article in *Atlantic Monthly* he wrote: "[t]hat Mars is inhabited is not the last, but the first word on the subject . . . man is but a detail in the evolution of the universe. . . . He learns that though he will probably never find his double anywhere, he is destined to discover any number of cousins scattered through space."[26]

Lowell was one of America's leading astronomers and the scientist most credited for the popular belief that canals existed on Mars.[27] He was called "the highest living authority on the subject of Mars"[28] and a "recognized Martian leader."[29] Lowell believed Mars was an old, dying planet whose inhabitants were desperately distributing the planet's meager water supplies through an elaborate system of canals.[30] Lowell's theories generated a great deal of scientific controversy and popular interest. Some scientists were unimpressed. One letter in *Science* described Lowell's work as "pseudo-science foisted upon a trusting public."[31] Others supported Lowell's theories. Waldemar Kaempffert, a journalist who specialized in reporting science, was so certain there were Martians he wrote that the idea of life on Mars was a "moot astronomical question."[32]

The discussions of intelligent life on Mars led to speculation that communication was possible, and a number of suggestions were made for contacting Mars. Several letters and editorials published in *Scientific American* discussed the various options available. Lowell believed he could communicate human intelligence by constructing huge, mathematically precise geometric forms in the Sinai Desert.[33] Professor R. W. Wood of Johns Hopkins University suggested placing a large black strip of cloth on the alkali plains of Texas. The strip could be rolled and unrolled at regular intervals to create signals.[34] In a series of letters in *Scientific American,* Professor William Pickering of Harvard University and others argued about the feasibility of using mirrors to flash signals.[35]

As early as 1901 wireless telegraphy was suggested as a means of communicating with Mars. Nikola Tesla, an eccentric scientist experimenting with wireless transmissions, announced that wireless signals from martians, or "inhabitants of whatever planet," were detected during his experiments. He wrote: "I can vividly recall the incident, and see my apparatus as though it were actually before me. My first observations positively terrified me, as there was present in them something mysterious, not to say supernatural, and I was alone in my laboratory at night."[36] Most scientists were not convinced. Astronomer Sir Robert Ball of Cambridge University concluded: "That beautiful invention with which the name of Marconi is associated has accomplished feats which transcend anything that could have been dreamed a few years ago. But significant advances would need to be made for the wireless to reach Mars."[37]

In 1907 Camille Flammarion of the Paris Observatory reported that Marconi's Cape Clear Station was receiving a signal every night between midnight and 1 A.M. that "consists of three points (. . .) which represent Marconi's S," the same signal Marconi sent in the first transatlantic wireless transmission. Flammarion concluded that because "Signor Marconi has not expressed any personal idea on the subject, it is probable he attaches no great importance to it."[38]

Professor David Todd, director of the Amherst Observatory, strongly believed that wireless technology could be used to contact Mars. He expressed hope that "a perfected ethereal telegraphy may, well within reason, permit intelligible speech from planet to planet, across the cosmic void. Quien sabe?"[39] Todd believed he could exchange signals with Mars by telegraphing from a hot-air balloon high in the atmosphere.[40] Todd tried his balloon experiment in 1912 but failed to establish contact. There was a great deal of popular interest in communicating with Mars, and radio was considered a viable technology for establishing contact. Although Marconi was mentioned in the discussions of Mars, he was not a significant figure. In 1916 *Scientific American* claimed that attempts to contact Mars had produced a "generation of unresolved discussion" where every so often "a self confessed 'scientist' from Podunk proposes to telegraph our neighbors in the ruddy planet."[41]

By the start of World War I, most modern scientists accepted the claims of the British Astronomical Society, the world's most influential group of astronomers, that the canals were simply illusions and dismissed the martian canals as a combination of poor visibility and Lowell's imagination.[42] While Lowell's theory of canal-digging Martians was largely rejected by the mainstream scientific community, his ideas still circulated in the popular press and fiction.[43] Lowell passed away in November 1916, and discussions of communicating with Mars diminished as World War I became the focus of the world's attention.

MARCONI'S MYSTERIOUS MESSAGES FROM MARS

The public's interest in communicating with Mars was renewed when the unfamiliar signals received by Marconi were reported in the popular press. The front-page article published in the *New York Times* reprinted part of an interview with Marconi that had been previously published in the *London Daily Chronicle*. The *New York Times* reprinted only the portion of the interview where Marconi discussed communication with the stars. Marconi was asked if he thought the "waves of the ether were eternal." Marconi replied: "Messages that I sent off ten years ago have not yet reached some of the nearest stars. . . . That is what makes me hope for a very big thing in the future. . . . Communication with intelligences on other stars." Marconi believed it was "silly" to assume life did not exist on other planets, and he believed any language barrier could be overcome. In the article Marconi mentioned he had received strong signals from someplace "outside the earth."[44] However, the planet Mars was never mentioned in the interview.

The following day an editorial suggested that because Marconi was known for accomplishing impossible tasks the idea of extraterrestrial communication warranted attention. The editorial discussed Marconi's interview only in terms of communicating with Mars and described similarities between the beliefs of Marconi and Lowell.[45] Marconi was now part of a renewed popular interest in Mars. He was in Europe when the *New York Times* article appeared, and his daughter Degna claims he "let out one of his rare shouts of laughter" when he read of his possible contact with Mars.[46]

The report of Marconi's mysterious messages rekindled the discussion of wireless communication with Mars. Nikola Tesla claimed that Marconi's signals confirmed Tesla's original report in 1901, that he was getting signals from Mars. Tesla remained convinced that wireless telegraphy was the most likely way to establish contact, because Mars was less than five minutes away by wireless.[47] An article in *Harper's* suggested that Marconi was simply receiving static but noted that some disturbances "are far off brotherly hands knocking at the door."[48]

The *New York Times* reported that Professor Todd, encouraged by the renewed interest in wireless signals from Mars, attempted to use his wireless apparatus to contact Martians. Todd claimed his instruments were perfected, and he expected successful contact if he could reach an altitude of thirty thousand feet. The article noted that Todd failed to gain the necessary altitude and once again failed to make contact.[49] William Rigge, an astronomer from Creighton University, raised several concerns about Todd's attempts to contact Mars. The wireless signal was not powerful enough to reach Mars, the balloon did not significantly reduce the distance between Mars and Earth, and "What language do the Martians speak?"[50] He speculated that Martians might be so far advanced they gave up trying to contact us, and he suggested the most compelling reason for no clear signal from Mars "is, of course, that there is no one there to send them."[51]

Several articles in *Scientific American* reported the reactions of scientists to possible signals from Mars. One editorial claimed there were "ready explanations" for the signals received by Marconi and that most scientists doubted that Martians were trying to contact Earth. However, the editorial concluded, "all in all, this matter deserves careful study when a scientist of Marconi's standing takes it so seriously."[52] A letter to the editor claimed that wireless technology made it possible to exchange signals with Mars and asked how we might "establish the interplanetary vocabulary."[53]

In March 1920 *Scientific American* published an interplanetary communication code based on the transmission of dots and dashes by wireless. The article introduced the code through the following scenario on Mars: "Your astronomers have just announced that signals are being received from the earth, consisting of dots and dashes regularly spaced. At the end of each block of, say, 20 signals, there is a pause, and after each 20 blocks a long delay, which apparently is the end of that message."[54]

The blocks could be used to build simple geometric forms that become progressively more complex over time. Eventually the code could be used to establish a common language for humans and Martians. The authors noted one requirement of Martian life: "You may be a hundred feet high, with the strength of a dozen elephants, or the size of a mouse with a score of legs. You must, however, be intelligent; that is a postulate of the problem."[55] By the end of 1920 it was a technical reality that wireless technology could be used to contact Mars, and a scientific code was offered for anyone willing to try.

On September 2, 1921, the *New York Times* once again gave Marconi front-page attention. The headline read, "Marconi Sure Mars Flashes Messages." The article reported that Marconi was convinced the signals he received on the *Elettra* were from Mars and resembled the letter "V" of the international code. The information was credited to J. H. C. McBeth, manager of the London division of Marconi Wireless Telegraph Company, Ltd., and not directly to Marconi. McBeth had addressed the New York City Rotary Club and stated the wavelengths of the signals received by Marconi were too long to be produced on Earth and were received regularly regardless of other interference. McBeth explained: "If life exists on that planet, it obviously follows that it is higher developed than on earth. Witness the intricate canal system, and if higher developed, then 150,000 meter waves [*sic*] lengths no longer become mysterious."[56] McBeth claimed Marconi shared his belief that the signals were from Mars.

An editorial in the *New York Times* the following day questioned the interpretation of the signals. To suggest martians "are trying to get into communication with us, that is going rather far, even for a savant as distinguished as Mr. Marconi."[57] The editorial claimed that Marconi, like Lowell before him, was dangerously close to losing his scientific credibility but also noted that Marconi's observations were important if true. Another editorial on the same page expressed more optimism: "[T]here is something dreamlike about all this, of course, but dreams have come true before now."[58]

A few days later another editorial offered a humorous reason why the Martian signals resembled the letter "V": "It stands for 'Volstead,' among other things, and may be the beginning of a warning against prohibition—or an exhortation to keep it up. . . . That the message is addressed to us is beyond question. Are we not the most important and interesting nations and people?"[59]

Scripp's Science Service, a newly established news service devoted exclusively to science, released a bulletin with a statement by Nikola Tesla claiming the signals were the result of radio undertones: "When a wireless station sends out a message . . . it also sends out undertones to the message."[60] The bulletin suggested a possible explanation for the signals was the effects of research conducted at the General Electric facilities in Schenectady, New York.

In May 1922 Marconi announced he was planning to sail the *Elettra* to the United States. A primary reason for his trip was to visit the "General Electric House of Magic" in Schenectady and examine new technological innovations in American radio. The GE plant employed some of the greatest scientific minds in wireless technology, and the scientists at GE looked forward to Marconi's arrival in mid-June.[61] Reporters also looked forward to his visit; this was not only Marconi's first visit to America since his initial in-volvement in the Mars discussions in 1919, but it was also reporters' first opportunity to directly question Marconi about his interest in messages from Mars.[62]

In an interview in Southampton, England, a few days before Marconi left for New York, a British reporter asked Marconi about the strange signals he had received. The *New York Times* reported his comments: "I shall be in America next month and shall certainly 'listen in' for these mysterious sounds. They have not been reported for some time and there is at the mo-ment no indication, so far as I am aware, that they are likely to begin again."[63]

A press photo of Marconi that was released as he crossed the Atlantic aboard the *Elettra* showed him surrounded by wireless equipment. *Current Opinion* published the photo and added a caption at the top that read: "He Expects to Hear from Mars."[64] The same photo appeared in *Radio News* and read "Senatore Guglielmo Marconi in the radio room of his yacht, 'Electra' [*sic*]. The loop was probably used in attempts to receive Mars."[65] The day before he was scheduled to arrive in New York, the Associated Press wired Marconi for a statement on the results of his experiments while crossing the Atlantic. He replied, "Have no sensational announcement to make." The *New York Times* interpreted this to mean the "Italian radio wizard has appar-ently failed to pick up any messages from Mars."[66] The *Elettra* arrived on June 16, 1922, and was met in the harbor by scores of reporters.[67] In his notable absence, Marconi's assistants answered questions about his wireless experiments and, according to the *New York Times*, reported Marconi had done "everything but communicate with Mars. Marconi is not doing that, and has never attempted such 'romantic futilities' . . . any suggestions of in-terplanetary communication were 'absurd' and 'ridiculous.' "[68]

During his stay in the United States, Marconi redirected reporters' ques-tions about Mars to the scientific advances he was making in his research. One reporter assigned to cover Marconi wrote: "But in all this there is not a word about communication with Mars, except the humorous remark of an engineer of the Radio Corporation that the first message to Mars will be a Mars-conigram."[69]

In July 1922, near the end of his visit to America, Marconi received the John Fritz Award from the American Institute of Electrical Engineers, reaffirming his scientific credibility. The text of his acceptance speech, published in *Radio Broadcast*, focused on the technical advances of wireless technology and his research into microwaves. He did not mention Mars.[70] He had effectively distanced himself from the discussions of Martian communication. The *New York Times* reported: "Those who were thrilled by the reports Marconi was trying to communicate with Mars may receive their antidote."[71] Apparently Marconi's fascination with radio was entirely terrestrial.

Late in July Marconi sailed back to England on the *Elettra*. He had toured many wireless stations in America and was particularly impressed with the work of scientists at the Schenectady General Electric plant. A bulletin from Scripp's Science Service released after Marconi left America announced that the alleged messages from Mars were produced at the GE plant in Schenectady. The bulletin stated: "The current of this wavelength was sent by Dr. Langmuir over the trolley lines between Schenectady and the famed Saratoga Springs, eighteen miles north of Electric City. The experiment was unannounced, and the powerful current evidently spread itself over the world. Senator Marconi denied the report that he had been in communication with Mars, and now proof is offered of the source of the 'signals.'"[72]

The bulletin marked the end of Marconi's involvement in the discussions of Mars. However, broader discussions of life on Mars and the use of wireless technology to contact Martians continued. Nikola Tesla remained interested in contacting Mars throughout most of his life.[73] In 1924 David Todd, now professor emeritus at Amherst, tried his balloon experiment again. This time he was interested primarily in receiving rather than sending messages. In his view, sending a message was "hardly probable," but "it is entirely within the bounds of reason to assume that Mars could communicate with the earth."[74] Once again he failed to make contact.

MARCONI'S POPULAR IMAGE

Most scholarly research concerning Marconi during the rise of broadcasting focuses on the transformation of the American Marconi Company into RCA rather than the transformation of Marconi's popular image. The story of Marconi and the messages from Mars provides a view of the change in Marconi's popular image from 1919 to 1922, the same period that witnessed the rise of American broadcasting. While the idea of communicating with

Mars seems absurd, the discussion provides an insightful view concerning how Marconi's popular image changed during the rise of American broadcasting.

Marconi was no longer an appropriate icon to represent radio, because he did not personify broadcasting and his influence in American radio had diminished. Marconi did not hear his first American broadcast until his trip to America in 1922, and he concluded: "The wireless tells me that New York is a lively place. There is evidence . . . in the methods of broadcasting and in the public interest in radio, that the United States is far ahead of Europe."[75] By 1922 American broadcasting was establishing itself as a powerful new force in radio, one with no direct connection to Marconi's use of radio. This left the press and its readers with an uncertain view of Marconi's place in the modern world of American radio.

There is little direct evidence that Marconi attempted to contact Mars; however, he did little to suggest otherwise. Marconi fueled the controversy by giving the press short, vague, and open-ended comments that begged speculation. For nearly three years, he would neither confirm nor deny reports that he was attempting to communicate with Mars. The research for this essay found no evidence that Marconi ever used the word "Mars" in public. It was the popular press who claimed Marconi's strange signals were from Mars and linked him with the Mars envisioned by Lowell. Marconi's ambiguous comments allowed the press and popular audiences a wide range of interpretations. The ambiguity of Marconi's comments also reflected a genuine scientific uncertainty. When interviewed by Orrin Dunlap in the late 1930s, Marconi said: "Who can affirm signals from Mars? How can I know? How can anyone know? Of course, the signals may come from space outside the earth. They may come from the upper reaches of the atmosphere. They may be caused by magnetic disturbances on the sun; they may come from Mars or Venus."[76] His popular image was losing power in the modern world of American broadcasting, so the popular press used his scientific voice as a substitute for Lowell's. The stories reinvigorated theories of possible intelligent life on Mars but positioned Marconi at the fringe of the scientific community. Linking Marconi to the discussion of Mars effectively distanced him from the modern scientific community that rejected such frivolous ideas.

Marconi's individual mastery and control of wireless technology created a popular image that was valued by early American radio enthusiasts who needed to learn the technology and construct their own equipment. Mastery of complex wireless technology became unnecessary as manufactured receiving sets became readily available and easy to use. The inaugural issue of *Radio Broadcast* in 1922 featured a portrait of Marconi on the first page, but the significance assigned him was historical and concerned his early role in the development of radio.[77] The emerging broadcasting culture regarded Marconi as part of the old order that viewed radio as a means of point-to-point communication, and the discussions about communication with Mars characterized the old order of wireless telegraphy. The interplanetary code used the old system of dots and dashes and required skilled technicians and specialized equipment to bridge the enormous distances, a system that was similar to Marconi's ship-to-shore operations. No one suggested broadcasting jazz to the Martians. Communication with Mars served as another potential situation in which Marconi could demonstrate his ability to send and receive signals over distances that were deemed impossible, and in this mission he seemed, finally, to fail. His mysterious messages linked him to the older popular discussion of life on Mars, not to the modern practice of radio broadcasting.

The announcement by Scripp's Science Service that the mysterious messages from Mars were in fact from GE's Schenectady plant demonstrated for the public the advanced state of American radio technology. The GE experiments produced radio waves so technologically advanced that even a great scientist like Marconi, who invented the technology, did not recognize the signals and assumed they were extraterrestrial. Marconi was no longer in step with the new direction American radio was taking. The discussions of Marconi's communication with Mars in the popular press demonstrated how much American broadcasting diverged from the previous use of radio as point-to-point communication. The old concept of wireless telegraphy appeared alien as broadcasting became the dominant and uniquely American application of wireless technology. The power of modern American radio was broadcasting and did not involve Marconi. The discussions about radio messages from Mars proved to be an effective way for American popular culture to reposition Marconi. He no longer personified American radio, and the discussion of radio signals from Mars symbolized a change in his image from popular icon to historical figure.

By the end of his visit to America, Marconi's scientific credibility was reestablished, but he was no longer a central figure in American popular radio. It was as if he had been banished to Mars. In an interview in 1938 Marconi claimed he was simply the victim of "reportorial enthusiasm," and when he was asked "foolish question No. 1. . . . Have you ever sent messages to other planets?" Marconi replied with his usual ambiguity: "I've sent lots of messages that never got anywhere."[78]

NOTES

1. The basic review of radio history comes from Eric Barnouw, *A Tower in Babel: A History of American Broadcasting* (New York: Oxford UP, 1966); Daniel Czitrom, *Media and the American Mind* (Chapel Hill: U of North Carolina P, 1982); Susan Douglas, *Inventing American Broadcasting* (Baltimore, MD: Johns Hopkins UP, 1987); Michelle Hilmes, *Only Connect: A Cultural History of Broadcasting in the United States* (Belmont, CA: Wadsworth, 2002); Susan Smulyan, *Selling Radio* (Washington, DC: Smithsonian Institution Press, 1994); Christopher H. Sterling and John Michael Kittross, *Stay Tuned: A History of American Broadcasting* (Mahwah, NJ: Lawrence Erlbaum, 2002).

2. Waldemar Kaempffert, *Radio Simply Explained*, vol. 2, *Easy Course in Home Radio*, ed. Gen. George Squire (New York: Martin Ray and Review of Reviews, 1922), 40.

3. Robert Lochte, "Invention and Innovation of Early Radio Technology," *Journal of Radio Studies* 7, no. 1 (2000): 93–115.

4. Barnouw, Czitrom, and Douglas provide basic information about Marconi. A recent biography is G. Massini, *Marconi* (New York: Marsilio, 1995). A good technical review of his contribution can be found in Hugh Aitken, *Syntony and Spark* (New York: John Wiley, 1976). Degna Marconi, *My Father Marconi* (New York: McGraw Hill, 1962), provides a daughter's perspective. Orrin Dunlap's book *Marconi: The Man and His Wireless* (New York: Macmillan, 1937) was reviewed by Marconi prior to publication and includes a preface by Marconi.

5. Douglas, *Inventing American Broadcasting*, 286.

6. Peter Dahlgren and Colin Sparks, *Journalism and Popular Culture* (Newbury Park, CA: Sage, 1992).

7. Douglas, *Inventing American Broadcasting*, xvii.

8. Ibid., 305.

9. "Scientific Standing of the Theory of Intelligent Life on Mars," *Current Opinion*, January 1917, 36.

10. Sharon Friedman, Sharon Dunwoody, and Carol Rogers, eds., *Scientists and Journalists: Reporting Science as News* (New York: Free Press, 1986); Dorothy Nelkin, *Selling Science: How the Press Covers Science and Technology* (New York: W. H. Freeman, 1995).

11. Jacques Barzun, *The Culture We Deserve* (Middletown, CT: Wesleyan UP, 1989), vii.

12. Robert Berkhofer Jr., *Beyond the Great Story: History as Text and Discourse* (Cambridge, MA: Harvard UP, 1995).

13. H. Aram Veeser, ed., *The New Historicism* (New York: Routledge, 1989); H. Aram Veeser, ed., *The New Historicism Reader* (New York: Routledge, 1994).

14. John Brannigan, "New Historicism," in *Literary Theories,* ed. J. Wolfreys (New York: New York UP, 1999), 417–59; Alun Munslow, *Deconstructing History* (London: Routledge, 1997).

15. Douglas, *Inventing American Broadcasting,* 3.

16. "Boy Wizard," *New York World,* August 8, 1897, 12.

17. "New Possibilities," *New York Times,* May 26, 1897, 6; January 23, 1898, 3.

18. "Wireless Telegraphy," *New York Times,* March 16, 1899, 1.

19. "Telegraphing without Wires," *McClure's,* March 1897, 383.

20. Aitken, *Syntony and Spark,* 191.

21. "The Wireless," *New York Times,* April 9, 1899, 22.

22. "Wireless Signals Across the Ocean," *New York Times,* December 15, 1901, 1.

23. "Unjust and Ungenerous," *Scientific American,* April 19, 1902, 287.

24. "Sci Am Marconi Disclaimer," *Scientific American,* August 8, 1902, 84. Other foreign scientists played a key role in the development of radio, but Marconi seemed to have the most popular appeal. Comparing Marconi's public image in the American press to that of Tesla, Steinmetz, Pupin, Popov, and others would provide useful insight into the relationship between scientists and popular culture.

25. Marconi operated an extensive network of ship-to-shore stations from the United States, Canada, and Great Britain, with additional offices in Brussels, Paris, Rome, and Buenos Aires. For an excellent essay on his Canadian stations see Donald Godfrey and David Spencer, "Canadian Marconi: CFCF Television from Signal Hill to the Canadian Television Network," *Journal of Broadcasting and Electronic Media* 44, no. 3 (2000): 437–55.

26. Percival Lowell, "Mars IV, Oases," *Atlantic Monthly,* August 1895, 222.

27. William Graves Hoyt, *Lowell and Mars* (Tucson: U of Arizona P, 1976); William Sheehan, *Planets and Perception* (Tucson: U of Arizona P, 1988).

28. "Why the Dwellers of Mars Do Not Make War," *Current Opinion,* February 1907, 211.

29. *Book Review Digest* (1907): 269.

20. Percival Lowell, *Mars* (New York: Macmillan, 1895); Percival Lowell, *Mars: The Abode of Life* (New York: Macmillan, 1910).

31. E. Blackwelder, "Mars as the Abode of Life," *Science,* April 23, 1909, 659.

32. Waldemar Kaempffert, "Mars—Things Known and Surmised," *Cosmopolitan,* October 1909, 611.

33. "More about Signaling to Mars," *Scientific American,* May 15, 1909, 371.

34. "Signaling Mars," *Scientific American,* May 8, 1909, 364.

35. George Fleming, "Signaling to Mars with Mirrors," *Scientific American,* May 29, 1909, 407; Wilfred Griffin, "Signaling Mars," *Scientific American,* June 5, 1909, 423; Edgar Larkin, "Signaling to Mars," *Scientific American Supplement,* June 19, 1909, 387; William Pickering, "Signaling to Mars," *Scientific American,* July 17, 1909, 43.

36. Nikola Tesla, "Talking with the Planets," *Current Literature,* March 1901, 359.

37. Sir Robert Ball, "Signaling to Mars," *Scientific American Supplement,* June 8, 1901, 212.

38. "Camille Flammarion's Latest Views on Martian Signaling," *Scientific American Supplement,* August 31, 1907, 137.

39. David Todd, "Professor Todd's Own Story of the Mars Expedition," *Cosmopolitan,* March 1908, 351.

40. "Prof. Todd's Plan of Receiving Martian Messages," *Scientific American,* June 5, 1909, 423.

41. "The Perennial Martians," *Scientific American,* February 12, 1916, 172.

42. Henry Paradyne, "The Mythical Canals of Mars," *Harper's,* January 15, 1910, 8.

43. For example, Edgar Rice Burroughs wrote a series of twelve novels starting with *The Princess of Mars* (New York: Grosset & Dunlap, 1917) and created a fictional Martian world modeled after Lowell's descriptions.

44. "Radio to the Stars Marconi's Hope, Gets Strange Signals Now," *New York Times,* January 20, 1919, 1.

45. "Let the Stars Alone," *New York Times,* January 21, 1919, 8.

46. D. Marconi, *My Father Marconi,* 234. There is little evidence about how Marconi reacted personally to the news that he was getting messages from Mars. Most of his public comments were ambiguous and suggested he remained focused on his research.

47. "That Prospective Communication with Another Planet," *Current Opinion,* March 1919, 170.

48. Buckner Speed, "Voices of the Universe," *Harper's,* April 1919, 615.

49. "Will Try to Talk with Mars," *New York Times,* July 9, 1919, 5.

50. William Rigge, "Wireless Signals to Mars," *Popular Astronomy,* April 1920, 306.

51. William Rigge, "The Signals from Mars," *Popular Astronomy,* May 1920, 369.

52. "Those Martian Radio Signals," *Scientific American,* February 14, 1920, 156.

53. "Who Can Answer This?" *Scientific American,* March 8, 1920, 245.

54. H. Nieman and C. Nieman, "What Shall We Say to Mars?" *Scientific American,* March 20, 1920, 298.

55. Ibid.

56. "Marconi Sure Mars Flashes Messages," *New York Times,* September 2, 1921, 1.

57. "Are Messages Coming from Mars?" *New York Times,* September 3, 1921, 8.

58. "Understanding Is Not Possible," *New York Times,* September 3, 1921, 8.

59. "A Letter with Meaning," *New York Times,* September 5, 1921, 10.

60. "Messages from Mars Scouted by Experts," *New York Times,* September 3, 1921, 4.

61. Degna Marconi claims that her father and the GE scientists were excited about the visit (*My Father Marconi,* 243).

62. "Ambitious Radio Possibilities," *Literary Digest,* July 8, 1922, 23.

63. "Developing Secret Wireless Service," *New York Times,* May 6, 1922, 6.

64. "He Expects to Hear from Mars," *Current Opinion,* August 1922, 187.

65. *Radio News,* September 1922, 433.

66. "No Mars Message Yet," *New York Times,* June 16, 1922, 5.

67. Dunlap, *Marconi,* 264.

68. "Marconi Here, Hopes to Conquer Static," *New York Times,* June 17, 1922, 8.

69. "Even Marconi Awed by Future of Radio," *New York Times,* June 22, 1922, 5.

70. "Marconi's Address to the AIEE," *Radio Broadcast,* August 1922, 341.

71. "Radio's Great Tomorrow," *New York Times,* July 9, 1922, section 7, D1.

72. "From Schenectady, Not Mars," *Literary Digest,* August 5, 1922, 33.

73. Marc Seifer, *Wizard: The Life and Times of Nikola Tesla* (Secaucus, NJ: Carol, 1996); Margaret Cheney, *Tesla: Man Out of Time* (New York: Simon & Schuster, 2001).

74. "Radio Messages from Mars?" *Literary Digest,* September 6, 1924, 28.

75. Dunlap, *Marconi,* 261.

76. Ibid., 267.

77. "Guglielmo Marconi," *Radio Broadcast,* May 1922, frontispiece.

78. Dunlap, *Marconi,* 334.

2 / The Davis Amendment and the Federal Radio Act of 1927

Evaluating External Pressures in Policy Making

FRITZ MESSERE

In March 1927 the new Federal Radio Commission (FRC) began sorting out the interference problems and setting a regulatory agenda that would shape the nascent broadcasting business in the United States, a business that was less than seven years old. Conceived by Congress as a hurried solution to the interference problems of 1926, the Federal Radio Commission undertook the unenviable task of creating a new regulatory agency without any resources allocated to it. Ironically, the Senate did not ratify the full membership of the commission, which lost two of its members within the first year. Not surprisingly, by the end of its first year the work of the FRC was meeting with dissatisfaction among members of Congress, distrust by the public, and attempts to rifle specific agendas through by large broadcasting and radio manufacturing interests.

The original legislation creating the Federal Radio Commission called for a one-year tenure for the agency, subject to reauthorization by Congress. During the reauthorization hearings, Representative Ewin Davis (R) of Tennessee charged that the FRC was doing the bidding of the large broadcast interests and that the agency had failed to meet its mandate to create service for all Americans.

Davis introduced an amendment to the reauthorization bill that declared all Americans were entitled to equality of radio broadcasting service, in terms of both transmission and reception. The amendment also called for equitable allocation of licenses, wavelengths, time, and station power to each of the states according to population within each zone. The purpose of the amendment was to make the intentions of Congress clear to the members of the Federal Radio Commission.

Before and after the amendment's adoption, public relations campaigns both for and against the implementation of the amendment's provisions heightened public awareness of the Federal Radio Commission and the problems that it faced. Posturing about the difficulty involved in trying to implement the equality of service provisions led the FRC to become reactive to the influence of various members of Congress, to the pressures of the electronics industry, and to the needs of smaller regional broadcasters. The reactive stance helped set the mode of operation and the public posture for the commission for the first years of its existence. The outcome of the FRC's work between the years 1927 and 1933 and the legacy of the Davis Amendment can be seen in the creation of a local/regional broadcasting service that relied heavily on a system of large and small broadcast stations that carried network-provided, commercially oriented radio programs designed primarily for commercial entertainment. The standard broadcast band, the predominant radio band for fifty years after the creation of the Federal Radio Commission, was shaped by the recommendations that came about as a result of the Davis Amendment.

While some might say that the trials and tribulations of an upstart federal bureaucracy might make for an interesting, even nostalgic look at the birth of radio regulation, others could question the importance of studying the adoption and implementation of the Davis Amendment today. Broadcasting historian Susan Douglas reminds us that we can look at "old articles about radio fever as fanciful and misguided stories of little consequence, or we can take them seriously, and analyze the connections they reveal between technology and ideology."[1] Even as the FRC was being created, powerful institutional forces sought to influence the decision-making process. Their roots were political, economic, technological, and social, and the interaction between those influences produced a situation calling out for regulatory control. Congress responded with compromise legislation, written broadly, allowing independent commissioners the freedom to develop a new systematic paradigm for regulating broadcasting in the United States.

In *The End of Liberalism*, Theodore Lowi writes that the compromise legislation that marked the beginnings of many regulatory agencies often called for unclear, contradictory goals. Lowi found many regulatory statutes were void of meaningful guidelines beyond the abstract requirements to serve the "public interest."[2] Did the vague, compromised language that created the Federal Radio Commission make it impossible for a new structure of broadcasting to develop? Would the FRC commissioners have the ability to separate their regulatory responsibilities from their political ones? Were the technical limitations of the medium destined to define the solutions possible to the equalization clause?

Through an examination of the issues and problems that compelled the Federal Radio Commission to adopt certain policy decisions that met the legislative requirements of the Davis Amendment, this essay attempts to illuminate some of the unintended consequences of deliberate legislative acts. The FRC began the regulation of wireless communication, and today's industry is still bound by some of the regulatory stances carved out during these early days. For example, today's Federal Communications Commission uses many regulatory procedures started by the FRC. Could a study of the initial controversies illuminate our knowledge about the FRC's expectations for structuring the industry, along with the resultant outcomes for reducing interference? As a corollary, can we discover any insights regarding the industry's expectations from the FRC?

Karl Popper suggests that the study of linkages between intentions and outcomes can produce insights into why the actions of historical actors who set out to accomplish one set of goals might produce unanticipated or contrary results.[3] Popper's suggestion holds promise for the study of broadcast regulation. For example, did the commission's desire to create a quick solution to meet the rigid requirements of the Davis Amendment contribute to the notable reduction of nonprofit broadcast stations?[4] Was there a concern by the FRC or consulting engineers that the new technical plan described in General Order 40 could be met only by commercial stations that were able to buy expensive new equipment to meet a set of more stringent technical regulations? Such a proposition, though not definitively accepted in the current literature, is not without possibility.[5] Still, such a proposition opens a speculative but viable set of explanations as to why commercial broadcasting emerged during the earliest days of radio and why a more public-service orientation in radio did not surface until the creation of the FM band.

Surprisingly, while some scholars have focused on either the history or the workings of the Federal Radio Commission, few have focused on the significance of the external pressures on the commission that may have prevented it from resolving the interference and technical problems in its own way and within its own time frame.[6] If we examine the interests, motivations, and behaviors in the institutional setting of the FRC against the interdependent interests and motivations of Congress, the large broadcast trust, and the National Association of Broadcasters, will we gain insights into the decisions and the decision-making process?

This essay briefly outlines the events that occurred before, during, and after the passage of the Davis Amendment; looks at the interaction among the various players; and identifies the interests they sought to advance. Finally, it examines the decision-making process and looks at some of the possible influences on the FRC in deciding how to implement the equality of service requirements of the Davis Amendment.

THE FEDERAL RADIO COMMISSION: THE FIRST YEAR

According to the first *Annual Report of the Federal Radio Commission,* "a wholly new Federal body was called into being to deal with a condition which had become almost hopelessly involved during the months following July 3, 1926."[7] Congress had failed to create proper legislative oversight earlier in 1912 when it gave supervisory responsibility to the secretary of commerce and labor. This failure to provide proper regulatory oversight came back to haunt Congress a decade later when Secretary Herbert Hoover found he lacked the authority to revoke station licenses or to assign power levels or times of operation.[8] Radio's growth was explosive.

Congress needed to do something fast; the question was what to do. Lowi reminds us that regulation is only one of several ways governments seek to control society and individual conduct. And since there are some specific purposes that are best pursued through regulatory techniques, we should be able to observe a distinct set of political-process consequences associated with this kind of government commitment.[9] Scholars disagree as to why legislators wanted an independent commission. Some legislators may have had some reluctance to trust the secretary of commerce and labor, since Hoover was seen as being closely aligned with large broadcast interests.[10] After consideration, perhaps Congress decided that an independent regulatory commission could best deal with the seemingly intractable interference problems that had developed as a result of the breakdown of the Radio Act of 1912.[11] Or perhaps Congress was reluctant to adopt any of the earlier bills retaining the supervision of the secretary of commerce, since they failed to gain bipartisan support in Congress. However, when Attorney General William Donovan declared the existing regulation unconstitutional, the mounting interference crisis made radio reception almost impossible in many parts of the country. Amid mounting complaints from the rapidly growing broadcasting industry and local constituents who were eagerly trying to listen, legislators moved to create emergency legislation.[12]

Representative Wallace H. White (R-ME) sponsored a bill in the Sixty-ninth Congress giving authority to the secretary of commerce to grant licenses, assign wavelengths, and allot time to broadcasters, while Clarence C. Dill (D-WA) sponsored a bill in the Senate that created an independent five-member commission to oversee broadcasting. Though both bills passed in their respective houses, the conference committee was unable to reconcile the difference before adjournment of the first legislative session.[13]

Continuing public outcry about the deteriorating listening situation around the country forced legislators into action. A compromise was reached early in the new year; the Radio Act of 1927 passed and was signed into law by the president on February 23, 1927. The act incorporated parts of both House and Senate bills by creating the five-member commission on a temporary one-year basis to assign broadcast licenses and bring order to the chaos of the airwaves. After the initial one-year period, licensing authority would revert back to the secretary of commerce, while the FRC would act as a sort of court of appeals for broadcasters. According to provisions of the act, certain nonpolicy functions were to remain with the Commerce Department.[14]

The Radio Act of 1927 gave the commission authority to grant or deny licenses as would best serve the public interest, and to assign frequencies, times of operation, and power output. Section 9 of the act instructed the commission to remove inequalities in geographic distribution of broadcast facilities that had developed prior to the act. Congress succeeded in appointing three of the five commissioners, and *The Outlook,* a news magazine of the period, claims that politics played a part in preventing several of the commissioners from gaining confirmation. At the end of the legislative session the Federal Radio Commission was only partly filled and had no appropriations budget. Other government agencies assisted with personnel and space as the FRC struggled to begin the task of creating a new federal agency without resources.[15]

Documents of the early days of the Federal Radio Commission show that one of the first issues discussed was a plan for frequency allocation and a timetable for implementation. This was necessary because section 1 of the act automatically terminated all existing licenses.[16] Following a precedent set by Secretary of Commerce Hoover, the FRC held hearings in late March to solicit opinions from broadcasters. The focus of these discussions centered on the issues of allocation and the engineering concerns surrounding the interference problem. Robert McChesney notes that these sessions were dominated by testimony of corporate-affiliated radio engineers.[17]

The outcomes of these discussions are reflected in the actions of the FRC and a plan they begin to implement. For example, General Order 11 (amended by General Order 13), issued on May 21, 1927, terminated all licenses, required all stations to file applications concerning their current status, and made radio stations subject to the provisions of the Radio Act of 1927. Included in the minutes for the meeting of May 21 is a statement that recognizes that "no scheme of reallocation which does not at the very outset eliminate at least four hundred broadcast stations can possibly put an end to interference."[18] This early declaration by the commission suggests that the FRC recognized the need to clear broadcasting interference through attrition of stations, reallocation of assignments, and reauthorization of power outputs. However, the actions of the FRC during this first year illustrate a much more conservative body.[19] It may be that given the tenuous nature of the commissioners' appointments and the lack of funding, the newly formed agency did not want to rock the boat. It may be that coercive actions from Congress or industry made the commission tread lightly, but during the first years few station licenses were revoked.

Throughout much of 1927, the FRC acted less like a regulatory body and more like a technical agency. Documents indicate the FRC moved congested stations to less-congested spots (frequency assignments) on the radio dial rather than reducing the number of licenses. A series of channel assignment changes made during this period helped some; however, the overall problem of overcrowding and interference was not eliminated.[20] Early commission orders moved various stations from one allocation to another to alleviate problems for "local listeners." However, as winter approached, rural areas still suffered from significant interference. General Order 19 provided for the large-scale transfer of station assignments to clear all frequencies between 600 kHz and 1000 kHz from heterodynes and other interference.[21]

The intention of the commission was to hold the industry in status quo while the agency sought recognition and money from Congress to execute its charge. Testifying to an oversight committee of the House, Commissioner Eugene Sykes stated: "[W]e concluded it was our responsibility under the law to first give a fair trial and see if it were possible to let all of these stations live. . . . [I]f we had denied 150 or 200 station licenses at that time, in my judgment and in the judgment of the commission, we would have had so many law suits and possibly temporary injunctions granted against us that practically the whole of the broadcast band would have been tied up."[22]

Analysis of FRC general orders and minutes during its first year indicates that the commission attempted to resolve the various interference problems on an ad hoc basis.[23] These attempts produced mixed results in the various regions of the country. FRC rulings seemed to ignore the commission's responsibilities under section 9 of the act and instead ensconced commercial broadcast interests, particularly the large chain broadcasting stations and affiliates.[24] Members of Congress charged the commission with favoring large broadcasters from the East while discriminating against the listeners in the South and West.[25] Commissioners vigorously denied the charges, but when the new Congress convened, oversight hearings and newspaper accounts of public reaction to the FRC indicate that it had not succeeded in fulfilling its goals.[26] A House report reflected the displeasure of its members: "The set-up in the broadcasting field which it was believed at the time the radio act was passed could be worked out in a year's time had not been effected. We are confronted with the dilemma of continuing the commission in authority for another year during which it is hoped the situation may be improved."[27]

In hindsight, it appears that the Federal Radio Commission did not see that political problems would develop as a result of its policy of maintaining the status quo while trying to resolve most interference questions on a case-by-case basis. One could argue that without proper funding and a fully confirmed slate of commissioners, the FRC lacked the political clout to resolve the technical problems it had been created to fix; thus the commission argued that it tried to avoid legal challenges that might further prevent implementation of the act.[28] Congress, on the other hand, recognized the dissatisfaction among its constituents very clearly and sought to rectify the situation during the commission's reauthorization process. Led by members from the South and the West, Congress amended the FRC's reauthorization bill to correct broadcasting's geographical imbalance.

THE FIGHT OVER THE DAVIS AMENDMENT

The Seventieth Congress took no pity on its stepchild. Philip Rosen says the two members most responsible for the creation of the FRC fiercely attacked its lack of accomplishments. Clarence Dill chided the "cowards and dullards" for their inability to develop a plan to reduce broadcast stations while allowing themselves to succumb to the influence of the radio trust. Representative White complained that the FRC policies had complicated the situation. Both White and Dill echoed their colleagues by insisting that the only solution to the interference problem was the elimination of some broadcast stations. Led by Representative Ewin Davis, legislators from underrepresented regions of the country protested that the FRC had failed to distribute facilities equally among the states.[29]

During an oversight hearing, Representative Davis served notice to Commissioner Sykes that he intended to change language in the act to remove any vagueness about the commission's responsibility.

> *Mr. Kading:* [D]o you not think it would be very important to act upon the suggestion of the chairman of preparing an amendment to be introduced in Congress clarifying the matter [interpreting equality of service]?
>
> *Commissioner Sykes:* Personally, I would be glad, of course, if Congress would clarify it. I would not like to have to undertake to draw the amendment, though; I would have to leave that to you gentlemen.
>
> *Mr. Davis:* In other words, your opinion is, naturally, even from the point of view of the commission itself, it is highly important for whatever statutory provisions are enacted for your guidance to be unambiguous and about which there can be no controversy or conflict of opinion.
>
> *Commissioner Sykes:* I would be delighted, Judge, to see it at my rest.
>
> *Mr. Davis:* I want to state I am in thorough accord with that and, so far as I am concerned, will undertake to effect that result.[30]

With the introduction of the Davis Amendment to section 9 of the act's reauthorization bill, a political debate ensued over the precise meaning of the "equality of service clause" and whether passage of the reauthorization with its inclusion would create a better radio service or hamstring the commission in its work. Depending on what interests one held, the amendment was designed to either destroy broadcasting or save it. There seemed to be little middle ground. For example, Senator Dill said the language of the new bill made it unworkable and impracticable and blamed the FRC for disregarding the equitable service provisions of the 1927 law.[31]

Industry leaders lobbied heavily against the amendment provisions. David Sarnoff, vice president of Radio Corporation of America, stated: "[I]t is my hope that Congress will not pass a bill, the technical provisions of which, to my mind cannot be of help either to the listening public or to broadcasting stations."[32] Even members of the Federal Radio Commission got into the fray. Commissioner O. H. Caldwell stated that the "rider would wreck our present wonderful radio broadcasting structure" and claimed the amendment "is not practical and must be discarded in the search for a way to reduce the number of stations." Meanwhile the *New York Times* speculated, "[W]ill the Ides of March in 1928 go down in history as a turning point in 'radio'?"[33]

The heated debate crossed party lines, making it difficult to assess relative support for the bill, which appeared to be tied to supporting regional constituent desires for either more radio service or for maintaining the status quo. For example, Representative White, a powerful Republican from Maine, aligned himself with Representative Davis, a Democrat from Tennessee. House Democrat Thomas McKeown from Oklahoma stated that if the "house failed to adopt the 'equitable distribution' provision, he would offer a resolution call for an investigation of the [radio] 'trust.'"[34] All of these congressmen had constituents who desired better local service, but House Democrat Emanuel Cellar from New York said, "[T]he amendment which the committee made to the Senate bill, to my mind, will put radio art into a straitjacket."[35] During February the FRC undertook several measures to appease southern supporters of the Davis Amendment.[36]

Outside organizations with an interest in radio also lobbied Congress against adoption of the amendment. The *New York Times* covered the reauthorization bill extensively. At one point it described the political maneuvering in Congress as if it were describing a battle scene: "Honors are even in the radio war being waged in Congress. Commissioner Caldwell opened the hostilities with an attack on the Watson bill. A few days later Senator Dill raided the Commissioner's position. Reinforcements in the form of Representative Davis, Tennessee, came to the Senator's aid. Just when it seemed the Commissioner might be forced to beat a strategic retreat, the National Association of Broadcasters, Inc. (NAB) hurled its shock troops in the breach caused by Davis' flank attack on the Commissioner's left while Senator Dill was hammering his front. It appears radio is in politics!"[37]

Despite the best efforts of the NAB, the radio "trust," and members who opposed it, the reauthorization that included the Davis Amendment's "equitable distribution" requirements passed by a large margin on March 28, 1928.[38] The clause amended section 2 of the radio act to read

> that the people of all zones . . . are entitled to equality of radio broadcasting service, both of transmission and of reception, and in order to provide said equality the licensing authority shall as nearly as possible make and maintain an equal allocation of broadcasting licenses, of bands of frequency or wave lengths, of periods of time for operation, and of station power, to each of said zones when and in so far as there are applications therefore and shall make a fair and equitable allocation of licenses, wave lengths, time for operation, and station power to each of the States, The District of Columbia, the Territories and possessions of the United States within each zone, according to population.[39]

The FRC was directed to carry out the equality of service requirement by granting or refusing licenses or renewals of licenses. As if to make it clear that the commission should do its bidding, Congress set all the commissioners' terms for expiration on February 23, 1929. The message from Congress seemed to be, "Get it done in a year or we'll get new commissioners."

With all of the apparent opposition to the Davis Amendment, why did this version of the reauthorization bill emerge from committee and pass? Rosen suggests that it passed to appease southerners who threatened to delay a vote on the reauthorization legislation. It may be that some members worried that a defunct FRC would mean that the United States would plunge further into broadcasting chaos without a regulatory body. Legislators did not want to face that eventuality, and since the commission's authority had already expired, this appeasement may have been the expedient political accommodation necessary to reinstate the FRC. Other members of Congress were concerned that without passage of the reauthorization, administration of radio would revert back into the hands of the Department of Commerce.[40]

THE DAVIS AMENDMENT AND THE ALLOCATION PLAN

With the passage of the amendment, the commission members now faced the problem of implementing a plan they had publicly criticized. However, faced with the reality of the situation, the commission had to formulate a plan to meet the specific requirements of the amendment. Louis Caldwell, chief counsel of the Federal Radio Commission, wrote, "[I]t would be hard to conceive of a more baffling problem than the one which Congress imposed upon the Federal Radio Commission by the so-called Davis Amendment."[41] Caldwell complained that before the amendment the act allowed the commission a certain latitude in making its license distribution among the different states; the flexibility was now gone because of the rigid requirements set forth by the new language.

Nevertheless, faced with the specific requirements of the Davis Amendment, the FRC undertook steps to devise an allocation policy that would bring station assignments into compliance with the newly amended radio act. There was disagreement among the commissioners as to the precise meaning of the amendment. The majority of the commission construed it as requiring immediate reallocation of the broadcast band, while Commissioner Ira Robinson claimed the amendment required the FRC to adopt a policy to be followed in the future where equalization would be attained wherever possible. The commission also grappled with the question of whether the amendment required an equality of the number of licensed stations without regard to division of time or whether two or more stations dividing time could be balanced against one full-time station in another zone.[42] Each interpretation created a problem for the FRC, since each interpretation called for a different engineering calculus.

At the end of March a working group from the Institute of Radio Engineers (IRE) submitted a memorandum to the commission describing a plan for classifying the ninety broadcast channels into three groups of licenses. The plan called for the creation of national, regional, and local broadcasting services. Under this scheme licensees would be apportioned equally to all five zones.[43] The study was reported out on April 6, 1928, when the commission asked radio engineers, under the supervision of Dr. J. H. Dellinger of the U.S. Bureau of Standards, for their recommendations to implement the allocation plan.[44]

Also during this time the Federal Radio Commission began to solicit the expert opinion from members of the Institute of Radio Engineers, such as L. E. Whittemore, in addition to using experts at the U.S. Bureau of Standards, Captain Guy Hill from the Army Signal Corps, and the other engineers from consultative or technical groups.[45] The obvious complications of the equalization clause required the commission to attempt to become more sophisticated in its approach to solving the radio interference problem. But now the commission found itself facing increasing pressure from Congress.[46]

By April 1928 the initial plan proposed by the Institute of Radio Engineers was fleshed out. Briefly, the plan created a zone-based allotment scheme for the ninety channels available in the standard broadcast band. It called for the creation of fifty high-powered stations that would operate on "cleared channels." Ten stations were to be assigned to each zone of the country. Because these stations were assigned the sole use of the channel (clear channel) during the nighttime, no heterodyne interference would occur, and reception of these high-powered stations would reach into the farthest sections of rural America. The remaining thirty-six channels would be divided between stations that served the regional and local needs of the various zones. Each zone would receive ten of these secondary channels. Because these secondary stations were lower in power, engineers believed it would be possible to assign more than one station to each region of the country.[47]

The IRE's plan did not meet with widespread approval from either Congress or the broadcasting industry. There were two major problems with the plan. First, it called for a maximum of 340 stations, which was a reduction of nearly 350 stations from the current allocation. Secondly, new higher-powered clear channel stations did not fit into the scheme envisioned by members of Congress seeking to appease their constituents. Ewin Davis, author of the equalization amendment, lamented that "the tentative plan is overloaded with so-called national stations."[48] Later that April the National Association of Broadcasters, the Federal Radio Trades Association, and the Radio Manufacturers' Association proposed a wholly different interpretation of the Davis Amendment. The NAB, fearing a reduction in the number of licenses, offered a plan that attempted to maintain the status quo of assignments as much as possible. The National Electric Manufacturers' Association (NEMA) and other broadcasting station groups also submitted various allocation plans to the commission.[49] No one plan seemed to meet the specific requirements of the equal allocation clause. While the IRE's plan seemed to have the inside track because it had the support of J. H. Dellinger, the *New York Times* reported members of the National Association of Broadcasters were disenchanted with the proposal, calling it too theoretical. The NAB and NEMA also called for an investigation of the agreements made by members of the radio trust.[50]

Why was a logically designed plan, incorporating some of the best engineering theory of the day, unacceptable to those with political or industry influence? There were major obstacles to implementing the engineers' proposed solution. First, equalization would require the commission either to target zones with more stations and reduce the number of licenses in those zones, or to increase the number of licenses in the zones that were underserved, thereby increasing the number of stations and the interference level overall. The former plan would rile Congress by eliminating many constituent radio stations. And while the latter plan might be politically expedient, it would not eliminate the interference problems that the FRC was created to resolve. In either case, there was also some concern that whatever plan was adopted, the plan would permanently freeze the number of broadcasting stations.

Similarly, the equalization clause required making the number of licenses allotted to the various zones proportional to the populations of the states within each zone. Thus it was possible that even though a zone may have the correct number of licenses, once the FRC decided whether to increase or decrease the number of licenses, the zones would have to redistribute those licenses among the states if their number did not reflect the correct population ratios. Further, while the engineer group's scheme began to address one of the equalization requirements of the Davis Amendment, the division of power allocations among the zones, their plan also needed to address station power and time division within the zone and among the states based on population.[51]

The FRC felt obligated to start the process of reducing the number of licenses in order to implement the new allotment scheme.[52] General Order 32, issued on May 25, 1928, asked for 164 broadcasting stations to show cause as to why they should continue to be licensed. Most of these stations were located in highly populated states in the East and Midwest. No stations from the South were included in the order. Over the summer a number of licenses were disposed, and other stations included in this group had their hours of operation or power sharply curtailed.[53] While the engineering staff under Dellinger grappled with the difficult problems posed by the equalization clause, the commission provided an outwardly visible demonstration that it was dealing with the questions of allocation and division of service by eliminating small and marginal broadcasters.[54] Ready to avoid controversy for its actions, the FRC issued two lengthy documents on August 23 and September 1, 1928, describing the commission's application of a vague public interest standard in reviewing the stations examined in General Order 32.[55]

Hugh Slotten contends that the engineers' view became dominant because key members of the commission believed that rancorous political debate would be avoided if the solution were based primarily on the use of technical reason. Engineers interpreted the "public interest" standard as one that provided the best possible service based on engineering standards and technical efficiency.[56] Since Congress failed to define the meaning of "public interest," the technical definition could be construed as easily as any other definition. Supporting this thesis is the fact that some commission members argued that equalization and reallocation were fundamentally technical problems demanding technological solutions.[57]

Slotten's thesis is enticing but not wholly supported by the engineering facts reported in the Federal Radio Commission's annual reports for 1928 through 1931. For example, the broadcast section of the FRC's annual reports of 1930 and 1931 under C. B. Jolliffe and V. Ford Greaves details a much more complex matrix of engineering data than previously included under Dellinger in General Order 40. Also, the commission abandoned the quota system that it applied in 1928. Starting with General Order 92, issued June 17, 1930, a "unit system" of evaluation to determine equalization compliance was adopted that included information about type of channel, power, hours of operation, and other considerations. The unit system provided a richer data set for analysis, but it also provided some indication that true equalization would never be achieved.[58]

GENERAL ORDER 40:
MAKING LEMONADE OUT OF A LEMON

On August 30, 1928, the Federal Radio Commission issued General Order 40, a plan outlining a quota system for the reallocation of broadcasting stations. Immediately the commission began a public relations offensive to convince politicians, broadcasters, and the public alike that the scheme was the best possible solution to meet the equalization requirements specified in the amendment.[59] On September 4, 1928, Chief Engineer J. H. Dellinger submitted a memorandum to engineers detailing the principles of the allocation plan. Three days later Dellinger issued a second engineering analysis of the plan. The second analysis, made by John V. L. Hogan, a well-known radio consulting engineer, supported Dellinger's engineering assertions. Hogan states: "I feel you and your Commissioners are to be congratulated upon having withstood criticism until this time when you are prepared to rearrange the broadcasters with the least possible disturbance of established services and the greatest improvement of the status of listeners, consistent with the law."[60]

Dellinger's memoranda and the supporting engineering opinions are significant for several reasons. First, they were meant to reassure those broadcasters who survived the earlier round of cuts that the status quo would be maintained as much as possible by providing a permanent, definite basis of station assignments for each zone and locality. Thus, any station that survived the license hearings of the past summer would find an allocation on the allotment table under General Order 40.[61] Second, Dellinger outlined a strategy for implementing forty high-powered stations on clear channels, a plan meant to bring greater listening choice to rural America while further entrenching the interests of the radio trust. Third, the plan placed several blocks of regional and local services on different parts of the dial to minimize interchannel interference. This reallocation allowed larger metropolitan areas to have more station assignments. Finally, by using the "borrowing" clause of the Davis Amendment, some commissioners hoped to keep licenses for stations in zones that were currently over quota by borrowing those frequencies from other states in the same zone that were under quota. This maneuver was meant to placate broadcasters and audiences in metropolitan areas who were used to having a diverse number of stations to choose from.[62]

While the plan implemented guidelines specified in the report of the Institute of Radio Engineers generally, General Order 40 specifically acknowledged the importance of meeting its political obligations as well as adhering to the commission's earlier decision that no existing stations would be abolished as a result of the new allocation. To reinforce the notion that it was meeting its responsibilities as a regulatory arm of Congress, the FRC's second annual report specifically outlined the outcome of license reductions as part of its attempt to meet the requirements of the Davis Amendment. Documents of the commission show that this strategy was developed in August before the actual announcement of General Order 40.[63]

In implementing the equalization plan, the FRC needed to meet specific regulatory requirements in the act allowing stations an opportunity to appeal the frequency assignment change if they were displeased with their new frequency. Such a move would reduce litigation and possible court challenges to the allocation scheme. The commission stated it would give stations an opportunity to examine the new assignments and challenge the potential changes; thus, all station licenses were extended until November 11, 1928. The details of the plan were sent to broadcast licensees on September 11. In that memorandum, Acting Chairman Sykes tried to assure broadcasters that the order was a starting point, not a final solution. "[I]t is the desire of the Commission that any broadcasting station which is dissatisfied with its assignment under the reallocation should have an opportunity to be heard and to demonstrate that public interest, convenience or necessity would be served by a better assignment," he notes.[64] In addition to proffering goodwill for the new plan and hoping to head off numerous court challenges, the commission wanted to examine the effects of the reallocation, which up to this point were only theorized on paper. A second temporary licensing period was established to allow the engineering staff time to correct unforeseen problems after the stations moved to their new frequency assignment.[65]

The commission used several strategies to disseminate positive information about the equalization plan to the general public. For example, the October issue of *Congressional Digest* was given over entirely to a discussion of the problems of radio reallocation. On the day of the reallocation, Commissioner Orestes Caldwell issued a lengthy statement to the public stressing several previously mentioned points that: (1) engineering experts created the plan, (2) small-town and remote listeners would benefit greatly, (3) dissatisfied broadcasters could challenge the assignment, and (4) some time would be required to evaluate the effects of the change.[66] At the same time, Dellinger issued a press release attempting to explain the benefits of the plan to both general and technically sophisticated readers. In the *New York Herald Tribune,* Dellinger suggested that listeners would find it helpful to make lists of the old and new dial assignments side-by-side for easy comparison, while in the *Journal of the Institute for Radio Engineers* he analyzed the allocation scheme for the technically minded.[67]

Outwardly the commission appeared pleased with the response to reallocation, although almost immediately following the announcement of General Order 40 numerous complaints were filed with the commission. Boasting about the benefits of the new allocation scheme under General Order 40, Commissioner O. H. Caldwell stated: "Congress handed us a lemon and we have proceeded to make lemonade out of it."[68] Immediately following the issuance of the commission's reallocation scheme, broadcasting stations began to protest the plan. Many complained that the plan did not constitute an equalization as required by the Davis Amendment. The commission had to set several hundred cases for hearing. Meanwhile political pressure mounted in Congress at the same time as various interest groups expressed displeasure with General Order 40. On November 22, 1928, a resolution passed requiring the FRC to report back to the Senate on or before December 15, 1929, detailing the number of licenses, power allocations, number of frequencies, and periods of time for operation among all five zones.[69]

AFTER EQUALIZATION:
ANALYSIS OF THE COMMISSION'S CHOICES

Analysis of the implementation of General Order 40 poses several problems for broadcast historians and legal, science, or political policy analysts. Mark Gilderhaus reminds us that the historian displays a bias through the mere choice of subject matter.[70] What the historian chooses reflects what he or she thinks is important. Yet, public interest theory, the basis upon which we provide assessment of regulatory success or failure, is predicated precisely on those fault lines—for example, on interpretive views of the events, legislative histories, the people circumscribing the agencies, and the specific laws analyzed during specific time periods. Robert Brett Horwitz notes that within this perspective, the public interest is assessed as either a theoretical standard or as a historical fact of the regulatory agency's birth.[71]

The Federal Radio Commission's birth was a difficult one. It was the result of rancorous debate, inadequate funding, and political manipulation. The FRC was created to deal with immediate and long-term structural problems. Thus, given the circumstances of the commission's birth, the amazing growth of radio as a means of communication and as a social institution, and the powerful lobbying interests of the radio trust and the NAB, the implementation of the Davis Amendment provides significant material to analyze. Several different theoretical frameworks provide potential for conceptualizing the importance of the events, for analyzing their long-term significance, and for explaining the behavior of the regulating agency.[72] Public interest theory provides us with the opportunity to view the events surrounding the implementation of the Davis Amendment as that of the resolution between the conflict of the needs of private corporations and the needs of the general public. We could deduce this based on the above-stated history surrounding the passage of the Davis Amendment.

While applying public interest theory would allow the reader a historical understanding of those events, the application of such an analysis fails to provide a richness of detail in defining the various influences that played upon the commission. For example, the growth of the radio industry during the 1920s seems to fail to conform to the mold of the small, individual producer as embodied in the Jeffersonian idealism of public interest theory. During this time, radio was primarily controlled by large industrialized companies such as RCA, Westinghouse, AT&T, and General Electric.[73]

The application of the "progressive" phase of public interest theory reflects the altered economic conditions created by large corporations, situations not unlike the growth of radio during the period leading up to the formation of the FRC; but the technical interference problems and the "equalization" requirements of the Davis Amendment effectively remove this means of analysis as a viable explanation for the promulgation of regulatory policy as embodied in General Order 40. On the face of it, the specific actions of the FRC generally seem to support the large radio interests as opposed to reflecting the work of an interventionist-type commission designed to protect powerless consumers.[74] Thus, the FRC does not seem to act like the Federal Trade Commission or other similar regulatory agencies.

In "Four Systems of Policy, Politics, and Choice," Theodore J. Lowi defines a model of capture theory that details likely policy outcomes based on the influences and types of coercion applied in given circumstances. This kind of analysis is useful because it allows one to look at the behavior of the actors and apply a schema to explain the events or outcomes as a result of the application of coercion, policy directives, or politics upon the regulating body. Lowi describes the four potential policies (and illustrations of their political effects) that had to be adopted by an independent commission such as the Federal Radio Commission as a result of the various potential influences as being:

- *Distributive policy* (e.g., nineteenth-century land policies, tariffs, subsidies)
- *Constituent policy* (e.g., reapportionment, setting up a new regulatory agency, propaganda)
- *Regulatory policy* (e.g., elimination of substandard goods, unfair competition, fraudulent corporate behavior)
- *Redistributive policy* (e.g., Federal controls of credit, social security)

Under such a schema, if one looked at the policy it would be possible to gauge the immediate influences upon that policy or upon trying to change that policy. For instance, distributive policy would be likely to influence individual conduct as opposed to the environment of conduct throughout a whole segment of an industry or industrial sector.[75]

To apply this schema to the Federal Radio Commission, one could analyze the nature of radio licensing and assess its potential benefit to the licensee. After doing so, it is possible to deduce the type of policies being applied to the broadcasting industry. For example, one could analyze the effects of the application of federal policy with the onset of radio licensing starting about 1912. The Radio Act of 1912 provided for little regulatory oversight. Licensing, primarily a record-keeping function assigned to the commerce department, would be considered "distributive" policy. In this case government is giving away (or licensing) a property right. The determinations made for a distributive policy type generally depend on individual conduct (e.g., is the applicant a suitable license holder?). One would conclude that the likelihood of coercion upon the policy maker, the giver of the license, is as remote as the likelihood of coercion by the government upon the licensee. Since the secretary of commerce essentially granted radio licenses when the individual or party applied for one, we can see that in real life little coercion would have been applied. Why? The answer is that no test was required for licensing and the license was not a limited resource in 1912.

Using this schema to look at changes in the types of policy illustrates that the Federal Radio Commission's actions do not fall into the regulatory policy arena as easily as the policies of other governmental agencies such as the Federal Trade Commission (FTC) or the Interstate Commerce Commission (ICC). Both the FTC and ICC were created to use "regulatory policy" to eliminate unfair practices or reduce the problematic of poorly made or unsafe goods. Clearly the FTC could apply coercion to firms through the use of "cease and desist orders" and "consent decrees." Similarly, the trust-busting ability of the FTC could move to decentralize and disaggregate large trusts.[76] Applying Lowi's schema illustrates the fact that there is a great likelihood of pressure or coercion applied to the regulatory agency when large trusts attempt to maintain the status quo.

The plight of the FRC appears somewhat different from traditional regulatory agencies, though, when we attempt to plot the influences on it. The 1927 Federal Radio Commission found itself in a different situation than the secretary of commerce did in 1912. For example, if the FRC attempted to use "regulatory" policy to break up the increasingly powerful radio trust, it was likely to face the threat of immediate coercion from considerable lobby efforts of the powerful corporations involved in the radio trust. Worse yet, because the FRC was not a permanently established independent regulatory commission, it found itself heavily influenced by various "constituent" policy initiatives of Congress since it faced a yearly renewal. Many in Congress were looking for the FRC to reapportion frequencies favorable to them—a bit of redistributive policy with a constituent interest bent. Conversely, other members of Congress from the East and Midwest looked to maintaining the status quo. Still others looked for the agency to develop policies that would permit local stations to transmit without the interference problems that plagued radio after 1926. There appeared to be no clear-cut constituent decision the commission could adopt that would please the majority of Congress. And educational leaders were interested in having the FRC develop redistributive policies that would create the necessary conditions for the long-term growth of radio for educational and informational purposes. Other special interest groups wanted to affect policy too. Commercial interests wanted to maintain the current system of broadcasting, ensuring the growth of powerful radio networks.

The divergent set of interests provided too many countervailing pressures on the infant, unstable Federal Radio Commission. As noted earlier, it was necessary for the commission to respond to party pressures and interest group pressures of various congressional constituents, mindful that Congress had (1) failed to confirm several commissioners who were friendly to Hoover,

(2) failed to provide funds for the agency's operation, and (3) anticipated that the commission would expire at the end of its term of appointment. Redrafting Lowi's four types of policies, showing the potential outcomes of such policies, would look like this:

- *Distributive*—granting new licenses and new classes of services
- *Constituent*—reapportioning radio licenses to meet constituent needs and desires
- *Regulatory*—regulating network behavior, regulating against unwanted advertising, instituting new ownership requirements
- *Redistributive*—asserting new federal licensing controls to ensure introduction of services not currently provided or to redirect current offerings to new constituents

Within the framework of this redrawn policy schema, one can conclude that the Federal Radio Commission is caught between several competing factions. The traditional congressional needs versus special interests needs are obvious. On one hand, some congressional members, such as Ewin Davis from the South, are applying constituent coercion on the commissioners and would like to see the commission equalize the number of radio licenses between the northern U.S. cities and southern cities. The pressures put on the commission by the congressional membership follows traditional logrolling behavior. Adoption of the Davis Amendment's equalization language requires the FRC to act to meet the regional needs of the South and the West. Other congressmen, such as Congressman Dill, wanted the commission to redistribute the radio spectrum for special interests such as alternative and educational users. Different interest groups applying various forms of lobbying pressure would try to force the commission to move in a specific policy direction. In choosing any political solution, the Federal Radio Commission would be forced to favor one interest group at the expense of another, regardless of which policy it chose.

The FRC was faced with many potential influences outside of Congress as well. The radio trust and some members of the NAB were at odds over potential regulatory policies for radio broadcasting. RCA, for example, was anxious to contain the application of FRC policy that could hamper the sales of radio receivers, since it held the patents on the devices or circuits needed to build radios. For example, licensing fees as a means of paying for programs, such as those imposed by Great Britain, were seen as a deterrent to the sale of radio receivers. And by 1927, the members of the radio trust held the most powerful radio stations, developed chain broadcasting, and had the engineering expertise to improve these stations quickly and dramatically.[77] RCA opposed constituent and redistributive policies that disfavored large stations and its radio network. Obversely, smaller broadcasters were afraid of the potential and power of the RCA trust. These smaller NAB members needed substantial revenues from advertising sales to build and expand their program offerings and broadcast facilities. These different factions attempted to coerce the FRC into adopting policies favorable to local or affiliated stations. While RCA would have favored a regulatory commission to ensure high engineering standards and the elimination of smaller nuisance stations, smaller NAB members would have favored a redistributive policy that required the delivery of programming at the local level.

The FRC tried to avoid upsetting the large station interests of the big broadcasters while at the same time trying to please the party or regional constituents' interests of Congress.[78] This strategy can be seen in the allocation scheme devised for General Order 40. The best channels favored large broadcast interests through the creation of "clear channel" station allotments, while the less powerful regional and local channel allotments could mollify many listeners concerned about their favorite local affiliated stations.[79] Given those countervailing forces, the strategy for implementing General Order 32 can be seen clearly. General Order 32 essentially reduced or eliminated marginal stations, including educational and special interest or "propaganda" stations as the FRC referred to them. As a result of the FRC's general policies and the implementation of General Order 32, these stations found their power levels slashed and their hours of operation sharply curtailed. Clearly the actions of the commission are traced along the regulatory and redistributive trajectory; by reducing the influences of special interest groups such as educators and religious groups, the commission eliminated some of the complexity and pressure of resolving the equalization problem that faced them.

Lowi's taxonomy provides a useful way for using the historical record to assess the normative and empirical implications of radio regulation. This analysis contradicts the notion that implementation of the Davis Amendment would be best served using the very best engineering principles available. Looking at the outcomes, the implementation of the equalization principles becomes an amalgamation of both constituent and redistributive policies. For example, the intention to provide equalization of services to all regions of the country cuts across constituent boundaries. However, Davis's criticism of the commission for failing to reallocate power and frequency assignments of the large radio monopolies suggests the FRC should respond to Congress's desire to apply constituent policies, while Dill's criticism that the FRC had not acted boldly enough suggests redistributive policies. Similarly Congress's refusal to confirm Commissioners Caldwell and Bellows suggests that members of Congress were uneasy with the close relationship between those two nominees and the powerful radio industry that was closely aligned with Herbert Hoover. These policy assumptions indicate normative policy goals Congress would have considered in voting the legislation for equalization up or down. However, along with normative assumptions, were there congressional concerns about formative outcomes too? Did members of Congress assume that the likelihood of coercion on these commissioners would be so great that they would do the bidding of the radio trust? Such a fear demonstrates one of the classic problems associated with the public interest—capture theory.

In capture theory, any institution with sufficient political influence will attempt to manipulate the policies of the agency. This may be too simplistic an explanation to understand the decision-making processes of the FRC. Any specific policy the FRC developed to help only one segment of the industry, say the large radio trusts, would meet the disapproval of those congressmen who supported a different constituency, such as small, local stations. Again, the commission's actions suggest that it was being pulled along *several* paths simultaneously. At the end of the first year, the influences upon the commission did not diminish. With the addition of specific equalization requirements in the Davis Amendment, the task that lay before the commission was more complex politically and technically than ever. The Federal Radio Commission needed to develop an initiative that would free it from the constraints of developing a strategy for meeting the needs of just one of the four traditional sets of influences described above. Instead, the commission decided to focus on a technological solution to the administrative dilemma of having too many political interests clamoring for different policy solutions.

GENERAL ORDER 40: MIXING TECHNOLOGY WITH POLITICS

Capture theory can be applied to scientific assessments as well as political influence peddling. Sheila Jasanoff states that bias in scientific assessment is commonly the result of conscious deception by "experts" or of uncritical acceptance of the industry's viewpoint by agency officials.[80] Whatever regulations the Federal Radio Commission decided to effect regarding the interference problem, it was faced with the reality that broadcasting had established an important place in the social consciousness of America. Michal McMahon notes that by the time Congress established the FRC in 1927, advertising had become the dominant mode of financing, despite listener preferences for alternative ways to support radio programming.[81] Clearly the broadcasting networks had programming that the public wanted to listen to, and two members of the commission had industry ties. But it was the recommendations of the Institute of Radio Engineers that essentially assured the continuance of the large broadcasters by setting up the allocation scheme for large, powerful clear channel stations in each zone of the country. In many cases these large stations were already owned by or affiliated with the broadcasting networks, either NBC or the newly formed Columbia Broadcasting System.

The decision-making process, at first blush, was seemingly based on engineering principles, but it appears to be influenced by political and economic decisions, as well as engineering requirements. For example, during the first years of the FRC, Alfred Goldsmith was both president of the Institute of Radio Engineers and the chief broadcast engineer of RCA. Thus, the recommendations of the radio engineers presented to the commission must have reflected, at least to some degree, the beliefs of how to best deal with the interference problem from the perspective of the special committee and RCA's chief engineer.[82] Other members of the IRE committee that was set up to study the implementation of the Davis Amendment included C. W. Horn of Westinghouse Electric, R. H. Marriot of International News Corporation, and L. E. Whittemore of the Bureau of Standards.

Several members of the commission spoke against the acceptance of the recommendations of the engineers. On August 17, 1928, Louis Caldwell, general counsel, notes in a memorandum to the commissioners:

> 3 a. The small stations are *not* being treated well under the proposed reallocation: it is foolish to think that they will be fooled into believing the contrary. . . .
>
> 5. One manifest injustice in the proposed reallocation is the fact that on the whole all the so-called trust stations receive the very best treatment (in some cases the same corporation preserves two or three

full-time assignments on the best channels) while the big independent stations in the Middle West are forced to divide time.

7. As a matter of fact, even the proposed reallocation does not come anywhere near complying with the Davis Amendment, under the heading of equality in number of stations.[83]

Also taking issue with the engineers' report, Commissioner Sam Pickard, of Zone 4, wrote: "I feel it is unfortunate that my views on that subject (using the borrowing clause under equalization) are not shared by a majority of the Commission. . . . My apprehension is that the present effort to approach the ideal . . . abruptly limits the facilities of this zone to a margin where stations, previously recognized as rendering worthwhile service by this Commission, cannot exist."[84]

Representative Ewin Davis, author of the amendment, also took exception to the engineers' allocation scheme, writing: "[E]ven from the standpoint of getting the National Broadcasting Company chain programs to the various sections of the country, there is no occasion for granting to such stations a monopoly of power or desirable and cleared channels, not to speak of the fact that such an allocation would deprive stations broadcasting independent programs of the share to which they are entitled."[85]

Even after adoption of the allocation scheme, various influential people spoke out about the adoption of a commercially based system as mapped out by the IRE and adopted by the commission. Speaking to the American Academy of Air Law in April 1931, Bethuel Webster Jr., former general counsel to the Federal Radio Commission, stated: "One may praise many of the performances of the National Broadcasting, the Columbia Broadcasting System, and originated by some of the chain and a few of the unaffiliated stations, and at the same time deprecate legislative policy and administrative weakness that permit the use of the ether under federal franchise for self-advertising stunts, for the sale of quack medicine, and the exposition of religious or social creeds in which the public generally has no interest."[86] Whether or not the recommendations of the Institute of Radio Engineers represented the very best solution to the equalization clause conundrum embodied in the Davis Amendment is open to interpretation. Many debated the implementation and the outcomes until the commission finally abandoned enforcement of the amendment in 1932. The final outcome, an allotment scheme that provided radio stations of varying powers to serve the

United States, worked substantially well until after the heyday of AM radio. What is at issue is not whether the allocation scheme worked but whether the Federal Radio Commission exercised due diligence in accepting the policy recommendations of a body that was biased in favor of the industry that created it.

One could argue that the FRC did not have the ability to proceed in such a technical task, since it did not establish its own engineering department until after the recommendations of the Institute of Radio Engineers on August 17, 1928.[87] But that criticism would not reflect the reality that J. H. Dellinger, who was chief engineer at the Bureau of Standards, oversaw the commission's technical needs during the interim period and ultimately became the chief engineer for the commission. While Dellinger's title changed, his work responsibilities did not.

Perhaps of greater importance are the questions that revolve around the way the commission solicited and accepted scientific advice. Members of the scientific community use a variety of boundary-defining strategies to establish their authority and enhance their stature within scientific areas and their professional circle. This behavior can be traced in the relatively new, rapidly expanding field of electrical engineering. Members of the IRE did this by building professional communities that claimed expertise, defining and excluding nonmembers, competing for and asserting primacy of knowledge, and asserting their authority against those who held divergent opinions. For example, between 1915 and 1920 the IRE board, under its secretary, David Sarnoff, attempted to influence policy makers to keep radio in the hands of private capital. That effort continued as RCA's chief engineer, Alfred Goldsmith, succeeded Sarnoff as secretary and then as president of the IRE. McMahon says that IRE's pronouncements confidently stated that "government interference always impedes technological creativity. The Board's assertions left no room for exceptions."[88] Thus the IRE's policy pronouncements from 1915 through 1930 seemed to reinforce the agenda for corporate entities that ultimately became part of the RCA "radio trust."

During the 1930s historian Charles Beard noted that "few indeed are the duties of government in this age which can be discharged with the mere equipment of historic morals and commonsense. Whenever, with respect to any significant matter, Congress legislates, the Court interprets, and the President executes, they must have something more than good intentions; they must command technical competence."[89] In this case, the building of a national broadcasting system really required significant regulation before the technical knowledge existed on how best to build and regulate it. Perhaps McMahon provides the best overview of the significance of the IRE's role in the technical decision-making process when he concludes that in addition to participating in the invention and development of radio, engineers made it feasible for corporate leaders to achieve vast organizational and physical systems. They shaped both the bureaucratic context in which they worked and, in part, the social uses of the technology they helped to create.[90]

Does the analysis of the political and technological implications of the Davis Amendment hold significance and meaning for regulators and policy makers of today, particularly in areas where technology is rapidly changing the environment to be regulated? In *The Fifth Branch,* Jasanoff says the notion that the scientific component of decision making can be separated from the political and entrusted to independent experts has been discredited. To prove useful, those making regulatory decisions need to be informed by an accurate knowledge of the internal dynamics of *both* science and regulation. She cautions that however rhetorically appealing it may be, no simple formula exists to allow for injecting expert opinion into public policy debate.[91] This caution should be inscribed for future communication policy makers to remember. In recent years the courts have often viewed FCC decisions as arbitrary and capricious, frequently lacking in sufficient economic or technological analysis to become the basis for viable regulation.

Today the Federal Communications Commission faces technical, political, social, and economic pressures both when establishing new services and when redirecting policy efforts for established services. The pace of innovation of technology again calls in to question the ability of regulators to make adequate decisions about which technologies hold promise for consumers and at what cost, what the effects of implementing new technology might be, and what impact these choices will have on current broadcast and telecommunications institutions. In many ways, the same pressures on policy makers existed during the formative period of the Federal Radio Commission. The passage of the Davis Amendment provided us with substantive material to analyze the external influences on policy making. Scholars could apply similar analysis to current FCC issues such as digital must-carry, multiple-ownership rules, and a host of other contemporary regulatory problems.

While the intent of the Davis Amendment was to create a legislative mandate for the FRC to treat different geographical areas of the United States with equality, in reality it allowed the commission little flexibility for developing a long-term plan for expanded services via radio. The amendment was repealed on June 5, 1936, allowing the FCC to expand services to meet the needs of new population areas around the country.[92]

Regulation restricts users' choice of activities and outcomes through the institutional consolidation of legislative, executive, and judicial power in the single apparatus of independent commission. The mode of action can be informal through the companion use of consultative bodies; the adjudication is flexible on a case-by-case basis; and the rule-making procedures can be formal, defining the way participation in a proceeding will occur. Given the ability of the institution to set rules, the complex interaction of influences on the regulatory process, and the flexible authority of the independent commission, scholars and consumers alike would be well advised to understand the contingent and socially constructed character of regulatory decision making.

NOTES

1. Susan J. Douglas, *Inventing American Broadcasting, 1899–1922* (Baltimore, MD: Johns Hopkins UP, 1987), xix.

2. See Theodore Lowi, *The End of Liberalism*, 2nd. ed. (New York: Norton, 1979). Also see Robert Britt Horwitz, *The Irony of Regulatory Reform: The Deregulation of American Telecommunications* (New York: Oxford UP, 1989), 31.

3. Karl Popper, "Prediction and Prophecy in the Social Sciences," in *Theories of History* (New York: Free Press, 1959), 276–85.

4. Robert W. McChesney, *Telecommunications, Mass Media, and Democracy: The Battle for the Control of U.S. Broadcasting, 1928–1935* (Oxford: Oxford UP, 1993), 18–21.

5. Christopher H. Sterling and John M. Kittross, *Stay Tuned: A Concise History of American Broadcasting* (Belmont, CA: Wadsworth, 1990), 111.

6. See Philip T. Rosen, *The Modern Stentors: Radio Broadcasting and the Federal Government, 1920–1934* (Westport, CT: Greenwood Press, 1980). Rosen looks at the beginning of radio broadcasting and its relationship to government over an expansive time period, covering the FRC's implementation of the Davis Amendment as a small part of the total work. Louise Benjamin's wonderfully documented book *Freedom of the Air and the Public Interest: First Amendment Rights in Broadcasting to 1935* (Carbondale: Southern Illinois UP, 2001) reviews the passage of the Radio Act of 1927 in light of the issues of freedom of the air, and *Congressional Digest*'s October 1928 edition takes on

the Davis Amendment controversy by describing the problems involved in implementing the specific requirements of the amendment (*Congressional Digest,* vol. 7, no. 10 [October 1928], 255–86).

7. Federal Radio Commission, *First Annual Report,* from Annual Reports, Numbers 1–7, 1927–1933. Washington, DC: U.S. Government Printing Office.

8. *United States v. Zenith Radio Corporation,* 12 F2nd 614 (1926).

9. Theodore J. Lowi, "Four Systems of Policy, Politics, and Choice," *Public Administration Review,* Summer 1972, 299.

10. Dixon Merrit, "To Unscramble the Air," *Outlook* 145, January 19, 1927, 75–76.

11. It appears that Congress understood the problems involved in this area. See Committee on Interstate Commerce, Sixty-ninth Congress, Report 772, May 6, 1926: "If the channels of radio transmission were unlimited in number, the importance of the regulatory body would be greatly lessened, but these channels are limited and restricted in number and the decision as to who shall be permitted to use them and on what terms and for what periods of time."

12. McChesney, *Telecommunications,* 16. On December 7, 1926, President Coolidge said, "[T]he whole service of this most important public function has drifted into such chaos as seems likely, if not remedied, to destroy its [radio's] great value. I urgently recommend that this legislation should be speedily enacted." See *Congressional Digest,* 257.

13. Public Act No. 632, 69th Congress, 2nd Session, February 23, 1927. "An act for the regulation of radio communications." Evidently both of the original bills appeared to be flawed in granting the regulatory party sufficient control or power over the licensee. The ABA noted that neither "deals adequately with the difficult problem of reducing interference" and that both bills ought to be amended "so as to provide for closing up superfluous stations and for paying just compensation to them." Air Law Committee, "Interim Report on Radio Legislation," *American Bar Association Journal,* vol. 12, no. 12 (December 1926), 848. For a discussion of the debate prior to passage of the act, see chapter 5 of Benjamin, *Freedom of the Air.*

14. Public Act No. 632, 69th Congress, 2nd Session, February 23, 1927. The law created a five-member panel appointed to overlapping six-year terms. Each commissioner was to be responsible for a geographical zone encompassing a large section of the country. However, the original authorization bill expired one year after passage. The Congress needed to reauthorize the commission in 1928. In 1929 Congress extended the commission indefinitely. See *Congressional Digest,* 265.

15. The commissioners included Rear Admiral W. H. G. Bullard for the second zone, Judge Eugene O. Sykes for the third zone, and Orestes H. Caldwell for the first zone. Both Henry A. Bellows of Minneapolis for the fourth zone and John F. Dillion for the fifth zone were confirmed by Congress. Though Caldwell actively sought appointment, he was not confirmed by the Sixty-ninth Congress. (*The Outlook* says that the

objection to both Caldwell and Bellows, according to Dill, was they were seen to be under the influence of Hoover. See *Outlook* 145, no. 12, March 23, 1927, 356.) According to Barnouw, Caldwell decided to start work under his interim appointment, without salary, hoping to be confirmed in the next session of Congress. Erik Barnouw, *A Tower in Babel: A History of Broadcasting in the United States,* vol. 1, *to 1933* (New York: Oxford UP, 1966), 213. Several other governmental agencies lent support to the orphaned commission. From the Department of Agriculture, Sam Pickard became the commission's secretary. The U.S. Navy lent the services of Captain Stanford Hooper, while the Department of Commerce offered the services of John H. Dellinger, chief of the department's radio division. See Benjamin, *Freedom of the Air,* 77.

16. Minutes of Discussion of the Federal Radio Commission, April 29,1927, National Archives and Records Administration (hereafter NA), RG-173, Box 128, DOA-Executive Director, General Correspondence.

17. McChesney, *Telecommunications,* 19.

18. General Order 11. Issued by the Federal Radio Commission, May 21, 1927, NA, RG-173, Box 128, DOA-Executive Director, General Correspondence. While it does not call for the elimination of any stations, the FRC clearly states that it believes elimination of interference can be accomplished only by reducing the number of broadcasting stations by 40 percent. General Order 11 draws special attention to the fact that there are no unallocated frequencies from which to draw upon. Hence, the commission indicates that it will be reassigning many stations to different frequencies.

19. Laurence F. Schmeckebier, *The Federal Radio Commission: Its History, Activities, and Organization,* Service Monographs of the United States Government, no. 65 (Washington, DC: Brookings Institution, 1932), 23.

20. Federal Radio Commission, *Annual Report,* 9.

21. Minutes of the Federal Radio Commission, June 7, 1927, NA, RG-173, Box 128, DOA-Executive Director, General Correspondence; General Order 19 issued by the Federal Radio Commission, November 14, 1927, NA, RG-173, Box 128, DOA-Executive Director, General Correspondence. Note that Special Order 211 issued by the Federal Radio Commission effected the reassignment of many stations to help with the interference problem in rural areas. See Federal Radio Commission, Special Order 211, November 16, 1927, NA, RG-173, Box 128, DOA-Executive Director, General Correspondence.

22. United States Congress, House of Representatives, Committee on the Merchant Marine and Fisheries, *Hearings on the Federal Radio Commission,* 70th Congress, 1st Session, January 26, 1928, 3.

23. This statement is not meant to suggest that the FRC had no plan or organizational conception of what it wanted to accomplish. For example, one of its first actions was to place all stations on even ten-kilocycle spacing. Similarly, during the summer of 1927 the FRC separated stations in the same locality by at least five channels. Both of

these techniques required some overarching plan. However, most problems were examined on a case-by-case basis. See "How the Federal Radio Commission Brought Order out of Chaos," *Congressional Digest,* 266.

24. See General Orders 10, 11, 12; Special Orders 5, 6, 7, 8, 9, Special Order 211. Federal Radio Commission, (various dates) NA, RG-173, Box 128, DOA-Executive Director, General Correspondence; see also J. M. Herring, "Equalization of Broadcasting Facilities within the United States," *Harvard Business Review* 9 (1930): 417–30.

25. "Urges Fixing Power of the Radio Board," *New York Times,* January 31, 1928, 18.

26. Rosen, *Modern Stentors,* 129. See also Schmeckebier, *Federal Radio Commission,* 25. And *Time* magazine wrote that the large broadcast interests would be displeased with the actions of Congress during the reauthorization of the FRC because: "[T]he effect may be to cut the franchises of the rich, long-established stations in New and Chicago zones to benefit the Southern and lower-Midwestern stations" ("Radio: Opportunity for Service," *Time,* April 9, 1928, 45).

27. United States Congress, House of Representatives, Committee on the Merchant Marine and Fisheries, *Report on the Federal Radio Commission to Accompany S. 2317. Report No. 800,* 70th Congress, 1st Session, February 29, 1928, 2.

28. Barnouw, *Tower in Babel,* 215.

29. Rosen, *Modern Stentors,* 129.

30. United States Congress, *Hearings on the Federal Radio Commission,* 31.

31. "Senate Demands Radio Bill Parley," *New York Times,* March 14, 1928, 6–7.

32. "Radio Men to Fight Bill in Washington," *New York Times,* March 7, 1928, 30.

33. "Radio War Rages Around 'Equal Division' Amendment," *New York Times,* March 4, 1928, 19; "Ides of March Loom as Day Approaches," *New York Times,* March 11, 1928, 15.

34. "Battle in Congress Opens on Radio Bill," *New York Times,* March 2, 1928, 22.

35. *Congressional Digest,* 268.

36. Minutes of the meeting of the Federal Radio Commission, February 17, 1928, NA, RG-173, Box 128, DOA-Executive Director, General Correspondence.

37. *New York Times,* March 4, 1928, 19. It should be noted that the *New York Times* was probably not an impartial observer. Since its main readership was the people of New York City, the *Times* reflected the indignation that the city might lose some radio stations during a reallocation of the Davis Amendment. See "Radio Men Unmoved by Davis Measure," *New York Times,* March 3, 1928, 10.

38. After a prolonged debate, the bill passed 235 to 135. The vote was split along geographical lines, with the majority of the opposition from the heavily populated states of the East and Midwest. See Schmeckebier, *Federal Radio Commission,* 28.

39. 45 Stat. L., 373, section 9.

40. Rosen, *Modern Stentors,* 130.

41. *Congressional Digest,* 262.

42. Federal Radio Commission, *Second Annual Report,* 12.

43. Ibid., 13.

44. "Report of Radio Engineers to the Federal Radio Commission," *Journal of the Institute of Electrical Engineers* 17(1928): 556. See also Press Release of the Federal Radio Commission, April 11, 1928, NA, RG-173, Box 128, DOA-Executive Director, General Correspondence. When the FRC came into being in 1927, it used the same techniques that the secretary of commerce had used in the National Radio Conference of the 1920s. Then the commission asked broadcasters for input to a possible solution to the interference problem. See Federal Radio Commission, *Second Annual Report,* 3. However, most of the input reflected commercial broadcasting interests. See McChesney, *Telecommunications,* 19.

45. Minutes of the meeting of the Federal Radio Commission, April 11, 1928, NA, RG-173, Box 128, DOA-Executive Director, General Correspondence.

46. At one oversight hearing, Chairman Ira Robinson complained of "political pressure constantly exercised . . . in all manner of cases" by members of Congress. See Schmeckebier, *Federal Radio Commission,* 57. This pressure, coupled with Congress's passage of the one-year-term clause in the 1928 reauthorization certainly illustrated the coercive potential of the legislature on the independent body. See Barnouw, *Tower in Babel,* 217.

47. Federal Radio Commission, Press Release.

48. Federal Radio Commission, *Second Annual Report,* Appendix "E," 133.

49. Ibid., 142–50. J. H. Dellinger attempted to discredit the plan submitted by the National Association of Broadcasters because it strayed too far from engineering considerations. In writing an analysis of the broadcasters' plan, Dellinger wrote: "Several speakers at the hearing emphasized that engineering considerations are not the only ones involved, and that other matters, financial problems, local conditions, etc. make some of the engineering recommendations impracticable. While it is true that the problem of broadcast allocation is too complex to be solved by straight engineering calculation, nevertheless its solution can not be right if it disregards any valid engineering principle."

50. "Radio Allies Offer Allocation Plan," *New York Times,* April 23, 1928, 18.

51. Federal Radio Commission. *Second Annual Report,* Appendix "E." "Summary of the conference of engineers on April 6, 1928, by J. H. Dellinger," 133. Dellinger states: "[S]ince the law requires equality of the number of hours and licenses among the zones, and, according to population, among the States within each zone, if time is divided on a given channel among several stations in any one State, this division must be duplicated on some channel in every other zone and proportionally in every State." Note that Dellinger says that the requirement for equalization is based on zones and the allocation of the licenses and power levels of the states within the zones.

52. Increasing the number of stations as a political expedient would have required the FRC to rescind General Orders 92 and 102, which set forth the method by which

equalization would be brought about. General Order 102 prohibited the FRC from allocating more stations to zones that already used its prorated share of facilities.

53. Federal Radio Commission, *Second Annual Report,* 150.

54. While Commissioner La Fount moved for the adoption of the basic principles of the Engineer's Plan on July 24, this was really a formality, since the commission had been working on the basic plan since April (Harold A. Lafount, Memorandum, July 24, 1928, NA, RG-173, Box 128, DOA-Executive Director, General Correspondence).

55. Federal Radio Commission, *Second Annual Report,* 163.

56. Hugh Slotten, *Radio and Television Regulation: Broadcast Technology in the United States, 1920–1960* (Baltimore, MD: Johns Hopkins UP, 2001), 54–55.

57. During this period and through the fall of 1928, commission members sought public support for the engineers' report. For example, on a tour of western states, fifth zone commissioner Harold LaFount supported the clear channel concept by stating: "We hear a lot about freakish characteristics of radio, but we know enough about it to realize that one station on a channel produces the desired results." See "West Unworried over New Waves," *New York Times,* May 6, 1928, Sec. xx, 21.

58. Herring, "Equalization of Broadcasting Facilities," 423.

59. While four commissioners supported the plan, Ira Robinson voted against the order, believing that the Davis Amendment did not require immediate action (Federal Radio Commission, *Second Annual Report*).

60. "Radio Engineer Analyzes New Broadcasting-Allocation Plan," NA, RG-173, Box 128, DOA-Executive Director, General Correspondence.

61. Memorandum to Broadcasting Committee, NA, RG-173, Box 128, DOA-Executive Director, General Correspondence; General Order 40 issued August 30, 1928, by the Federal Radio Commission, August 30, 1928, NA, RG-173, Box 128, DOA-Executive Director, General Correspondence.

62. Memorandum 180, "To All Persons Holding Licenses to Broadcast," Federal Radio Commission, September 11, 1928, NA, RG-173, Box 128, DOA-Executive Director, General Correspondence.

63. Memorandum to Eugene O. Sykes from G. Franklin Wisner, NA, RG-173, Box 128, DOA-Executive Director, General Correspondence.

64. Ibid.

65. *Congressional Digest,* 266.

66. Orestes H. Caldwell, "Why the Broadcasting Reallocation Was Made," NA, RG-173, Box 128, DOA-Executive Director, General Correspondence.

67. J. H. Dellinger, "The New Dial Settings:" NA, RG-167, Personal Papers of John H. Dellinger; see also J. H. Dellinger, "Analysis of Broadcasting Station Allocation," *Journal of the Institute of Radio Engineers* 16 (November 1928): 1477–85.

68. O. H. Caldwell, "Broadcasting Reallocation."

69. Herring, "Equalization of Broadcasting Facilities," 422.

70. Mark T. Gilderhaus, *History and Historians: A Historical Introduction,* 2nd ed. (Englewood Cliffs, NJ: Prentice Hall, 1995), 80.

71. Horwitz, *Irony of Regulatory Reform,* 27.

72. Ibid., 22. Horwitz provides an outstanding discussion of the different theories of regulation and their specific weaknesses and strengths.

73. By 1928 AT&T was out of the broadcasting business, having sold WEAF and its other radio holdings to Radio Corporation of America in 1926.

74. Horwitz, *Irony of Regulatory Reform,* 121.

75. See Lowi, *Public Administration Review,* for a complete discussion of this schema.

76. Hiram L. Jome, *Economics of the Radio Industry* (Chicago: A. W. Shaw, reprinted by Arno Press, New York, 1971), 53. The formation of the radio trust and the creation of RCA occurred largely because of government intervention that made the licensing of technology easier.

77. Michal McMahon, *The Making of a Profession: A Century of Electrical Engineering in America* (New York: Institute of Electrical and Electronics Engineers Press, 1984), 163. See also Jome, *Economics of the Radio Industry,* 251.

78. During the spring of 1928, the FRC quickly approved power increases and frequency changes for stations in the southern zone but withheld changes in allocation or allotment for stations in the East and Midwest. See NA, RG-173, Box 128, DOA-Executive Director, General Correspondence; FRC minutes, April 11, 1928.

79. See a "Memorandum to Mr. Caldwell," which states: "[A]ll the present high-powered stations are backed by large electric or radio interests and were established early in 1921 or 1922. At that time these were practically the only organizations that saw the possibilities of high-powered broadcasting, had the engineering backing and financial ability to undertake such station construction." Carl H. Butman, Secretary, Federal Radio Commission. NA, RG-167, Box 87, Personal Papers of J. H. Dellinger, February 2, 1928.

80. Sheila Jasanoff, *The Fifth Branch: Science Advisers as Policymakers* (Cambridge, MA: Harvard UP, 1990), 15.

81. McMahon, *Making of a Profession,* 163; Jome (*Economics of the Radio Industry,* 246) notes the probability that indirect advertising will support stations in 1926.

82. McMahon (*Making of a Profession,* 164) notes that the FRC and the IRE were so close during these early years that two of the five commissioners served as IRE board members too.

83. Louise G. Caldwell, NA, RG-167, Box 87, Personal Papers of J. H. Dellinger, August 17, 1928.

84. Sam Pickard, NA, RG-167, Box 87, Personal Papers of J. H. Dellinger, August 31, 1928.

85. Ewin Davis, letter to the Federal Radio Commission, Federal Radio Commission, *Second Annual Report,* 134.

86. Bethuel M. Webster Jr., "Our Stake in the Ether," address to the American Academy of Air Law and The School of Law (New York University, April 10, 1931), 9.

87. J. H. Dellinger, NA, RG-167, Box 37, Personal Papers of J. H. Dellinger, August 17, 1928.

88. McMahon, *Making of a Profession,* 152.

89. Charles A. Beard, *The American Leviathan: The Republic in the Machine Age* (New York: Oxford UP, 1941), 297.

90. McMahon, *Making of a Profession,* 157.

91. Jasanoff, *Fifth Branch,* 17.

92. Federal Communications Commission, *Second Annual Report of the Federal Communications Commission for the Fiscal Year ended June 30, 1936* (Washington, DC: U.S. Government Printing Office, 1936); Sterling and Kittross, *Stay Tuned,* 170.

3 / Wrestling with Corporate Identity

Defining Television Programming Strategy at NBC, 1945–1950

CHAD DELL

> Media organizations and occupations lie right at the heart of any study of
> mass communications, for they embody the processes through which the
> *output* of the media comes into being.
>
> — Margaret Gallagher, "Negotiation of Control
> in Media Organizations and Occupations"

Conventional historical accounts of the "early years" of television broadcasting generally begin in earnest in the post–"television freeze" period of
the early 1950s with the emergence of the so-called Golden Age of live television drama.[1] These historical approaches overlook a series of fundamental
influences that emerged in the 1940s and contributed to the shaping of television programming as we know it.

This essay examines the preparation for and the initial stages of commercial network television broadcasting operations in the years 1945 to 1950,
with particular emphasis on the corporation seemingly in the best position
to dominate the field—the National Broadcasting Company (NBC). I argue
that constraints operating both inside and outside NBC guided the fledgling
television network toward a series of programming and market strategies
that in 1949 contributed to a fiscal and programming crisis within the corporation. This crisis ultimately led to a solidification of the direction the
corporation was to take with regard to programming, moving decisively
away from sports and toward a fuller commitment to studio-based entertainment forms. This movement in turn allowed NBC (and the other networks)
to begin to wrest control of prime-time network programming from advertisers and their agencies, sponsors who had dictated the content of much of
radio network programming for the previous twenty years.

In researching this historical episode, I am interested less in the program
choices NBC made than in those it ultimately passed over. For it was these

neglected yet *popular,* inexpensive, advertiser-supported program types—professional wrestling and roller derby among them—that may very well have been in the organization's best *business* interest to program, were it not for the fact that they conflicted with NBC's corporate self-image. It is this sort of conflict I intend to illustrate.

For the purposes of this essay, I bracket much of the discussion of these program types—particularly with regard to class issues[2]—in order to focus primarily on the economic factors affecting NBC's decisions. Quasi-sports programs such as wrestling and roller derby were comparable to other sports program types in terms of production costs; the talent fees and broadcast rights were normally significantly lower than their "legitimate" sports counterparts. Such programs would therefore have been fiscally, if not programmatically, attractive.

ORGANIZATIONAL CONSTRAINTS

Corporations—particularly large ones such as NBC—cannot be analyzed as homogeneous, univocal corporate bodies. Rather, organizations are divided into various divisions of activity, spheres of influence, and thus into coalitions of individuals who represent a varied, sometimes shifting set of interests. These interests are manifest in the form of internal *constraints* placed upon the organization. As an organization increases in size, the constraints placed upon it—both from internal and external interests or sources—may become increasingly inconsistent or conflicted.[3]

As NBC prepared to compete as a television network in the 1940s, two types of internal constraints were readily apparent, either from NBC's public actions or from the tenor of its interoffice discourse. The first was likely NBC's corporate self-image, in which the network saw itself from the outset as the "number one" broadcast network in America. NBC's network radio operation was so dominant that it prompted some at rival network CBS to suggest that it cede the mass audience entirely and target a smaller, more educated niche (a suggestion rejected by its president, William Paley).[4] Not surprisingly, this was the image NBC wished to project for the emerging television network, both to maintain its corporate image and to differentiate itself from competing networks. By 1948 the slogan "NBC . . . America's No. 1 Television Network" appeared in the network's full-page advertisements in *Broadcasting* magazine.[5] One result of this self-image was an apparent conservatism with regard to programming: seeing itself in a dominant position in its field, NBC was less willing to take chances on program types, preferring to let others develop programs that NBC would lure away once they were sufficiently "seasoned." For example, DuMont's first successful program, *The Original Amateur Hour,* was coaxed to join NBC in 1949.[6]

In launching the television network, a second, related discourse emerged: NBC increasingly described its television programming strategy in terms of "quality telecasting," presenting "the best television shows available." Because the word "quality" played an integral role in NBC's public definition of its radio network, it is not surprising to see the image applied to NBC's televisual efforts as well.

NBC's corporate self-image was in many respects in conflict with the market strategy so crucial to the company's success, which was a second internal constraint that existed at the network. The prosperity of NBC's television network depended on a number of factors, including the continued profitability of its radio network, from which the initial financing of television's operation would come. But the cost of television programming alone promised to be many times that of radio. Network strategists had to reconcile, in their words, "the conflicting elements of high-quality telecasting and comparatively low costs."[7] With little chance of reaching profitability in the early years, NBC was forced to keep program costs to a minimum, a strategy that constrained NBC's expressed desire for "quality" programming, which tended to be more expensive. In the formative stages of network broadcasting, NBC would struggle to resolve these contradictory aims.

In addition to these internal influences, NBC was also constrained by interests outside the organization, not the least of which was the Federal Communications Commission's (FCC) insistence that station licensees broadcast a minimum of twenty-eight program hours per week. Additional demands accrued from NBC affiliates seeking programs that were both low cost *and* popular and from national advertisers seeking both nationwide and inexpensive advertising venues. Pressures rose as competing networks and program producers found popular and commercial success with inexpensive "low quality" program types, such as wrestling and roller derby.[8] Finally, NBC was at times under considerable pressure from RCA to show a profit— or at minimum an "acceptable" deficit. It was within this context of internal and external constraints that NBC television program strategies were formulated.

POSTWAR PREPARATIONS: 1945 AND BEYOND

In the early postwar years, NBC circulated an internal report detailing a proposed five-year master plan for NBC's efforts in television titled "Financial Prospects for NBC Telecasting, 1946–1950." This document proposed a careful strategy not only for launching a national television network but also for guiding it to profitability and recovering 80 percent of the losses sustained, all by the year 1950. Initial losses would be covered by anticipated profits from the NBC radio network, expected to amount to $20.9 million between 1946 and 1949, or about two and one-half times the anticipated capital requirements for station and network operations. Thus, NBC's television operation would be dependent on the fortunes of its radio network operations or, failing that, on equity capital provided by RCA rather than on a stable pool of borrowed capital.[9]

The long-range goal for NBC and the other networks was an advertiser-supported national network operation. However, as William Boddy points out, while the networks pressed advertisers and their agencies to participate in television, the networks were determined not to lose control over network programming as they had with radio. A 1945 article appearing in *Televiser* observed that the networks were opposed to outside program production, preferring to keep control of production in-house. While many early programs in fact were produced by outside agencies during the first few years of commercial television operation, regaining network program control was clearly a part of NBC's plans.[10]

Despite this long-term goal, the networks' early prosperity was tied to the construction and operation of network "owned and operated" television stations (O&Os). NBC's strategy for profitability depended heavily on the significant revenues generated by these stations.[11] NBC planned to anchor its television network with WNBT in New York, the only NBC television station in regular operation in 1946. Construction permits had been granted for stations in Washington, DC, Cleveland, and Chicago, and an application was pending for a fifth station (then the legal limit) in Los Angeles. NBC anticipated that by 1950 *all five* stations would be operating at a profit.[12]

Immediate external constraints—FCC regulations and as-yet-unavailable AT&T technology—combined to threaten the profitability of NBC's O&Os and compel the network to make decisions regarding programming. As a station operator, NBC was bound by the FCC under Section 3.661 to maintain a regular program schedule of not less than two hours per day nor less than twenty-eight hours per week, within a few months of commencing operation.[13] However, AT&T—which controlled and operated the coaxial landlines linking the stations—could not furnish the interconnections necessary for NBC to distribute network-originated programming to its affiliated stations. Though NBC did arrange for microwave interconnections with stations in Philadelphia and Schenectady, New York, the company was quick to point out that these were temporary links, stating publicly that it had "no plans for entering the network facilities business on a permanent basis" in competition with AT&T.[14] To compound the problem, there was as yet no reliable method of recording televised programs for distribution; the kinescope would not be a viable option until 1948. Thus, without coaxial lines each station would be forced to produce a substantial portion of its own programming—a costly endeavor. Ignoring any repercussions from the FCC with regard to "public service," NBC chose to delay the start of station operations in each city outside New York for as long as the FCC would allow, waiting until it could draw the bulk of network programming from WNBT when interconnections were established. In order to contain costs, NBC intended to limit locally originating programs to "films, remote pickups, and the minimum number of low-cost studio programs needed to serve the community needs."[15]

Network operations were thus seen as crucial, due primarily to the high cost of program production and concomitant with FCC constraints. NBC's "Financial Prospects" report noted: "Except for lower production by certain stations during the early months of operation, the 28-hour schedule represents a MUST for NBC. Therefore, the costs involved at this level of telecasting represent the expenditures which NBC will have to meet, regardless of how many programs are sponsored. Expansion beyond 28 hours will result from the addition of sponsored programs and the costs will be covered by the charges made to advertisers."[16] Network operations were also, in NBC's view, where the *real* profits lay. With network radio operations serving as a precedent, the organization could confidently predict that "revenue from national advertising will be the principal source of income to NBC from telecasting."[17]

Compelled to provide a minimum number of program hours, NBC had to reconcile the conflicting goals of "high quality telecasting and comparatively low cost."[18] Cost containment could best be achieved through "remote" telecasts of sporting events, political functions, and the like. Unlike studio productions, where settings and costumes had to be constructed, scripts written, and performances staged, remote broadcasts of sporting events could depend on performances staged in their natural environment.

However, though there was no explicit description of what constituted "high quality telecasting" in NBC's "Financial Prospects" report, it is clear that most within NBC equated quality with studio production. While the radio network made use of remote broadcast material, the foundation of its program schedule was grounded in studio-based entertainment genres: comedy, variety, drama, serials, and the like. And the report fully expected television programming to echo radio's programming style, arguing: "[I]n programming concepts, it must be constantly emphasized that television is an outgrowth of radio and not of motion pictures. The economic limitation on telecasting simply will not permit operations to follow the lavish Hollywood pattern."[19] Thus, planners at NBC anticipated that network program offerings would follow programming precedents set in radio, offering not filmed materials but rather "high quality 'live' shows and remote pickups of national interest."[20] Assuming that the latter program type would comprise sporting events, political conventions, and other one-time events, the remaining "high quality 'live' shows" would doubtlessly be produced in NBC's studios. Thus, it seems clear that at NBC, "quality" and "studio" were commensurate.

The course initially set out by NBC would necessarily be an expensive one. NBC's hourly studio production costs in 1946 were nearly four times the cost of remote broadcasts ($715.00 and $175.00 per hour, respectively), and NBC executives expected this ratio to widen: "Increased studio-program costs during the next few years anticipate improved programs and higher talent costs. Since the other NBC stations as well as the affiliates will depend on New York for the 'quality' programs they telecast, WNBT will have to furnish the 'top notch' shows."[21] While remote broadcasts would have provided an ample number of low-cost programming hours, the corporation's commitment to "quality" programming necessitated higher-cost studio programs.

However, this position was neither entirely universally held nor completely defensible. Beyond the obvious fiscal argument, some within NBC argued that sporting events *were* "quality" programming. A 1947 report on the status of television commented: "Public and special events, especially sporting events, are important factors in television programming. Columbia is making a great bid for prestige by trying to secure rights for numerous [sporting] events."[22] Others, including NBC's own research department, pointed to the "quantity" of audience such events attracted. A 1945 NBC survey of 1,070 New Yorkers found that 87.7 percent had seen a boxing program on television in the previous month. Thus, while most equated the notion of "quality" with studio programs, and thus with a desirable corporate self-image, there were also dissenting positions being expressed, advocating the value of sports programming.

It is clear from public positions the company took in 1946 that NBC took its five-year plan seriously. That year marked the NBC radio network's twentieth year in operation, and the company announced in *Broadcasting* magazine that the year would also be "marked by the launching of television on a national scale."[23] Later, at a press conference in Hollywood, NBC president Niles Trammell announced optimistically that NBC "hopes to break even by the end of the third year, and put television on a paying basis within five years."[24]

PROGRAMMING

If NBC was relatively clear as to what constituted "quality" television programming, its sponsors were considerably less so. Though nine commercial sponsors joined NBC in its first years of television experimentation, nearly a decade later, sponsors were still admittedly unsure as to what constituted appropriate programming for its newfound advertising medium. For example, the promotions director for Commonwealth Edison reported in 1946 the company had tried five different program types in the previous two years; *Telequizzicals* was but the latest in "a series of experimental ideas being tried out by the company."[25]

Even CBS demonstrated indecision regarding its programming direction. In the spring of 1947 the network announced it was closing its television studios, laying off studio production personnel and discontinuing all studio broadcasts, declaring its intention to "concentrate our efforts for the time being on actuality broadcasts, such as sports and special events."[26] *Broadcasting* reported the network's decision "aligns CBS with that part of the industry which believes that television's main appeal, at least for the immediate future, lies in its ability to bring into the homes of set owners visual reports of news and sports events while they are actually happening."[27] Less than a year later CBS made yet another abrupt turnaround, announcing its intention to "immediately" begin construction of the "largest television studio plant in the United States," in an effort to reintroduce studio programming to its schedule.[28] Needless to say, there was considerable debate as to just what type of programs would be appropriate to and successful on television.

Sports Programming

It was clear to some advocates of television that sports programming would and should dominate the medium. One proponent argued sports was "a natural for television," predicting that sports would comprise "about 60% of the program load of television for many years to come."[29] In its assessment of expanding advertiser interest in television in the fall of 1946, *Broadcasting* magazine asserted: "[S]porting events are today television's most professional entertainment. . . . Also, a ball game or fight card provides several hours of video program fare far more easily for the broadcaster than the same amount of time devoted to studio programs."[30] The article went on to describe the popularity of televised sports programs with audiences, which in turn, *Broadcasting* argued, accounted for the genre's attraction to sponsors.[31]

There is little question as to why broadcasters would have been drawn to the genre. Boxing and wrestling events were particularly easy to produce: the action takes place in a limited area and could be televised with only two cameras. Furthermore, many of the costs associated with studio production —including sets, props, and rising talent fees—could be avoided or minimized.

Not surprisingly, sports ranks among NBC's earliest programming efforts.[32] However, as historian Ron Powers points out, the real impetus came not from NBC but from one of its earliest sponsors: the Gillette Safety Razor Company. In 1939 Gillette advertising director A. Craig Smith proved the viability of sports as an advertising vehicle when he staked nearly one-fourth of the company's annual advertising budget on the Mutual Network's radio broadcast of the 1939 World Series—until that point a marginal advertising opportunity at best. Still, the World Series drew a sizable male audience, the target consumer for Gillette's product line. Though the series went only four games, the sales response was four times greater than anyone at the company had imagined and sealed Gillette's commitment to sports programming.[33]

Gillette continued sponsoring sporting events on radio in the following years and in 1944 initiated the *Gillette Cavalcade of Sports* boxing program on WNBT television in New York. In 1946 the program was among the first included in NBC's debut network broadcast schedule. Airing on Monday and Friday nights, *Cavalcade of Sports* accounted for about half of NBC's weekly network broadcast schedule. The program was created and produced by Smith and his associates; in fact, it was Gillette, and not NBC, that owned the broadcast rights to most of the sporting events—and all of the "prestige" events—on NBC's schedule throughout the 1950s.[34] While NBC was pleased to have Gillette as a paying sponsor, company executives no doubt chafed at the lack of control over its programming.

By the fall of 1947, NBC's WNBW in Washington, DC, was on the air three evenings a week, and affiliation agreements had been signed with stations in Philadelphia, Boston, and Schenectady, New York. Still, full network programming was a year away. Local field production for WNBT in New York accounted for over 60 percent of the station's programming—more than ninety hours per month, or one or two sporting events per day—and included New York Giants baseball and horse racing. However, of these programs, only boxing was offered through the network.[35]

NBC collected considerable data on its competitors during this period, particularly on the actions of CBS and DuMont. The monthly progress reports filed with top management contained detailed discussions of the activities of the competition, focusing in particular on the success its counterparts were experiencing with sports programming. NBC's competitor activity report for December 1947 noted that CBS "continue[s] to cover all big events in [Madison Square] Garden exclusive of boxing . . . events sponsored by Ford, General Foods, and Knox Hats," while DuMont was offering "boxing and wrestling on Tuesday and Friday evenings for American Shops (menswear), [and] boxing on Monday evening for [a] local television set dealer."[36]

While wrestling did not involve any of the characteristics of "quality" programming befitting NBC's self-image, competitive interest (as well as industrial necessity) led the organization to consider wrestling as a program option. In early 1948, NBC executive Doug Rodgers submitted a report stressing the profitability of roller derby, which he argued was "fast becoming one of the largest sporting events."[37] Furthermore, the sales department, anxious to secure advertising revenue, reported that R&H Beer had expressed some interest in sponsoring a professional wrestling program.[38]

Unlike its competitors, NBC had not produced a weekly wrestling program prior to 1948. However, a confluence of opportunities was presented to NBC as it sought to fill its program schedule, which the company acted on during the 1947–1948 season. Gillette was sponsoring a boxing program on Monday nights from St. Nicholas Arena in New York (along with the *Cavalcade of Sports* on Fridays from Madison Square Garden), for which NBC was providing remote production facilities. Though most published directories of prime-time network television programs do not indicate as much, there is evidence that NBC began airing the program *Wrestling from St. Nicholas Arena* on Tuesday nights in January or February 1948.[39] This was a fiscally prudent decision, particularly as the NBC remote unit equipment was already in place from the previous evening's boxing telecast. Furthermore, the cost of the series was attractive; while the cost of twenty-six hour-long boxing programs amounted to $44,790, the cost for the equivalent number of wrestling programs was $27,690, nearly half the expense. And both were a bargain when compared with studio programs: the half-hour program *Author Meets the Critics* ran $71,760 for twenty-six episodes, while estimates for the *NBC Television Music Hall* ran as high as $457,600 per season.[40] For an industry in the initial—and very costly—stages of development, faced with an inability to charge advertisers sufficiently to recover program costs, programs such as wrestling seemed the more tactical and judicious choice.

This programming genre ran counter to other plans under consideration at NBC. In April of 1948, two months after CBS announced plans to build new television studios in New York, NBC reported the opening of its newly constructed studio facility, Studio 8-G. Three times larger than its existing studio, NBC announced that the facility was "the world's most modern and best-equipped television studio," able to accommodate up to four programs produced in direct succession.[41] Furthermore, in keeping with its self-image, in the summer of 1948 NBC considered offering affiliates what they called "feature service programs," a supplementary offering of "quality" programming above and beyond NBC's regular service. This proposal was immediately met with resistance by affiliates, who contended program costs were already higher than they could afford. Easton C. Woolley, head of station relations, argued: "The cost of the feature service must be reduced to the individual affiliation; otherwise, this merchandise will continue to remain on the shelves. The affiliates generally tell us that the program costs are beyond their reach and are so high that they cannot be resold locally. The stations do not question the fact that we are putting the money into the productions. What they want is a lower grade production at a lesser figure at this stage."[42] Much like the networks, most individual stations, faced with enormous start-up expenses, were losing money.[43] And like a select few at NBC, affiliates longed for inexpensive programming to help them fill their twenty-eight-hour broadcast quota. NBC, apparently responding to the complaints, announced at its fall affiliates convention it was dropping the proposed service, explaining it had "not worked out satisfactorily."[44]

Looking back at the fledgling 1947–1948 television season, *Broadcasting* reported that advertisers had demonstrated a strong interest in sports, sponsoring 376 hours of sports programming in the month of February alone, nearly 60 percent of all broadcast time. In June, televised sports programs claimed half the spots in the "top ten" list published by Pulse. From the standpoint of both broadcasters and advertisers, boxing and wrestling programs were becoming "standard video material the year round."[45]

Heightened competition had some within NBC worried about the company's market position in television. In his monthly television report, NBC sales manager Reynold Kraft warned: "Competition is a thorn in our sides and will be more so as time goes on and additional stations come into the market. DuMont has shown higher Hooper ratings in its programs, than has either CBS or NBC, but advertisers do not believe this condition will obtain when NBC can expand its program service and schedules."[46] Similar worries were circulating in the station relations department. In a July 1948 memo to NBC president Trammell, Frank Russell told of a station owner in Baltimore who was securing program services from more than a half-dozen sources, including CBS, ABC, and DuMont. He reasoned that this example was "a very clear indication of what a large number of stations will do as soon as they have an opportunity to receive programs from more than one source. It is a development absolutely contrary to the interests of a single network such as NBC."[47] Russell warned that unless NBC's television programming changed markedly, both its television and radio operations could be at peril: "It stands to reason that NBC can only maintain its position of eminence by being the leader in television. . . . Unless we come up with a program of action which will result in our clearing time on our affiliates immediately, we will be in real trouble before the end of the year."[48] Clearly, a number of NBC executives felt that the company's future success was inexorably tied to its television programming decisions in the coming year. Those same executives saw storm clouds on the horizon.

THE 1948–1949 SEASON

A. Craig Smith and Gillette renewed their sponsorship of both Monday and Friday night boxing series for the 1948–1949 season, programs that had regularly rated in the top five by Hooper TV ratings in the New York area and that were consistently NBC's highest-rated programs. While even NBC viewed such numbers with some skepticism, it is significant that NBC Research consistently produced the information for top management.[49] NBC also committed to a full season of *Wrestling from St. Nicholas Arena,* no doubt due in part to its continued proximity to Gillette's Monday boxing program. Furthermore, the program was now sponsored on WNBT in the New York area by John F. Trommer, Inc., a regional brewery. By spring the program had found a second sponsor—Gunther Beer—in Washington, DC, which was paying one thousand dollars per month for its participation. NBC's prime-time schedule was not yet at capacity, but executives expected to have a "reasonably full schedule" by spring.[50]

Discernible sponsorship patterns began to emerge during the 1948–1949 season as more advertisers entered the field and as the results of programming decisions became clearer. Two trends emerged from the period: first, sponsored sports programming continued to dominate commercial television, accounting for over 50 percent of sponsored programming during the year. But as more television stations began operation across the country and more advertisers clamored to tie their advertising to sports events, sports programs became increasingly localized. Regional broadcasting rights for home games of area professional baseball and football teams were granted to local television outlets, and sponsorship of such programs by national, regional, and local advertisers increased measurably, though increasingly on a station-by-station basis. Sponsorship of network sports programming continued but was increasingly dwarfed by regional advertising placement.[51]

A second advertiser trend emerged, this concerning network program sponsorship. While national advertisers continued their experimentation with program types, it became increasingly clear that two entertainment program genres were gaining in popularity among television sponsors: drama and comedy/variety. In December 1948 *Broadcasting* observed: "Though there is still heavy emphasis on sports programming—other and more widespread forms of television entertainment are going on the air. . . . Dramatic programming, particularly, is on the increase."[52] Network sports programs for the previous month still led the field with sixty-six hours, but dramatic programming, accounting for forty-two network broadcast hours, was not far behind.[53]

NBC's research department offered a further reason for reevaluating sports programming, based on preliminary studies of television audiences. The department reported that while "the desire to see sports telecasts has been one of the chief reasons for the purchase of sets, there are increasing signs of more varied preferences on the part of the television audience."[54] Examining the preliminary ratings performance of sports programs, the department concluded that while sports such as baseball perform well on their own, when competing against "outstanding variety or dramatic programs, or with telecasts of well-known radio shows, their ratings suffer sharp decreases."[55]

Comedy/variety programming, as it was called, lagged in total network hours, but the genre's popularity with audiences was rapidly being established by the nascent rating services at the time. The 1948–1949 season marked the start of Milton Berle's *Texaco Star Theatre,* which by the end of the season had emerged as a runaway "hit" with set owners, regularly garnering 50 ratings or better.[56] Though sports programming still dominated the ratings charts—perhaps due to the sheer aggregate of program hours—the popularity of other program types among audiences was on the rise, and national advertisers were increasingly shifting their support to these emerging television genres.

THE CRISIS

Maxon Advertising, which represented Gillette, had warned NBC since the fall of 1948 that its client would likely drop the Monday night bouts due to budgetary constraints, though this was not likely to occur before early 1949. Thus, it came as no surprise when Gillette concluded its sponsorship of *Boxing from St. Nicholas Arena* with the May 9, 1949, broadcast—this despite the fact that ratings for the Monday evening program were regularly outdistancing the Friday edition.[57] NBC's contract for the Tuesday wrestling broadcasts lapsed the following evening, and NBC did not renew it. Both were replaced the following season with studio-based programs.

That same week, RCA chairman David Sarnoff warned stockholders that

1949 "will be a more difficult year" for the company than the year before, laying much of the responsibility on NBC's television division. *Broadcasting* magazine reported on May 9 that "the impact of television on the corporation's broadcasting operations imposes [in Sarnoff's words] 'no easy task during this conversion period.'"[58] In the same issue, the trade journal revealed that NBC had laid off sixty employees from its radio division, in an austerity measure aimed at reducing overhead by $1 million. NBC Central Division vice president I. E. Showerman was quoted as saying that the cost of television operations was "largely responsible" for the layoffs.[59]

A month later, fiscal difficulties deepened, precipitating a crisis at the National Broadcasting Company. In a report to RCA, executives at NBC estimated that overall profits for 1948 would be down by nearly 60 percent from the previous year—from $5 million to $2.1 million. NBC anticipated sustaining a loss in total company operations in July and August 1949—the first time such a loss had occurred since August 1935. Anticipated losses, NBC reported, were due to two factors: a larger number of program cancellations by summer radio sponsors than anticipated, coupled with larger-than-expected deficits in television operations—an estimated deficit increase of $1.35 million over 1948, and an increase of nearly $750,000 over the loss budgeted for the year. The television division now anticipated a total deficit for 1949 of $4.5 million.[60]

NBC executives assured RCA that they were moving quickly to reverse the course and keep the television division's losses below the $4 million mark. They reported plans to eliminate daytime programming and considered eliminating or fiscally restricting a number of "rather expensive sustaining programs," replacing them with less-expensive live shows.[61] RCA also reorganized its program department in an effort to streamline the chain of command and gain better control over program budgets.[62]

DECISIONS

Given the serious fiscal constraints being experienced, it is significant that the summer of 1949 was also the last time that roller derby and wrestling were seriously considered as program options. NBC received information that the Chesterfield cigarette company had expressed an interest in sponsoring roller derby nationally during the upcoming 1949–1950 season. Assistant sports director James Dolan approached New York promoter Leo Seltzer in hopes of luring his organization away from ABC. However, while Seltzer was interested, he was bound to a five-year contract with ABC, with little hope of release.[63]

Dolan was also contacted about renewing *Wrestling from St. Nicholas Arena,* but his response was initially negative. In a memo to NBC director of television operations Carleton Smith, Dolan reported: "I just wanted to be sure that we all agreed that wrestling has no place in our program schedule." Smith's response was handwritten and unexpected: "What day of wk? Saturday? How much? I'm *interested*—."[64] Surprised no doubt by the reply, Dolan inquired further into the matter. Finding that the event was available in its previously scheduled Tuesday time period, Dolan queried: "Should I check further on this for you?"[65] The response came a week later, this time from operations manager Fred Shawn: "You are right. We are not interested in wrestling."[66] Though the issue was revisited periodically throughout the fall, wrestling never returned to NBC's prime-time schedule.

NBC might have seriously considered wrestling and roller derby as program options in the summer of 1949. The company had reached a critical point in its efforts to dominate a new entertainment distribution system, precisely at a point when it was in need of inexpensive programming as a means of cutting costs. However, several factors prevented such an occurrence. On the one hand, NBC's corporate self-image was generally stronger than a market strategy that might have included such "debased" entertainment forms. Undoubtedly, by 1949 wrestling as a performance genre was too far outside NBC's corporate self-image and commitment to "quality programming" to be reconsidered as a viable program option. NBC's prime-time schedule was filled to capacity for the 1949–1950 season, with *Gillette Cavalcade of Sports* the single prime-time sports entry. Though the other three networks continued to schedule sports programming in prime time—totaling over thirteen hours of boxing, wrestling, and roller derby each week—NBC continued to move aggressively toward studio production, despite the significantly higher costs associated with it.[67]

Additionally, in pressing forward with studio programming, NBC sought to distinguish itself from its competitors. While ABC and DuMont were achieving ratings success with wrestling and roller derby, NBC had committed to product differentiation, in an attempt to establish itself as the "leader" in television programming.

However, other factors no doubt contributed to the course NBC chose to pursue. NBC ignored both its own growing group of affiliates, who continued to ask for less costly programming they could more successfully market to local advertisers, and program suppliers, who could offer just that type of inexpensive programming at a time when NBC had a genuine need for it. Instead, NBC gambled that it had more successfully defined the interests of the one group the company perhaps could not ignore: national advertisers. Though sports sponsorship continued to dominate aggregate television advertising across the nation, *network* advertisers were continuing to move away from sports as a national programming option, in favor of more expensive studio and filmed programs. Variety, comedy, and dramatic programs, which had begun to show promise during the 1948 season, were emerging in 1949 as generic forms well suited to television and popular with audiences, and the nation's top sponsors were supporting them in increasing numbers. By the fall of 1949, drama and comedy/variety programming surpassed sports as the program types dominating the rating charts; during the 1950 season, NBC's *Gillette Cavalcade of Sports* was the sole network sports program entry in Nielsen's Top 25 for the year, where it ranked sixth.[68]

Moreover, NBC's commitment to expensive studio programming ultimately served another company goal: to break with the radio model of sponsor control over prime-time programming. By moving resolutely to expensive program genres, and building or leasing studio production facilities, NBC was bidding to retain control over the process of production and to keep a measure of control over its schedule. As the "Future Prospects" report pointed out, NBC knew that production and talent costs would continue to rise precipitously, eventually becoming prohibitively expensive for all but a few sponsors. While sponsors would doubtlessly be drawn to the popular programming, they would no longer be able to afford to individually sponsor, and thus control, an entire television series.

This in turn puts the hiring of Sylvester "Pat" Weaver, long pointed to by historians as an "innovator" in television, in clearer perspective. Two weeks after the budget crisis erupted at NBC, the company announced that Weaver had been retained to fill the position of vice president in charge of television, to begin on August 1, 1949. In his first major memorandum to his staff, Weaver proposed that NBC should move away from the radio model of single-sponsor programs and toward what he called a "magazine" style of advertising, with multiple advertisers purchasing time adjacent to NBC programming. NBC would be responsible for attracting viewers through its "program ingenuity." It then would be up to sponsors to "prepare advertising that will maintain the viewing during the commercial periods."[69] Weaver's proposals, not surprisingly, were remarkably consistent with the direction NBC had taken over the past four years. Weaver may not have been the initiator of many of the innovations with which he is credited, as, for instance, Michele Hilmes's insightful critique points out.[70] Nevertheless, he was perfectly suited to champion NBC's goal of program autonomy and its commitment to "quality" programming.

CONCLUSION

NBC chose a long-term view in responding to its fiscal crisis in the summer of 1949, electing to maintain its investment in the type of expensive studio-based programs to which advertisers were beginning to gravitate rather than resorting to inexpensive program types that would have eased the company's fiscal difficulties in the short term. While sports programs were popular with both advertisers and audiences at the time, as I have established, national advertisers were increasingly attracted to comedy/variety and dramatic programs, genres that NBC recognized and chose to invest in despite its fiscal constraints. Finally, the timing and duration of the FCC's 1948 television "freeze" no doubt bolstered NBC's decision: artificially limiting the pool of potential affiliate stations in turn reduced the number of television networks that could survive, while creating near-monopoly conditions for the survivors. And the pre-freeze television licensees doubtlessly were attracted by NBC's commitment to expensive programming—much as NBC's radio affiliates were in the 1930s—elevating NBC's market position. The freeze could not have come at a more fortuitous time for NBC.

Hindsight easily demonstrates the success of NBC's strategy: though the network posted a deficit again in 1950, reporting a net loss of $3,894,000, NBC reported a profit of $8,645,000 in 1951 on billings of over $59 million.[71] In 1952 gross billings rose more than 40 percent to $83.2 million, 20 percent higher than CBS, NBC's nearest competitor. Though profitability came two years later than had been predicted in 1945, in most other ways the master plan was quite accurate.[72] Moreover, NBC's decision during the crisis of 1949 solidified the direction the network would take with entertainment television, one that the other networks would quickly follow. By 1951 network prime-time sports programming dropped 50 percent to five and a half hours a week. Professional wrestling disappeared entirely from network prime-time schedules in 1954; and by 1955 prime-time sports programming stood at two hours weekly, with the three remaining commercial television networks now firmly committed to studio-based programs. Finally, over the course of the decade, NBC and the other networks successfully wrested control over most sponsor-produced programming. NBC opened its West Coast studio facility in Burbank in 1952, the same year the company told a House subcommittee it was producing 59 percent of its entire program schedule.[73] In the wake of the quiz show scandals at the close of the decade, NBC and the other networks quickly achieved hegemony over their program schedules.

A number of conflicting discourses, factions, and constraints affected and guided one entertainment corporation in its bid to compete successfully in the emerging commercial television market. Unlike the television historians who argue that the significant decisions regarding television programming emerged in the 1950s, these decisions were made at NBC in the 1940s as a result of the discourses and constraints outlined here, decisions that helped to chart the course of television for decades to follow.

NOTES

1. Erik Barnouw, *The Golden Web: A History of Broadcasting in the United States,* vol. 2, *1933 to 1953* (New York: Oxford UP, 1968); Erik Barnouw, *Tube of Plenty: The Evolution of American Television* (Oxford: Oxford UP, 1975); Christopher Sterling and John Kittross, *Stay Tuned: A History of American Broadcasting,* 3rd ed. (Belmont, CA: Wadsworth, 2002); William Boddy, *Fifties Television: The Industry and Its Critics* (Urbana: Illinois UP, 1990), 15. Sterling and Kittross examine individual program genres beginning in 1948, but their reliance on an NAEB analysis of television programming (303–04) suggests that the important program decisions were fixed in the early 1950s. In his excellent examination of television history, historian William Boddy correctly points out that the broad *social* decisions about television broadcasting were in fact solidified in the 1930s and 1940s; still, he too only begins substantive discussion of television *programming* with the period of the 1950s.

2. Wrestling typically has been thought to attract a primarily working-class audience. However, the composition of the wrestling audience was changing and expanding dramatically in the postwar era. See Chad Dell, "Researching Historical Broadcast Audiences: Female Fandom of Professional Wrestling, 1945–60" (PhD diss., U of Wiscon-

sin–Madison, 1997). Wrestling was very popular among early TV set owners in the middle and late 1940s, and was available in most television markets nearly every evening. Research on set ownership revealed that the majority of purchasers were upper- or upper-middle-class families, a fact that calls into question traditional audience classifications. "Telefacts," *Broadcasting,* December 20, 1948, insert.

3. For a more in-depth discussion of corporate constraints, see Jeffrey Pfeffer and Gerald R. Salancik, *The External Control of Organizations: A Resource Dependence Perspective* (New York: Harper and Row, 1978), 14–29.

4. Barnouw, *Golden Web.* It is helpful to remember that prior to 1942, NBC had operated two powerful radio networks, NBC Red and NBC Blue. The latter carried more sustaining programming, while the former was considered more commercial (Erik Barnouw, *A Tower in Babel: A History of Broadcasting in the United States,* vol. 1, *to 1933* [New York: Oxford UP, 1966], 272). As a result of the FCC's chain broadcasting rules, upheld by the Supreme Court in 1943, NBC was forced to divest itself of one of the networks. It sold the less profitable NBC Blue to Lifesaver Company magnate Edward Noble. This episode suggests NBC's commitment to commercially dominant programming and likely served as an object lesson to Paley.

5. Advertising insert, *Broadcasting,* May 17, 1948, 86B-M.

6. Gary N. Hess, *An Historical Study of the DuMont Television Network* (New York: Arno Press, 1979). This strategy was also used in NBC's treatment of roller derby. NBC was perfectly content to have ABC and DuMont develop roller derby as a subgenre, preferring to use its position as the dominant network at the point when roller derby demonstrated its profitability. See James Dolan Papers, NBC box 341, folder 1, Wisconsin Historical Society Archives, Madison, WI (referred to hereafter as NBC [box #/folder #]); and William Stern Papers, NBC 346/4, for further discussion (reprinted courtesy of National Broadcasting Company, Inc. [NBC]).

7. "Financial Prospects for NBC Telecasting, 1946–1950," NBC 105/17, p. 16.

8. Stations also increasingly had inexpensive program materials made available to them from independent producers and syndicators such as Telecom Incorporated, founded in 1944, and Ziv Television Programs, which was formed in 1948. Boddy, *Fifties Television,* 69–70; Christopher Anderson, "Ziv Television Programs, Inc.," in the Museum of Broadcast Communications' *Encyclopedia of Television,* ed. Horace Newcomb (Chicago: Fitzroy Dearborn, 1997). Available at http://www.museum.tv/archives/etv/ Z/htmlZ/zivtelevisio/zivtelevisio.htm (accessed March 24, 2004).

9. "Financial Prospects," iii, 91.

10. Boddy, *Fifties Television,* 94–95.

11. Ibid., 114.

12. The call letters for NBC's O&O television stations followed the theme of "WNB–": WNBT-New York, WNBW-Washington, WNBH-Hollywood, and so on.

Hess (*DuMont Television Network*, 49) mentions a second NBC station, W3XPP in Philadelphia, operating in 1946. However, this was an experimental license and was not included in NBC's stated network plans. "Financial Prospects," iii.

13. "FCC Extends Waiver," *Broadcasting*, September 29, 1947, 20. The FCC postponed the rule's implementation every three months through 1946 and 1947. Nonetheless, the rule did hold considerable sway with broadcasters, as NBC's report demonstrates.

14. "NBC Installing Alternate Video Route," *Broadcasting*, January 12, 1948, 17.

15. "Financial Prospects," viii, vii.

16. Ibid., 16.

17. Ibid., 15.

18. Ibid., 93–94.

19. Ibid., x.

20. Ibid., 14.

21. Ibid., 93–94.

22. "*Cavalcade of Sports* TV Survey," May 29, 1945, NBC Research Division, TV Files, NBC 105/1; "Television NBC: A Nice Sunday Morning Subject," TV Files, NBC 105/26, p. 3.

23. "Trammell and Mullen See 1946 as Best in NBC's 20 Years," *Broadcasting*, January 7, 1946, 24.

24. While Trammell's publicly announced hopes of breaking even by the close of 1948 were a year earlier than predicted in NBC's report (which anticipated a $0.2 million loss in 1949), his latter assertion was consistent with it: the report predicted a cash surplus of over $7 million in 1950. "Financial Prospects," Chart 3, v-b; "Video Operations Deficits Will Range Up to $150,000 Monthly, Says Trammell," *Broadcasting*, April 8, 1946, 69.

25. Adrien B. Rodner, "Advertiser Tried Everything in Two Years of Television," *Broadcasting*, October 7, 1946, 49.

26. "CBS Not to Abandon Video Activities," *Broadcasting*, May 12, 1947, 17.

27. Ibid.

28. "CBS Video: Construction to Commence on Largest TV Plant," *Broadcasting*, February 23, 1948, 14.

29. "Sports on Video," *Broadcasting*, April 15, 1946, 104.

30. Bruce Robertson, "Autumn Expansion Is Seen for Video," *Broadcasting*, August 26, 1946, 15.

31. Ibid.

32. In 1939, NBC's first year of experimental station operation, the company's programming consisted primarily of remote pickups of "bicycle races, a baseball game, a tennis match, a football game, a hockey game, Macy's Thanksgiving Day parade, etc." ("TV Milestone," *Broadcasting*, April 25, 1949, 54).

33. Ron Powers, *Supertube: The Rise of Television Sports* (New York: Coward-McCann, 1984), 23–28. Gillette sold nearly four million razor sets, four times as many as they had hoped.

34. Ibid., 54–55; Tim Brooks and Earle Marsh, *The Complete Directory to Prime Time Network TV Shows, 1946–Present,* 7th ed. (New York: Ballantine, 1999), 122–23.

35. NBC Report—August 1947, TV Files, NBC 105/24.

36. See "NBC Sales Reports" for August through December 1949, TV Files, NBC 105/17, 105/24; "December 1947 Sales Report," TV Files, NBC 105/24, pp. 10, 14–15.

37. Doug Rodgers, "Program Material—Roller Skating," Reynold R. Kraft Papers, NBC 398/17. "Roller Derby" as such did not begin until 1949; Powers (*Supertube,* 48–49) claims that Dick Lane first created the sport in Los Angeles, broadcasting it on KTLA, a DuMont/Paramount O&O.

38. NBC Monthly Operation Analysis, January 1948, Kraft Papers, NBC 398/17, Section II—Sales.

39. Advance Program Schedule—WNBW—April 1948, Program Schedules, Kersta Papers, NBC 585/53; Kraft Papers, NBC 398/17.

40. "NBC Television Programs Offered to RCA Victor for Sponsorship, 1948," Kersta Papers, NBC 584/24.

41. Bruce Robertson, "CBS Video Construction to Commence on Largest TV Plant," *Broadcasting,* February 23, 1948, 14; "NBC's TV Studio 8-G Called 'Most Modern,'" *Broadcasting,* April 26, 1948, 27.

42. Easton C. Woolley, Interoffice memo to Charles R. Denny, July 22, 1948, Station Relations, NBC 574/15.

43. The FCC reported that in 1948 the four networks lost a total of $6.4 million, while the forty stations not owned by the networks lost $8.6 million. Network Financial Report, 1948, Federal Communications Commission, quoted in Hess, *DuMont Television Network,* 58.

44. "Sun Valley: NBC TV Affiliate Contract Unveiled," *Broadcasting,* September 27, 1948, 23.

45. Steve Flynn, Interoffice memo to J. Robert Myers, January 31, 1949, Carleton Smith Papers, NBC 214/26; Sterling and Kittross, *Stay Tuned,* 864; *Television Digest,* December 10, 1949, quoted in Hess, *DuMont Television Network,* 69; "Half of First Ten Pulse Ratings Taken by Sports," *Broadcasting,* July 12, 1948, 14; "Telestatus Report," *Broadcasting,* April 26, 1948, 9–10.

46. May Television Report, Reynold Kraft, June 15, 1948, TV Sales, NBC 398/17.

47. Frank N. Russell, Interoffice memo to Niles Trammell, July 9, 1948, Station Relations, NBC 574/15.

48. Ibid.

49. As Eileen Meehan argues, television ratings have never been an exact measure of actual viewership (Eileen Meehan, "Why We Don't Count: The Commodity Audience,"

in *Logics of Television: Essays in Cultural Criticism,* ed. Patricia Mellencamp [Blooming-ton: Indiana UP, 1990], 117–37). Ratings were, however, a regular part of the information flow at NBC, which as Pfeffer and Salancik (*External Control*) point out, is significant in understanding how the organization defines what information is important. Top Ten Programs, February and March 1948, TV Files, NBC 106/5.

50. Wrestling 1949–1952, James Dolan Papers, NBC 344/12; "New Business," *Broadcasting,* September 13, 1948, 6; Gunther Beer in Washington, Carleton Smith Papers, NBC 214/12, 214/26; George Sandefer, WNBW Report, February 1949, Carleton Smith Papers, NBC 214/27; Harry C. Kopf to Niles Trammell, Monthly Summary of Operations, January 11, 1949, Carleton Smith Papers, NBC 214/26.

51. "Telestatus Report," *Broadcasting,* April 26, 1948, 10; "Ford Completes TV Sports for Summer," *Broadcasting,* March 1, 1948, 17.

52. "Telestatus," *Broadcasting,* December 20, 1948, 37.

53. Ibid.

54. Bulletin 70, November 3, 1948, Research, NBC 184/1.

55. Ibid.

56. "Texaco Video Show Hits Record 63.2 Telerating," *Broadcasting,* November 1, 1948, 64; "Hooper: Berle Still Tops in N.Y.," *Broadcasting,* May 2, 1949, 40.

57. NBC's Monday boxing program was rated #1 in New York, with a 54.0 rating, and #2 in Philadelphia, with a rating of 46.7. NBC's Friday boxing series ranked eighth in both cities, with a 33.0 and 29.3 rating, respectively. "Pulse Telefacts," *Broadcasting,* November 22, 1948, insert.

58. "RCA Report: Sarnoff Denies Shakeup," *Broadcasting,* May 9, 1949, 30, 59.

59. "NBC Layoffs: Central Division Hardest Hit," *Broadcasting,* May 9, 1949, 51.

60. John H. MacDonald, 1949 NBC budget report to J. H. McConnell, VP, RCA, June 27, 1949, Carleton Smith Papers, NBC 214/32.

61. Ibid.

62. Carleton Smith, Interoffice memo to Niles Trammell, July 21, 1949, Carleton Smith Papers, NBC 214/28. There is evidence that sponsored programs also often exceeded their budgets, and efforts were made to keep spending under control.

63. William Stern, Interoffice memo to Norman Blackburn, June 17, 1949, William Stern Papers, NBC 346/4; James Dolan, Interoffice memo to George Frey, July 11, 1949, James Dolan Papers, NBC 341/1.

64. James Dolan, Interoffice memo to Carleton Smith, July 21, 1949, James Dolan Papers, NBC 344/12.

65. James Dolan, Interoffice memo to Carleton Smith, August 4, 1949, James Dolan Papers, NBC 344/12.

66. Fred Shawn, Interoffice memo to James Dolan, August 12, 1949, James Dolan Papers, NBC 344/12.

67. Brooks and Marsh, *Complete Directory,* 1154.

68. "August Telepulse," *Broadcasting,* August 22, 1949, 47; Brooks and Marsh, *Complete Directory,* 962.

69. Pat Weaver, Memorandum Number One, September 26, 1949, Weaver Papers, NBC 118/5.

70. Michele Hilmes, *Radio Voices: American Broadcasting, 1922–1952* (Minneapolis: Minnesota UP, 1997), especially chapter 5 and conclusion. Hilmes argues that the "magazine format" show (exemplified by *Today, Tonight,* and *Home*), as well as the concept of multiple sponsorship, had been familiar to American radio listeners since the 1930s. It is also interesting to note that another Weaver "innovation," the oft-touted "Operation Frontal Lobes" project, initiated in the early 1950s, mirrored NBC's failed "feature service" efforts from 1948.

71. FCC Form 324, quoted in Hess, *DuMont Television Network,* 75, 78.

72. January 30, 1953, Bulletin, NBC Research Bulletins, NBC 184/2.

73. Boddy, *Fifties Television,* 168–70.

4 / The Importance of Colorization of Motion Pictures and Syndicated Television Programs to Broadcasting, 1985–1990

Douglas Ferguson

Motion pictures originally filmed in black-and-white are being converted to color movies by a computer process known as *colorization*.[1] Unlike hand-tinting, which manually adds one or two colors to individual frames of film, colorization allows the choice of several thousand colors combined to render a full-color visual effect as if the film had been originally shot in color.[2] Although the process has been used to restore aging color movies, its primary application is for black-and-white motion pictures. This innovation has created controversy among media practitioners, even though black-and-white films like Fritz Lang's classic *Metropolis* had been tinted for rerelease into art house exhibition long before the advent of computer colorization.[3]

The impact of new technologies on mass communication sometimes arises in the most unexpected places. Just as media observers thirty years ago could never have anticipated the disruption to traditional television caused by VCRs, satellite/cable channels, and remote control devices, it would have been similarly inconceivable even twenty years ago that old movies could be made to look newer. The unpredictable nature of technological change in the mass media makes it increasingly important to study the ramifications of current developments so that public policy may adjust to unknown changes in the future.[4] To that end, this chapter traces the controversy regarding motion picture colorization.

This chapter explains the economic and aesthetic issues inherent to the colorization controversy, the stakeholders involved, and their political and legal activities. The controversy has wound down considerably since the summer of 1988, but it is far from dead. Opponents of colorization continue to battle for the moral rights perspective.[5] Briefly, the concept of moral rights is the European legal principle that protects "artistic copyright." The concept is suggested by the language of the Berne Convention for the Protection of Literary and Artistic Works (2 Martens [2nd] 173) dated September 9, 1886. Moral right was integrated into the Berne Convention at the Rome Conference of 1928.[6] It is noteworthy that the United States is not a signatory of the convention; in the United States, property rights are given higher regard than artistic rights.

SIGNIFICANCE TO BROADCASTING

Colorization was extremely important to broadcasting in the 1980s, because the appetite for filmed content grew immense with the proliferation of cable channels and the resulting competitive pressures. Previously, broadcasters were content to treat black-and-white materials as being too old to show, despite the intrinsic entertainment (and artistic) value of filmed series made prior to the network conversion to color in the mid-1960s. Prior to the arrival of multichannel television, broadcasters controlled what materials were seen on television and could thereby segregate materials not filmed in color to late-night time periods, if shown at all.

Television programming has changed significantly since the early 1970s. And since the early 1980s, the number of independent stations has grown, thus increasing the need for programming. Independent stations were particularly interested in movies but believed movies filmed in color would attract much larger audiences than those filmed in black-and-white. Further, multichannel moguls like Ted Turner were willing to find new homes for old programming, thereby increasing older shows' value in syndication. Older movies were of special interest because entire channels could be devoted to classic movies (e.g., Turner Classic Movies). Older series (e.g., *Gilligan's Island, McHale's Navy*), however, had limited appeal, because contemporary audiences expected color instead of black-and-white. The arrival of computer technologies that could paint color onto black-and-white film coincided with a historic point in the demand and supply for dozens of cable channels and hundreds of new television stations not affiliated with a net-work. Hence, the potential profitability of content once thought to be use-less increased.

A SHORT HISTORY OF COLORIZATION

Film color began with hand-stenciling at the turn of the century "by battal-ions of women who, with the aid of magnifying glasses, colored each frame individually" with the permission of French and German directors.[7] Con-ventional color came in the 1920s with the Technicolor two-strip variety for features like *The Black Pirate* (1926) and was improved in the 1930s with the three-color Technicolor process for *Becky Sharp* (1935).[8] The process was very expensive, making it more sensible for the film studios to produce thou-sands of films in black-and-white instead of color. Computerized coloriza-tion did not develop until the 1970s.

The significant technological accomplishment of the moon landing in 1969 played a role in the development of colorization, leading to the birth of a new industry.[9] Wilson Markle began colorizing the video of Apollo as-tronauts in the early 1970s but was bound by a ten-year agreement to work only for NASA. In 1981 Markle joined with brothers Morris and Earl Glick to form a computer graphics firm that by 1983 had become Colorization, Inc.[10] The company was owned by Hal Roach Studios and by Color Systems Technology (CST); each owned 50 percent.[11] In July 1985, American Film Technologies (AFT) was formed to compete with CST. Colorization did not appear to be a moneymaker, however, and by December 1987 AFT man-aged to lose $4.7 million.[12]

The potential for significant profit for colorization was going unrealized until entrepreneur Ted Turner purchased the MGM library (3,300 titles) in 1986. Turner simultaneously announced his intention to colorize as many as 280 films, a declaration that served as an important watershed event for the colorization industry. Both AFT and CST had an important economic agenda to pursue in their attempts to transform the large number of black-and-white films into color.[13] A further technical development announced in August 1987 provided another boost for the colorization industry. CST de-veloped a method for computerized colorization that was three times faster than previous methods.[14] Although this had little impact on cost, it short-ened the time needed to get an "enhanced" film to television syndication. By

1987, then, the improving colorization technology made it relatively easy to recast black-and-white images into color, a fact that served as the catalyst for a controversy to develop between stakeholders.

THE CONTROVERSY

The controversy surrounding film colorization centered on the dispute between the copyright owner of the motion picture and the various creators of the motion picture, most often the director. Directors are virtually unanimous in their opposition to what they term the "coloroids."[15] The late Orson Welles left instructions that Ted Turner not use "crayons" on *Citizen Kane*.[16] At the same time, copyright owners see the films as their property and want to market them to a public that presumably does not want to see them in monochrome. Ted Turner drew attention with his remark, "The last time I checked, I owned those films."[17] The fundamental question may well be whether the motion picture is art, commodity, or both.[18] Attempts to resolve the controversy have involved stakeholders, and eventually Congress and the courts.

Aesthetic Assumptions

A central issue in the controversy is an aesthetic judgment that colorized movies constitute an assault on the senses. Bernard Beck outlined "the aesthetic concerns at stake" for the artist, the art world, and what was called "general human concerns," specifically dealing with the nature of work.[19] Beck wrote: "In the arts, work is still defined in a way that includes personal meaningfulness as an intrinsic property. This does not mean that artists can count on maintaining such personal integrity, but [it is] a paramount goal."[20]

Beck attributed the establishment of the hegemony of color to "the major innovation that threatened the mass popularity of all movies and gave movies the final push into artistic respectability: the arrival of television."[21] As television became the new target for scorn, motion pictures "seemed more artistic."[22] The supposed demand for colorization, however, presents "a dilemma to any putative guardians of the sacred status of black-and-white movies as an authentic art medium."[23]

What caused the aesthetic sanctification of black-and-white films? R. N. Wilson theorized that nostalgia played a significant role by asserting that in a more general sense, both filmmakers and members of the audience may react as if their memories had been violated by coloring. Memory is crucial to a concept of self and to a grasp of continuity, of meaningful personal chronology. If a remembered movie, as art and artifact, is altered, viewers of a certain age may feel their past has been betrayed.[24] Wilson pointed out that art, unlike life, can be "had again" as an aesthetic experience. Even though still photography began in black-and-white because of technical limitations, "photographers turned necessity into a virtue and exalted black-and-white as the only faithful medium for photography as an art form."[25] Similarly, some movie directors have claimed "certain emotions may only be truly captured in colorless terms."[26] According to Barry Sherman and Joseph Dominick, black-and-white evokes different emotions: "colorization takes away the sharp edges from an image, blurring it, making it less distinct, if not less real."[27]

Artistic authenticity is an important element of the colorization debate. Dorothy Nelkin noted that authenticity is a necessary condition of aesthetic value, writing that the dark, brooding styles and glistening wet streets of 1940s film noir are expressed in the subtleties of shading and contrast that are intrinsic to black-and-white. Color applied to black-and-white film imposes its own dimensions, its own quality, that violate the intent of the artist and the integrity of the film.[28] Michael Schudson, however, disputed Nelkin's demand for authenticity. Instead, the issue became how works of art are updated: "We perform Shakespeare in modern dress. We read the Bible in translations. . . . Our symphony orchestras play Bach's music on instruments he never heard and in secular halls of culture he never intended or imagined. We silently read and study as 'literature' poetry originally created for oral performance."[29] Indeed, Schudson wondered if all literary translation should be prohibited, because—like the film colorist—a translator makes aesthetic decisions on every page without consulting the author.

Robert Russett made a case for colorization by discussing the aesthetics of video versus film, explaining that there is "a clear distinction between the inherent qualities of projected film and the type of imagery that is generated when a motion picture is electronically transmitted."[30] Russett wondered about the millions of existing black-and-white TV sets that eliminate the beautiful chromatic tone of color films: why no outcry about decolorization? For Russett, the opponents of colorization miss the fundamental alteration of film when it is televised: "The only way to experience film in its pure and original form is to view it projected in a theater."[31]

Another important aspect of the art versus commodity argument is the basic premise that the moral rights of the creators, especially those approaching the status of the auteur, are more important than the financial rights of the copyright holders. Several observers of this controversy have noted the collaborative nature of motion pictures.[32] Although the artist who creates a painting (or a concerto) usually toils as a lone creator, the director of commercial feature films necessarily engages in a cooperative effort. When the director says, "Don't touch *my* film!" the other individuals who conceived, helped create, or financed the motion picture can logically ask, "*Whose* film?" Indeed, some films (e.g., *The Wizard of Oz*) have more than one director.[33] Mayer suggested that most of the films involved in the colorization controversy are not "director films" but "studio films," for which the screenwriter was more responsible than the director for the creative vision.[34] As suggested earlier, this is a problematic assumption in light of the U.S. legal system, where copyright laws are recognized over moral rights.[35]

Yet another substantive issue is whether the public genuinely dislikes black-and-white movies on video. The research evidence is mixed. This preference for the original, uncut version is presumed to be particularly keen among film aficionados, although Sherman and Dominick found no differences in attitude toward colorization among college students who were judged to fit or not fit the "fan" category.[36] The answer most likely depends on the historical context in which the question is asked.[37] At a time in media history when color television was still diffusing, there probably was a disdain for black-and-white content, because color was seen as "more modern" (often synonymous with "better," though not necessarily). For example, the marketability of old television shows in black-and-white was at a low point in the 1970s. Many of the pro-colorization companies lived through that era, an experience that may "color" their current feelings. Now that color television is the norm, it could be that modern audiences are more accepting of monochrome materials, witnessed by the large number of contemporary motion pictures (and music videos) being made (or simulated) in black-and-white.[38] If this is true, Frank Lovece correctly observed that colorization is only a fad, like 3-D.[39] Several film directors predicted: "Ultimately, of course, the colorizers will lose this battle . . . future generations will discard these cheesy, artificial symbols of one society's greed."[40]

No discussion of aesthetics is complete without addressing the "color knob" argument.[41] Proponents of colorization argue that opponents can turn down the color control on their television sets if they want to see programs and films in black-and-white. Opponents have noted, however, that many color television sets do not permit the adjustment of chroma levels. Furthermore, once the image has been colorized, it is not as sharp as if it had remained in black-and-white. But it is no surprise that non-artists fail to see the difference between real black-and-white and ersatz black-and-white any more than the fact that most television viewers are not deeply offended by the phony look of colorization.

Finally, in answer to the art-or-commodity issue, the author of this chapter assumes that motion pictures are both an art and a commodity. This premise is useful for understanding the eventual compromise that was entered into between the stakeholders of the industry debate.

Stakeholders

The colorization controversy began with opposing camps, both of whom were significant stakeholders in the art versus commodity dilemma.[42] Representing the artists were the American Film Institute, the Directors Guild of America, the Writers Guild, the American Society of Cinematographers, and the Screen Actors Guild. The most active and visible among these artistic organizations was the Directors Guild of America (DGA).

While the Directors Guild of America was appealing to Congress in 1987 about the colorization of past films, it was also looking to the future. In May 1987 the DGA began film and television contract negotiations with the Alliance of Motion Picture and Television Producers (AMPTP). In parallel talks starting the same month, the DGA began direct negotiations with the management of the major studios regarding "creative rights."[43] Opposition to colorization was only one of twenty creative rights proposals. The DGA sought "to prohibit any material alteration of a motion picture after delivery of the answer print [director's cut]."[44] Other proposals required the director's permission for television editing, panning and scanning, and changing to allow 3-D exhibition.

On the other side, the Motion Picture Association of America (MPAA) allied itself with the National Association of Broadcasters (NAB), Turner Entertainment Company (a licensee of superstation WTBS), the Association of Independent Television Stations, and the Video Software Dealers of America.[45] The teaming of the MPAA and the NAB (normally enemies) made for strange bedfellows, but the film studios have a tradition of being at cross-purposes with the creative community. George Lipsitz wrote: "The historic battle between artists and entrepreneurs extends back to the beginning of the industry."[46]

Behind the industry proponents is the colorization industry itself. These companies are American Film Technologies, Inc. (AFT), Color Systems Technology, Inc. (CST), and Tintoretto. Their arguments in favor of colorization were among the most forceful during the earliest congressional subcommittee hearings on colorization.[47] For example, they argued that low demand for color movies by television stations (virtually the only remaining mass exhibitor of classic films until the popularization of VCRs) was preventing old movies from being shown.

As with so many aspects of life, this alignment of artist versus corporation is not so simple. For example, movie studios like MCA, Paramount, and Warner do not colorize their libraries, reportedly to avoid offending the directors with whom they wish to work.[48] Disney and Twentieth Century Fox, however, are not above tinting the black-and-white films in their vaults. Disney films (e.g., *The Absent-Minded Professor*) are assumed to be in little demand among young people, who "reject black-and-white films with near unanimity."[49]

The Economics of Film Alteration and Enhancement

To further complicate the issues addressed here, it is necessary to consider that colorization is not the only way that films have been altered or enhanced.[50] Motion pictures are routinely subjected to panning and scanning, time compression, and editing. Moreover, films themselves are remade by other film directors. Beck argued there was "no hint of shame or scandal" with the remaking of film classics.[51]

With the advent of wide-screen motion pictures in the 1950s, the amount of material that can be displayed on television screens had already become a problem before colorization was developed (ironically, the wide-screen process was the film industry's response to competition from television). In order to show all the action, especially where directors made full use of the wide screen, television versions of such movies have been forced to pan and scan the image.[52] Films such as *Lawrence of Arabia* and *Rebel Without a Cause* are difficult to watch on television, even with panning and scanning. The "letterbox" format, which reduces the entire cinematic frame to preserve the width (at the expense of using the full height of the television screen), has been a recent response to the problem. The reverse process (reframing an old film for wide-screen exhibition) for theatrical releases has not created a similar controversy; one famous example is the reframing of *Gone With the Wind*.[53]

A wide variety of technological alterations are used on films currently, and there may be more in the future. Television stations have long resorted to chopping movies to conform to commercial breaks or time slots.[54] Some motion pictures have been electronically "sped up" (a process called *lexiconning*) to make them fit a shorter time slot.[55] Such editing has long been an issue but never led to congressional hearings on the infringements of film directors' moral rights. Likewise, motion pictures have been enhanced to permit stereophonic sound.[56] There has been little hue and cry about sound issues. Apparently, there is a lack of customer interest, not unlike the disinterest shown by the public toward the colorization controversy.[57] Indeed, colorization may not be the last affront to film purists. David Robb noted the potential in the future for 3-D and holography to change the aesthetics of motion pictures. It is one thing to put a veneer of color on *Casablanca,* but it may be a greater shock to have Rick, Ilsa, and Sam literally in one's living room.[58]

Woody Allen, a film director who makes contemporary films in black-and-white, called film colorization "the straw that broke the camel's back."[59] Indeed, the initial use of more noticeable film classics like *It's a Wonderful Life* and *Casablanca* has attracted more negative attention to the process than the colorizing of less-appreciated films like *Sands of Iwo Jima* or old TV shows like *McHale's Navy.*[60] Ironically for Woody Allen, his first film success was *What's Up, Tiger Lily?*—in which he took a Japanese B-movie and used new sound, dialogue, and footage for humorous effect.[61] One wonders if the Japanese director was outraged.

A separate area of concern deals with nontechnological alterations involving motion pictures. David Blum argued that film directors like John Huston and Alfred Hitchcock have taken great liberties with the novels they adapt.[62] He cites *The Maltese Falcon* as a prime example of "how movie directors alter other artists' work for their own benefit."[63] Could it be that Dashiell Hammett's original work is "filmized" in the same sense that John Huston's original work is colorized?

It is difficult to avoid judging the colorization controversy in terms other than its being a "simple exercise in greed,"[64] and many technological devices are undertaken with an eye toward increasing audiences, hence profits.[65] Certainly there was a potential for Ted Turner to make a great deal of money from colorization. Dempsey estimated that the $300,000 cost for colorizing each motion picture is substantially less than the conservative estimate of $500,000 revenue per title.[66] Turner's library of one hundred classic movies could thus yield $20 million. Unfortunately, 99 percent of home video renters do not care about old movies, whether they are colorized or uncolorized.[67] Officials at Turner's company admitted that the timetable for completing the colorization allowed no times for a home video window.[68]

To date, the financial payoff has been with television syndication of colorized movies. At the heart of the economic situation is the ability of colorized programs to attain higher ratings than black-and-white programs; color programs on television have 80 percent higher ratings than comparable ones in black-and-white.[69] Television syndication of old classic television programs would be the "final test" of the financial success of the colorization process.[70]

Initially, the firms that invested in colorization lost large sums of money. There was a time when it looked as if the process was not profitable. However, the finances of companies such as AFT (American Film Technologies, Inc.) had improved substantially by 1990.[71] But just one year later the financial picture was less profitable for AFT.[72] Indeed, colorization was abandoned in the early 1990s because it was no longer considered cost-effective.

Political and Legal Issues

There is a strong bond between members of the entertainment industry and politicians. The entertainment industry often uses its "star appeal" to influence the political process. The motion picture, television, and recording businesses are uniquely able to bring highly recognizable people to testify on their behalf in congressional hearings, a strategy that was used in the colorization debate when the DGA arranged appearances of James Stewart and Ginger Rogers, neither of whom was a director. More significantly, members of the entertainment industry are also large political contributors. Aside from the money given to campaigns, the same "star appeal" can enhance political campaigns. One of the presidential hopefuls in 1988 was Representative Richard Gephardt (D-MO), who on May 13, 1987, offered a bill that promised to "provide artistic authors exclusive rights to control material alteration including colorization of motion pictures."[73] A key provision would

require the director (or the director's heirs) to give permission for colorization. Senator Daniel Patrick Moynihan (D-NY) similarly announced he was
"considering" offering a bill similar to Gephardt's "Film Integrity Act of
1987" (H.R. 2400), though neither was given much chance for success. It
could be argued that an organization with less highly visible members would
not be able to convene a congressional subcommittee on its behalf. On the
other hand, Senator Patrick Leahy (D-VT), who chaired the 1987 subcommittee, was apparently not swayed by the movie stars. Even so, presidential
hopefuls like Gephardt may have been influenced by the high-profile nature
of the colorization imbroglio.

Conversely, the political climate was ripe in the 1980s for commercial
interests to cast aside the aesthetic interests of those who consider film to be
art. Ronald Reagan was in the White House presiding over a fundamental
shift away from close federal regulation of American broadcasting. This de-
regulatory mood probably influenced companies to consider economic alter-
natives that would have seemed unthinkable in previous decades, although
deregulation began to take root toward the end of the Carter presidency.

With political influence supporting both sides of the art versus commodity issue, in May 1987 the DGA began their "social negotiation of
rights" before the Senate subcommittee chaired by Senator Patrick Leahy.[74]
The directors were represented by prominent artists such as Woody Allen
and Milos Forman.[75] On the other side stood the colorization industry and
Turner's forces.[76] The hearings had no immediate impact, aside from the
introduction of the Film Preservation Act of 1987 by Senator Gephardt,
discussed above. Representative Leahy saw little harm in alteration of a film
when the original motion picture, like an adapted novel, was still available.[77]
The two sides were uncompromising.

The critical period in the history of film colorization came during the
summer of 1988. The initial indications pointed to a victory for the DGA,[78]
but this proved premature. In June 1988 legislators and Jack Valenti of the
MPAA successfully hammered out a compromise, similar to Valenti's successful work with the movie rating system twenty years earlier.[79] The compromise, principally sponsored by Representative Bob Mrazek (D-NY),
called for colorized films to display a disclaimer stating that directors had
not been consulted regarding the alteration of the motion picture.[80] An
original pre-colorized video copy of each title would be sent to the Library
of Congress. A film preservation board was created to choose twenty-five

motion pictures per year that would designate certain films as "classics" and further require disclaimer labels for such films when subjected to material alterations such as colorization.[81] The full House of Representatives approved the bill unanimously on June 29, 1988. The DGA hailed the measure as a "tremendous victory for film lovers everywhere."[82] In August 1988 the Senate made minor changes to the film preservation bill, and the first twenty-five titles of the National Film Registry were selected by the board in September 1988.[83] The list was culled from one thousand titles nominated by mail and finally selected by James Billington, librarian of Congress. The film preservation bill was signed by President Ronald Reagan in October 1988.[84] The legislative outcome of the summer of 1988 was Ted Turner's colorized telecast of *Casablanca* on November 8, 1988. The fate of *Citizen Kane* was different. Under an interpretation of the contract Orson Welles had signed to direct the film, Ted Turner agreed not to colorize *Kane*.[85]

The latest phase of the DGA's quest for "moral rights" began during congressional hearings in October 1989. Although Senate subcommittee members were sympathetic to filmmaker concerns, they were equally committed to maintaining the status quo for the film studios, "an industry that contributes mightily to the U.S. balance of trade."[86] Senator Orrin Hatch (R-UT) said he was "generally opposed to the imposition of moral rights concepts by federal statute rather than through the bargaining of the parties to a transaction."[87] In February 1990 the DGA had better fortune with the House of Representatives, where a congressional panel passed a bill granting "enforceable rights" to visual artists. Representative Robert Kastenmeier (D-WI) sponsored the measure and chaired the subcommittee, but he said the bill was narrowly focused on painters, sculptors, and graphic artists, such that film directors' rights would be "issues for another day."[88]

The art versus commodity colorization issue has been fought in courtrooms as well as in legislative hearing rooms. Scholars have argued that colorization is not really a legal issue, given the current status of copyright in the United States.[89] The only cases dealing with colorization were ones that involved ownership, not artistic rights.[90] Directors did not donate their work to the studios but were very well paid.[91]

W. S. Strong outlined the copyright considerations in layperson's terms.[92] A colorized videotape is, by law, a derivative work rather than a mere copy. He noted that once a film is in the public domain (i.e., no longer under copyright), the legal right of the colorization companies to create a derivative work is protected by copyright laws. Norman Glick of Colorization, Inc., asked rhetorically: "If the directors cared so much about their films, why did they let their copyrights lapse in the first place?"[93]

The colorization industry achieved its first important legal victory in June 1987, when the copyright office of the Library of Congress agreed that colorized films were "derivative works" eligible for copyright protection. The decision turned on two key elements: human intervention (rather than by computer alone) and the wide range of colors used (four thousand per frame from a palette of sixteen thousand). The DGA had opposed separate copyright protection, arguing that the colorized versions were not sufficiently different from the originals.[94] The ruling concurred with arguments by Hal Roach Studios that color choices would be "based on artistic experience, expertise, and judgment."[95] In April 1990 the DGA found a way to prevent Turner Entertainment Company from colorizing *The Haunting,* a 1963 film directed by Robert Wise. Wise's contract contained a clause that specified the motion picture be filmed in black-and-white and that no substantial changes could be made without Wise's consent.[96]

During that same month the Supreme Court ruled in *Abend v. MCA* that MCA, James Stewart, and the Alfred Hitchcock estate had violated the copyright of a literary researcher when it rereleased *Rear Window* in 1983 without his consent. Sheldon Abend owned the rights to a story on which *Rear Window* had been based.[97] By May 1990, Turner Entertainment Company had decided to delay its decision to show *The Haunting* (which it had already paid to colorize) because of the Supreme Court ruling. For his part, Abend hoped to form a kind of "literary ASCAP" to protect authors from alteration by filmmakers.

CONCLUSION

The fate of colorization was actually sealed by 1991, and the whole issue is now an interesting footnote in broadcast history prior to 1990. An official at AFT was quoted as saying colorization movie syndication is "in the toilet," with only $22,000 profit per title.[98] Perhaps colorization went out with a whimper. The colorization controversy has moved from a narrow issue of colorization to a broader one that deals with the rights of artists. This chapter has addressed the underlying issues along with the sequence of events that led to the state of colorization by 1990. Several conclusions may be drawn from the issues and events.

First, it is unlikely that the "camel's back" will ever be the same, given the current trends in copyright law.[99] New communication technologies yet to be developed will likely continue an assault on works of art, at least in the eyes of traditionalists. Even modern motion pictures will eventually fall into the public domain and be subject to "enhancements" beyond our present imagination. In this sense it is useful to study the course of events for motion picture colorization, because it serves as an example of how problems may arise and subsequently be resolved.

Second, it is probably disingenuous for proponents (and opponents) of colorization to hide behind the argument that all alterations and enhancements of films are either all good, all neutral, or all bad. Moreover, the analogy between the colorization of a black-and-white motion picture and the film adaptation of a literary work is overworked. The public *knows* the difference between an adaptation and an alteration, even though it still has trouble telling the difference between video and film. On the other hand, the argument that most or all of the classic films in question were intended to be released in black-and-white is equally overstated. One could make a reasonable argument that no photography or cinematography would have been done in black-and-white had the color process been available inexpensively. Others would argue that some black-and-white films *still* would have been an artistic choice, but it remains difficult to imagine such "choice" occurring on the scale of pre-1960s Hollywood.

Finally, it is still unclear how important the colorization controversy is to the general public. Although public opinion should not ultimately decide whether colorization is an acceptable practice, the lack of concern among the audience for movies is at least an indicator of whether colorization is an important controversy. The public will not likely suffer, regardless of the outcome. It is unlikely that motion picture directors will be less willing to create masterpieces. Nor is it probable that black-and-white classics will become less available to those who want to see them. The 91 percent penetration of VCRs (not to mention DVDs) in the United States has taken the decision away from the traditional distribution systems.[100]

NOTES

1. R. N. Wilson, "Green and Other Colors," *Society* (May/June 1987): 21–23. The term "colorization" becomes a problem when put in its gerund form, "colorizing." A more appropriate term would be "coloring," but the former version has worked its way

into the American lexicon. Turner Entertainment called the process "colorimaging" to avoid the grammarians (see *Broadcasting,* October 24, 1988, 45).

2. Bruce Klopfenstein, *The Technology of Colorization* (Chicago, IL: Speech Communication Association, 1991).

3. Bernard Beck, "Inglorious Color," *Society* (May/June 1987): 4–12. The Killiam Connection is a private library of early black-and-white films available for 16mm rental. The latest catalogue indicates that many of the titles (e.g., *The Birth of a Nation* and *Intolerance*) are tinted, or as Killiam phrases it: "When appropriate, COLOR TINTS are added."

4. Beck, "Inglorious Color," 4–12.

5. David J. Kohs, "Paint Your Wagon—Please! Colorization, Copyright, and the Search for Moral Rights," *Federal Communications Law Journal* 40 (1988): 1–38.

6. Michael Sissine Wantuck, "Artistic Integrity, Public Policy, and Copyright: Colorization Reduced to Black and White," *Ohio State Law Journal* 50 (1989): 1013–33.

7. "Tinting and Toning," *The Economist,* April 2, 1988, 83.

8. Herbert T. Kalmus, "Technicolor Adventures in Cinemaland," *SMPTE Journal* 100 (March 1991): 182–90.

9. The first moon pictures were available only in black-and-white, for technical reasons.

10. M. Sheridan, "Black and White in Living Color," *Canadian Business,* February 1987, 57–63.

11. "Hollywood Color Wars Attract Risk Takers to Do the Planning," *Television/Radio Age,* April 4, 1988, 121, 126.

12. Ibid., 121.

13. According to the author's survey of the Internet Movie Database at http://www.imdb.com/, the proportion of non-animated U.S. feature films released in color for each respective decade from the 1920s through the 1980s was the following: 1%, 13%, 13%, 34%, 60%, 95%, and 97%.

14. "Color Systems Outfit Devises Faster Method of Colorizing Pics, TV," *Variety,* April 2, 1987, 3, 43.

15. Sheridan, "Black and White in Living Color," 57–63. Ironically, Frank Capra was originally supportive of the idea and approved the colorization work done by others on a ten-minute segment of *It's a Wonderful Life.* Later, he reconsidered when he was denied creative control. The colorization firm had discovered that Capra had let the copyright lapse years before.

16. Morrie Gelman, "Colorization of 'Kane' Halted," *Variety,* February 22, 1989, 419–20.

17. "Hollywood Color Wars," 121, 126.

18. Beck, "Inglorious Color," 4–12.

19. Ibid.

20. Ibid, 5.

21. Ibid, 6.

22. Ibid.

23. Ibid, 10.

24. Wilson, "Green and Other Colors," 22.

25. Ibid.

26. Ibid.

27. Barry L. Sherman and Joseph R. Dominick, "Perceptions of Colorization," *Journalism Quarterly* 65 (1988): 976–80.

28. Dorothy Nelkin, "Show and Sell," *Society* (May/June 1987): 16.

29. Michael Schudson, "Colorization and Authenticity," *Society* (May/June 1987): 18.

30. Robert Russett, "A Case for Colorization," *Audio-Visual Communications,* June 1987, 52.

31. Ibid., 69.

32. "Colorizing Bill Seen Dying," *TV Digest,* June 27, 1988, 9; Paul Harris, "Top Director in D.C. to Speak Out against Colorizing," *Variety,* May 13, 1987, 3, 48; R. L. Mayer, R. Word, and B. Young, "Colorization: The Arguments For," *Journal of Arts Management and Law* 17 (1987): 64–78.

33. Mayer et al., "Colorization," 64–78.

34. Ibid., 76.

35. Kohs, "Paint Your Wagon," 1–38; Wantuck, "Artistic Integrity," 1013–33.

36. Sherman and Dominick, "Perceptions of Colorization," 976–80.

37. Indeed, colorization has been abandoned because it is no longer considered cost-effective. Companies that charged three thousand dollars per minute to colorize films were not making enough money. By the time such companies raised their prices in the 1990s, their initial customers had become disenchanted with the return on their original investment. Ted Turner quietly discontinued colorizing his film library.

38. Wantuck, "Artistic Integrity," 1013–33.

39. Frank Lovece, "CBS/Fox Releases Intensify Colorization Debate," *Billboard,* January 31, 1987, 52–53.

40. Woody Allen, Milos Forman, Sydney Pollack, Ginger Rogers, and Elliot Silverstein, "Colorization: The Arguments For," *Journal of Arts Management and Law* 17 (1987): 79–93.

41. Ibid.

42. "Hollywood Color Wars"; Lovece, "CBS/Fox Releases," 52–53.

43. David Robb, "Directors Push to Protect Their Pix," *Variety,* May 27, 1987, 5, 37.

44. Ibid., 5.

45. Drew Voros, "Anti-colorization Crusade in Uphill Battle," *Variety,* September 1, 1989, 9, 12.

46. George Lipsitz, "Blue Money," *Society* (May/June 1987): 14–15.

47. Mayer et al., "Colorization," 64–78.

48. John Dempsey, "Canadian Tax Loophole Lifts Colorizers, *Variety,* February 4, 1991, 31, 33.

49. B. Young, "Video Classics: Color Them Profitable," *Billboard,* June 13, 1987, 9.

50. Asa A. Berger, "Film Technology's Latest Frankenstein," *Society* (May/June 1987): 12–13.

51. Beck, "Inglorious Color," 4–12.

52. Dennis Wharton and James McBride, "Second Group of Pix Chosen for National Film Registry," *Variety,* October 22, 1990, 10.

53. Beck, "Inglorious Color," 4–12.

54. "House Hearing Covers Colorization Spectrum," *Broadcasting,* May 18, 1987, 78–79.

55. Gary Edgerton, "'The Germans Wore Gray, You Wore Blue,' Frank Capra, Casablanca, and the Colorization Controversy of the 1980s," *Journal of Popular Film and Television* 27 (Winter 2000): 24–32.

56. "House Hearing," 78.

57. Chris Morris and Earl Paige, "It's Not the Color of Money," *Billboard,* May 16, 1987, 1, 85.

58. Robb, "Directors Push," 5.

59. Allen et al., "Colorization," 79–93.

60. "Here's Looking at Hue, Kid," *Broadcasting,* June 13, 1988, 46–47.

61. Beck, "Inglorious Color," 4–12.

62. David Blum, "Emotion Pictures," *New Republic,* February 9, 1987, 13–15.

63. Ibid., 14.

64. Beck, "Inglorious Color," 11.

65. "Hollywood Color Wars"; Eugene Secunda, "Is Movie Colorization a Moral Issue for Broadcasters?" *Broadcasting,* May 25, 1987, 20; Sheridan, "Black and White in Living Color."

66. John Dempsey, "Distribs Find Pics the Color of Money," *Variety,* April 8, 1988, 43, 58.

67. Young, "Video Classics," 9.

68. R. Tyler, "Retailers Say Black & White More Popular Than Colorized Versions," *Variety,* August 3, 1988, 50.

69. Secunda, "Colorization a Moral Issue," 20; Tyler, "Black & White More Popular," 50.

70. Dempsey, "Distribs Find Pics," 43.

71. John Dempsey, "O'seas TV Viewers Getting 1st Look at Colorized Pix," *Variety,* January 31, 1990, 65.

72. Dempsey, "Canadian Tax Loophole," 31.

73. Harris, "Top Director," 3.

74. Beck, "Inglorious Color," 7; Harris, "Top Director," 3.

75. Allen et al., "Colorization," 79–93.

76. Mayer et al., "Colorization," 64–78.

77. Harris, "Top Director," 3.

78. Paul Harris, "Directors Win D.C. Victories on Colorization," *Variety*, June 22, 1988, 1, 77.

79. Jack Valenti reprised his role as the peacemaker. He was successful in portraying the government as the villain.

80. Paul Harris, "Pic Preservation Board Okayed by Prez; Win Against Colorizing," *Variety*, October 8, 1988, 2. The disclaimer read: "This is a colorized version of a film originally marketed and distributed in black & white. It has been altered without the participation of the principal director, screenwriter and other creators of the original film"; Paul Harris, "House Okays Film Registry Compromise," *Variety*, July 6, 1988, 5, 29.

81. The board comprised the presidents of the MPAA, NAB, AMPTP, Academy of Motion Picture Arts and Sciences, Screen Actors Guild, the Directors Guild, Writers Guild, National Society of Film Criticism, Society for Cinema Studies, American Film Institute, University Film and Video Association, and the chairpersons of the film departments at UCLA and New York University; "House Bill Calls for Labeling of Colorized Films," *Broadcasting*, July 4, 1988, 49.

82. Yet, the original DGA version of the bill would have prohibited the colorized film from being exhibited under its original title. Harris, "House Okays," 5.

83. "Bill Creating Panel to Label 'Classics' Closer to Passage," *Variety*, August 17, 1988, 1, 53; "Library of Congress Names 25 Titles to New Registry of Significant U.S. Movies," *Variety*, September 27, 1988, 10, 28.

84. National Film Preservation Act of 1988, Pub. L, No. 100–446, Title 1, 1988 U.S. Code Cong. & Admin. News (103 Stat.) 1782–88 (codified at 2 U.S.C.A. §§ 178–78(2) (West Supp. 1989); Harris, "Pic Preservation Board," 2.

85. Gelman, "Colorization of 'Kane' Halted," 419–20.

86. Voros, "Anti-colorization Crusade," 9.

87. Ibid.

88. Dennis Wharton, "Color DGA Encouraged by Bill," *Variety*, March 7, 1990, 7.

89. Secunda, "Colorization a Moral Issue," 20; Kohs, "Paint Your Wagon," 1–38.

90. S. Linfield, "The Color of Money," *American Film*, January/February 1987, 29–35, 52.

91. Mayer et al., "Colorization," 64–78.

92. W. S. Strong, "Legal Shadings," *Society* (May/June 1987): 19–21.

93. Sheridan, "Black and White in Living Color," 59.

94. 52 Fed. Reg. 23, 442–43 (February 4, 1987).

95. Paul Harris, "Win for Coloroids: Govt. Outlines Plan for Copyrighting," *Variety*, June 24, 1987, 1, 77.

96. James McBride, "Directors Look to Spook Colorizers via 'Haunting,'" *Variety*, April 25, 1990, 20, 29.

97. David Robb, "'Haunting' Through out the 'Window,'" *Variety*, May 9, 1990, 5, 38.

98. Dempsey, "Canadian Tax Loophole," 31.

99. Even more recent efforts to lengthen the number of years that copyrighted films can be kept from the public domain will not likely have any implications for film colorization. The Sonny Bono Copyright Term Extension Act of 1998 does not specify colorization issues, but the law does raise concerns that Disney characters may *never* enter the public domain. Likewise, films of the 1930s will wait longer and longer to be colorized, assuming their copyright holders see more value in the original black-and-white versions than in derivative colorized versions.

100. Television Bureau of Advertising Online. Available at http://www.tvb.org/rcentral/mediatrendstrack/tvbasics/04_Cable_and_VCR_HH.asp (accessed April 12, 2004).

5 / WAPI

Entertainment and Sports Broadcasting at an Educational Radio Station in the 1920s

SAMUEL J. BRUMBELOE AND J. EMMETT WINN

The first broadcasting station in Alabama, WMAV (We Make a Voice), "was installed for the primary purpose of broadcasting weather, market, and crop reports and other technical information . . . [with] broadcasting for pure entertainment . . . [as] a secondary nature."[1] Although originally intended for informational purposes, specifically useful to the farmers of Alabama, the radio station at Alabama Polytechnic Institute (API), in the small rural east Alabama town of Auburn, instead broadcast primarily entertaining sports and musical programs. P. O. Davis, who was then doing public relations work for the Alabama Extension Service, a statewide land grant agricultural outreach mission of API, was placed in charge of the station even though "he had never seen a broadcasting station [and had] never thought much about it."[2] Despite this, Davis took control of station WMAV and remained in charge when only a short time later the station was renamed WAPI, to honor the school.

Radio in Alabama was essentially the result of a congressional act. In 1914 Congress passed the Agricultural Extension Work Act, or Smith-Lever Act, which stated in Section 2 "that cooperative agricultural extension work shall consist of the giving of instruction and practical demonstrations in agricultural and home economics . . . and imparting . . . information on such subjects through field demonstrations, publications, and otherwise."[3] In the early 1920s, the new medium of radio was seen as a means of outreach to the isolated farmers of rural Alabama. Nonetheless, as it turned out, the station became, almost from its inception, a sports and entertainment broadcasting programmer. Historical records show that its listeners enjoyed the entertaining broadcasts and proved so by making the 1926 World Series "the most popular and appreciated feature yet broadcast" on the station.[4] While WAPI was never financially secure, due to API's poor state funding, it did manage to garner a relatively large audience that brought it to the attention of commercial interests in Alabama, eventually resulting in the station's moving to the larger metropolitan city of Birmingham, Alabama, approximately 120 miles to the northwest, at the end of the 1920s. The station also became one of the first successful joint ventures between API and its cross-state rival, the University of Alabama. Thus, the station helped pave the way for a renewal of athletic competition between the two colleges, a significant cultural event in its own right. In fact, it was not its educational mission but instead the combination of economic interests and the profitability of collegiate sports, particularly football, in Alabama that shaped this radio station. This case study of a specific radio station struggling to find its "voice" in programming in the 1920s elucidates how early radio outside the network system was influenced by social, cultural, and economic factors.

Media scholar and historian Douglas Gomery argues that the goal of broadcast history should be "localism" with a direct interest in "programming efforts at the community level."[5] WAPI's significance is derived from studying its programming choices and the influences that drove those choices. Since network programming was not an option for this educational station, it had to develop its own programming way. Further, investigating WAPI and its role in broadcasting popular music and sporting events provides a better understanding of the role of early broadcasting in the development of southern sports culture. Moreover, WAPI is historically significant as an early innovator in sports broadcasting. It broadcast its first football game within a year of KDKA's first-ever football broadcast and led the southern United States in development of play-by-play broadcasting of baseball and basketball games. The modern ubiquity of sports-related cable networks and sports programming on traditional networks has its roots in the early broadcasting experiments of stations such as WAPI.

Likewise, the importance of college football to the South cannot be underestimated. Although the football program at Auburn dates back to 1892,[6] 1917 witnessed an important step in Auburn's prominence as a football power and in southern college football's quest for national acceptance. That year, a small Auburn team tied a much more powerful team from Ohio State University, prompting the *Birmingham News* to report that Auburn confirmed "the feeling [that] still lingers way down deep in the heart of every Southerner that one fellow from Alabama can lick four Yankees."[7]

Radio at Auburn had an unusual beginning. According to Davis, the station's benefactor, newspaper business leader Victor Hanson, gave a one-time gift of $2,500, "but his total gift was tiny in relation to what was spent by the university's Agricultural Extension Service."[8] The *Birmingham News* reported that the gift made Auburn only the fifth institution of higher learning in the nation to have a radio station.[9]

The monetary gift for the radio station was made as a part of the Great Auburn Drive, which was a public attempt by API to find additional sources of funding aside from the money granted by the Alabama state legislature, which favored funding the University of Alabama.[10] Hanson, the editor of the *Birmingham News* and an API trustee, felt that Auburn's experience in wireless telegraphy would make it an excellent place for a radio broadcasting station.[11] The idea for the gift originated with two Auburn engineering alumni who had studied wireless telegraphy while at Auburn—Lonnie B. Munger and Hayden Brooks; however, there is no evidence to suggest that these two men ever had a direct relationship to the station.[12] Davis notes that after the initial monetary donation, the station scrambled "to find a competent radio engineer—one who could get [a radio station] ready to broadcast."[13] Davis further explains how the lack in funding hurt the early progress of radio at Auburn, noting that "no one on the Auburn faculty was interested in gratis work."[14] Perhaps more important, Davis points out that among the faculty, "no one was really qualified" in radio.[15] So as it turns out, Auburn's experience in wireless telegraphy was actually of little help to the new broadcasting station.

Nonetheless, API's student newspaper, *The Plainsman* (originally known as *The Orange and Blue*), praised the gift and stated, "it [was] wonderful to know that Auburn [would] be able to take the lead in the South . . . in radiophone broadcasting work."[16] Meanwhile, as the college suffered financially, the Auburn Athletic Association turned a sizable profit of more than $15,800 for the 1921–1922 season, with the popular and successful football team generating the majority of the profit margins.[17] After the donation it was announced that the station was intended to present "nightly programs of primary service to the farmer," including "scientific lectures," and that "the chief function of the broadcasting station [was] in instruction and [in the] graduation of operators and in scientific experimentation."[18] The *Birmingham News* stressed the prospective benefit of the station to agriculture in the state, emphasizing the station's educational potential as an extension of the Alabama Polytechnic Institute.[19] The director of the Alabama Extension Service, L. N. Duncan, expressed that it was "hoped that [the radio] service may be made of tremendous value to the farmers."[20] Duncan states in the 1922 annual report of the Alabama Cooperative Extension Service that the radio station would be used "to broadcast general agricultural information, instructions to county agents, marketing and weather reports as well as other timely information."[21]

Furthermore, Duncan laid a plan to put radio receivers in the county agricultural extension agents' offices and in the main office of the Farm Bureau, confirming that the station planned on benefiting Alabama's agricultural industry. Dr. Wayne Flynt, a noted Alabama historian, explains that the flourishing farmers of the state in the early 1920s were buying radio receivers as a sign of their affluence, gained from the increased production for World War I and good growing conditions throughout the 1910s.[22] Despite these lofty plans, the only regular programs for the station during its first years of operation were the Auburn football games.[23] In fact, the station was not "operated [in 1923] except to broadcast some of Auburn's football games . . . [and] the station operated on only one third of its rated power."[24] These sorts of sports broadcasts were certainly not a benefit to the state's agricultural industry as the station's intentions had promised. While there may have been brief time periods in late 1922 when weather reports were made[25] and in 1923 when weather and market reports were broadcast,[26] there is little evidence to suggest that the station was ever used primarily for agricultural purposes.

BRIDGING SEPARATE CULTURES

Wayne Flynt suggests that the conservative white farmers in Alabama in the early 1920s would not have approved of the lifestyle at the state's colleges, because they saw them as overtly liberal and amoral. The Alabama farmers in the 1920s were in stark opposition to the New South advocates who favored industrialization and urbanization. While the urban areas of the state, particularly Birmingham, began to flourish, the rural citizens were left feeling alienated, as the onset of the agricultural depression began as early as 1920. Therefore, the farmers would probably not have approved of the state's colleges, their social dances that were beginning to feature jazz music and flapper women, or the illegal drinking that was going on in places like Auburn, Birmingham, and Tuscaloosa (home of the University of Alabama).[27]

However, Flynt argues that at the same time, farmers would enjoy listening to a sports game or a musical program (as opposed to a scientific lecture) on the radio as they went about their daily business or during their brief periods of relaxation, such as each evening after supper.[28] These arguments suggest that the early sports and musical broadcasts of the Auburn radio station, while not necessarily of an educational benefit to Alabama's agricultural industry, did appeal to the farmers.

THE STRUGGLING SUCCESS OF AUBURN RADIO

In late November of 1923, WMAV announced plans to begin broadcasting a more regular schedule of programs to start on December 1, and claims were made that the station would finally operate at full power.[29] This date was pushed back to December 13 and then again to late February of 1924,[30] showing that the station was experiencing setbacks. These setbacks were probably due to a lack of talent, the shifting of bandwidths, and poor funding for the station.[31]

The shifting of bandwidths and the constant increasing and decreasing of power plagued radio at Auburn. The station's original bandwidth had been at 360 meters, but the opening program of WMAV in February of 1924 aired on 250 meters, the fourth different bandwidth the struggling, young station had used since first coming on the air. WMAV/WAPI shifted bandwidths at least eleven times, while reducing or increasing wattage power at least seven times. S. E. Frost points out that the "changes in power [and bandwidths] were caused by mechanical troubles" and by governmental urging.[32] Davis argues that in the early years of WMAV, the station "pecked and struggled as best [it] could with equipment that was almost obsolete by the time it was installed,"[33] suggesting that the continued lack of funding for new equipment was a serious problem faced by the radio station.

Finally, however, a regular schedule of programs did begin airing on Thursday and Saturday nights at 8:00 P.M. soon after the station's official dedication on the evening of February 21, 1924.[34] This schedule is the first significant indication of an attempt to provide educational programming for the state's agricultural industry beyond weather and market reports. While Thursday nights provided musical programming, "on Saturday evenings a program [was] run which [was] of special benefit to the farmers, [with] talks on agricultural subjects being made by faculty members of that department of the college."[35]

The earliest evidence suggesting that WMAV had some success in winning an audience was in May of 1924, although the audience was made up primarily of interested radio listeners from outside the state of Alabama.[36] One letter from South Dakota claimed that its listener had enjoyed a concert broadcast, while another letter from Connecticut asserted that its listener had enjoyed and "received the greater part of a lecture on Alabama."[37] Meanwhile, as Auburn and its radio station continued to suffer financially, the Auburn administration announced plans to build new practice fields for the football team, "as a result of the large attendance at football games [the previous] season."[38] In contrast to the radio station's monetary worries, the football program and the Auburn Athletic Association were prospering.

While radio represented entirely new opportunities as a burgeoning economic field in the early 1920s, Davis implied that not many in Auburn "had [any] real interest in radio broadcasting."[39] However, by the following term, the fall of 1924, a radio club formed for "all students interested in any phase of radio,"[40] in hopes of arousing more interest in radio at Auburn. Otherwise, Davis suggests that the station faced the very real threat of going off the air.[41] The radio club and the radio department of the agriculture college were able to make some progress in stimulating interest in radio by late 1924.[42] This progress was aided by an equipment donation from a Birmingham station, WSY (owned by the state's electrical utility, Alabama Power), and "by the addition of an advanced class . . . [in broadcast] engineering theory and practice."[43] Unfortunately, the equipment donated by Alabama Power was obsolete.[44]

The limited progress the station was making was frustrating to its operators, and claims were being made that the merging of the "educational" WMAV and the commercial WSY would allow for "educational and musical programs [to] be broadcasted regularly for the benefit of America's huge radio audience."[45] The equipment from WSY was donated to Auburn in January 1925 but did not reach Auburn until late March of that year.[46] In the meantime, plans for a building to house the radio station were made, and people assigned to the project were sent to radio stations in several large cities throughout the southern and midwestern United States to obtain ideas for a plan for a proper radio station.[47]

Once the equipment from Alabama Power arrived, radio at Auburn had an influential new sponsor—Auburn's athletic director, Roy Dimmitt. Dimmitt announced the arrival of the equipment and promised that "there will be a radio house built somewhere on the campus."[48] While the Auburn Athletic Association had no formal relationship with Auburn radio, Dimmitt's involvement suggests that the association was quick to recognize the benefits of having a radio station to broadcast their profitable athletic contests to a growing fan base.

Davis argued that the donation of WSY ultimately proved of little use to WMAV other than for spare parts and to aid in the realization that radio at Auburn needed a technological upgrade in order to continue broadcasting.[49] Therefore, the Agricultural Extension Service, "under the advice and guidance of . . . [API's] Department of Electrical Engineering," decided to purchase "the latest model 1000-Watt Western Electric Station."[50] Two two-hundred-foot towers were purchased and a radio building was built, while "a room 24 feet by 24 feet on the third floor of Comer Hall [was] converted into a very [modern] studio."[51] Thus, Davis contends that WAPI was created from the remnants of WMAV, new equipment, and parts from WSY for the expensive sum of approximately $40,000.[52] Davis also argues that WMAV's major value was as a precursor for WAPI.[53]

WAPI: NOT AN EDUCATIONAL STATION

WAPI was to be a more powerful station than WMAV with a more comprehensive plan for the extension of education through regular broadcasting.[54] In the 1925 annual report of the extension service, Duncan states, "the main purpose of this station will be to give to the people of Alabama an all-round educational program of great magnitude and importance."[55] This is the definitive explanation of WAPI's educational and agricultural extension mission. Plans were made for the station to be operational by December of 1925. Furthermore, reporter J. M. Wilder claimed that the new station would help to put Alabama Polytechnic Institute among the nation's leaders in radio education.[56]

However, the new station never primarily served an educational purpose. The first documented broadcast of WAPI, or "The Voice of Auburn," was "the Birmingham Southern–Auburn [football] game . . . play by play."[57] This road game, broadcast in late September of 1925 with details provided from descriptions sent over a telegraph wire to the station, was the first game broadcast that year, and plans were immediately made to continue to broadcast the entire season of games. Meanwhile, a call was made to the talented performers among the student body to volunteer their services to the station.[58] The favorable audience reaction demonstrated by the initial broadcast that season,[59] and by the Auburn team's success that year on the playing field,[60] suggests that the football games were broadcast, while the station remained otherwise silent for the remainder of 1925. The station made no educational broadcasts that year and served no instructional purpose of any magnitude.

An editorial in *The Plainsman* congratulated the University of Alabama on the South's first national football championship and their 1926 Rose Bowl victory.[61] The article also called for a renewal in athletic competition between the football teams from Auburn and Tuscaloosa.[62] Meanwhile, the date for the official opening of WAPI was pushed back from December of 1925 to February of 1926,[63] suggesting that WAPI was struggling from the same sorts of problems that had plagued WMAV. Eventually the station did have its formal opening on the evening of February 22, 1926, and was dedicated as the Victor Hanson Radio Broadcasting Station of the Alabama Polytechnic Institute.[64] It was claimed that the new station would feature programs that were both "entertaining and instructive, including all kinds of music and lectures by all members of all divisions of the faculty."[65]

Yet, WAPI's emphasis on entertainment is reflected in the station's opening program. While the program featured speeches from the college's president and the governor of Alabama, it also featured several musical selections from the radio station's orchestra.[66] The formal opening of WAPI proved to be a great success around the state, especially among API alumni, as several long-distance phone calls and telegrams were received from well-wishers to welcome the station to the airwaves and thank the station for an entertaining first program.[67]

The week after the station's opening, *The Plainsman* announced that Alabama's agriculture and industries commissioner had given an important address to the state's farmers on the station.[68] That same week's edition also announced the hosting of the station's first fraternity night, with the Alpha Tau Omega fraternity planning to present several musical features to be sung by members of the fraternity.[69] Eventually, WAPI chose Friday evenings for the entertaining fraternity night, later expanding it to include sororities and other school organizations.[70]

The musical programs from WAPI's fraternity night that spring were supplemented by other entertaining programs, most notably Auburn's baseball games.[71] The first documented baseball broadcast featured an exhibition game between Auburn and a popular professional minor league team the Birmingham Barons.[72] The exhibition game demonstrated the growing economic importance that the radio station played by drawing valuable public attention to Auburn sports for the Auburn Athletic Association, as "the net receipts of the day [were] used toward a scholarship fund for worthy athletes."[73]

Crop reports were broadcast by WAPI, and "by this method it was possible for the farmers to receive the reports at least twelve hours earlier than they could have done otherwise."[74] While twelve hours does not represent a significant amount of time or an advantage for most farmers, it did represent a great advantage for the illiterate farmers who received the broadcast. However, the predominance of entertaining programming over informational programming on WAPI illustrates that the station was primarily an entertaining broadcasting station despite its educational mission.

THE CONTINUED DIFFICULTIES OF BROADCASTING

Unfortunately, the station was again experiencing difficulties. While the purchase of the equipment from Western Electric was a significant upgrade, it was never able to deliver the clear signal for the predetermined distance of 135 miles.[75] The station was also suffering from interference with other stations that shared its frequency, most notably WIOD of Miami, Florida.[76] While WIOD and WAPI agreed not to broadcast programs at the same time,[77] interference would plague the Auburn station until the passing of the Radio Act of 1927, which addressed the interference problem.

About a month after WAPI's opening, a program was given simultaneously from Auburn's studio and the ballroom of the Tutwiler Hotel in downtown Birmingham.[78] The musical program was not extraordinarily different from many of the musical programs already on the air. However, it did demonstrate the growing interest for radio in the state's most populated urban area, Birmingham.[79] Thus, the popularity of the program reinforced the importance of Birmingham as a radio market.

In the fall of 1926 WAPI continued to demonstrate a willing effort to overcome adversity by reopening on a new wavelength in an attempt to find a home on the radio dial with less interference.[80] The opening program that fall was given by the studio orchestra, which had been "one of the most popular features of station WAPI" the previous term.[81] The station also announced plans to broadcast a regular schedule of programming every day of the week, including Sunday night, that would "include not only music but educational numbers, including popular lectures and dialogues by members of the faculty and other special lecturers . . . [while] plans [were also] underway for broadcasting athletic events."[82] These plans for educational and entertaining programming were confirmed by a brochure on WAPI printed for distribution by the extension service in the fall of 1926.[83]

The Agricultural Extension Service continued to maintain that "education [was] the chief purpose of Station WAPI." The service stated that while the station "was dedicated to education; along with education must be entertainment and other features to make a first-class broadcasting station." The service also noted that "good music . . . [was] the leading entertainment feature." This entertaining musical programming was supplemented by the broadcasting of athletic events, which included the broadcasting of baseball, basketball, and football games, making "Station WAPI . . . a major [contributor] to athletics."[84] The music and sports programming easily became, "the most popular features given by the station."[85] In fact, the station's sports programming continued to be the station's most popular programming, as evidenced by audience response.[86]

THE POPULARITY OF SPORTS PROGRAMMING ON WAPI

The fall of 1926 also saw several members of a unified Auburn community call for a renewal of competition between Auburn's and Alabama's athletic teams.[87] Several groups around the state joined in this quest to see a renewal in athletic competition, especially in football, between the state's two largest schools.[88] Meanwhile, WAPI broadcast its most popular program when trustee Victor Hanson asked for and received a broadcast relay of the 1926 World Series. Claims were made that "baseball fans throughout Alabama . . . were able to [follow] the first game of the series [between the St. Louis Cardinals and New York Yankees] and the Auburn-Clemson football game play by play by radio from their own firesides."[89] It was reported that the World Series broadcast received messages from more than 6,000 listeners, and it was "estimated that approximately 50,000 people of the state received a play-by-play report of the Yankee-Cardinal games from the radio station of Auburn."[90]

As the popular World Series programming came to an end, *The Plainsman* featured an editorial that questioned the potential ills college football teams might place on the academic missions of their institutions.[91] The article also recognized the benefits of college football and ultimately decided that the positives outweighed the negatives, while calling for "precaution [to] be taken by college and university officials to protect the game from further undesirable influences . . . that may be unfavorable to the institutions as educational centers."[92] Meanwhile, college football broadcasts on WAPI, which now featured the reigning national champion University of Alabama team along with a struggling Auburn team, were becoming extremely popular across the state.[93] Several fans, especially those of the University of Alabama, sent telegrams during the games noting the hundreds of listeners enjoying the broadcasts and thanking the station.[94] These broadcasts certainly added to the growing pride of the South in college football, as Alabama was once again invited to participate in the Rose Bowl at the conclusion of the 1926 season.[95] Football fans in Alabama were especially excited, because the University of Alabama's success in football meant "that the state of Alabama, and, consequently the South, [stood] pre-eminent in America's favorite sports competition."[96] Unwittingly, Auburn indirectly encouraged the growth in popularity of what would become their biggest sports rival, as WAPI's broadcasts of the successful Alabama team contributed to the growth of a huge fan base for the University of Alabama football team within the state. Also, unfortunately, these successes and Rose Bowl invitations by Alabama in 1925 and 1926, and in 1927 by Tulane, were not matched by Auburn, leading to the forced resignation of a popular Auburn coach, David Morey, and the ousting of the college's president, Dr. Spright Dowell.

By November of 1926, *The Plainsman* began printing a regular weekly schedule of programs to be aired on WAPI. One of the first of these schedules announced the airing of Auburn's annual Thanksgiving Day football game against Georgia Tech,[97] the school's main rival at the time. The game-day festivities featured several yearly traditions, including a parade. The schedules in the student newspaper continued into the next semester announcing plans for the airing of baseball and basketball broadcasts and a weekly sports discussion to be given by various members of the Auburn coaching staffs. The basketball games broadcast by WAPI were the first of their kind in the Southeast and some of the first nationally, although the pace of the game made it more difficult to follow over radio than play-by-play broadcasts of football or baseball.[98]

As WAPI was extending its schedule of sports programs, members of the senior class, along with fraternities, were supporting a plan for the building of a new football stadium at Auburn,[99] which led to an official investigation by the board of trustees on the viability of such a proposal,[100] despite the college's continued financial struggles.[101] The school was also seeing returns on their plans to renew competition with the University of Alabama, as *The Plainsman* printed University of Alabama president Dr. George Denny's letter wishing Auburn luck in the upcoming Southern Conference championship basketball tournament.[102] This economic focus on sports despite the college's funding problems highlights the importance of college athletics, especially football, to Alabama culture.

The station continued to expand its popular sports programming, with the World Series and college football broadcasts having served as a major catalyst to the continuing development of sports broadcasting on WAPI.[103] The expanded sports programming was highlighted by the airing of the scores and results of Major League Baseball and some of the local minor league teams from the Southern Association.[104] The station also featured broadcasts of the Southern States high school basketball tournament held in Auburn in February of 1928.[105]

The popularity of sports broadcasting on the radio station is further demonstrated by the fact that the schedule of programming for the station continued as a popular weekly feature of *The Plainsman* and that the station sustained plans for announcing the football games for Auburn and Alabama. These broadcasts continued to show the enormous popularity of football broadcasts, and they were beginning to pay dividends for the players as well, as "the Varsity Football men . . . were awarded [very expensive] fountain pens . . . [by boosters as] special gifts to the athletes."[106] The athletic association also noticed the growing popularity of the team and announced a nighttime football game to be played the following season, the first of its kind in the state of Alabama.[107] The basketball broadcasts also became very popular among listeners of the station as the 1928 basketball team finished the season with an outstanding record and a second-place finish in the conference tournament, losing the championship game by only one point. Letters were received from as far away as the Florida Everglades congratulating the Auburn broadcasts and the basketball team.[108] The station capped off its popular sports programming by managing to move its sports broadcasts outside its studio to give "field-side reports of [at least] six baseball games played on the Auburn campus."[109]

MUSICAL AND OTHER ENTERTAINING BROADCASTS

While sports broadcasts were the most popular, music was by far the most featured programming of WAPI. As Alabama Polytechnic Institute was setting another enrollment record,[110] the music on WAPI began to feature new performers along with the already immensely popular studio orchestra. The variations in the musical programming included a cappella vocal selections; piano, violin, and other instrumental solos; jazzy numbers from the newly formed Auburn Radio Tigers orchestra; and several guest musicians.

Music was also a common feature during other programs. For example, in a schedule of the station's programming from the late fall of 1926, details were given on a program that featured lectures from an Alabama congressman and an API professor, with supplemental music programming featured in between.[111] That schedule also gave news on the concert given by the Atlanta and West Point Railway Band that featured a twelve-year-old singing sensation.[112] Meanwhile, as the farmers of Alabama enjoyed WAPI's entertaining programs, they suffered through a debilitating drought and depression, forcing "a large reduction in cotton acreage . . . [as] their buying power . . . reached its lowest ebb since 1920 with debts made in making the [cotton] crop in 1926 still in the book."[113] Interestingly, WAPI did not seriously address these agricultural issues and instead chose to air entertaining programming, thus highlighting its abandonment of its educational charge.

As "the Alabama Polytechnic Institute [was] selected for the eighth consecutive year as a Distinguished College by the War Department," the beginning of the 1927 fall term witnessed the station's continued commitment to musical programming.[114] While the music programming on the station featured classical and jazz numbers, it also began to have a distinctive local sound. For example, the station featured fiddle and banjo music common to Appalachia as well as favorite southern hymns. The studio orchestra also would take requests received through fan mail. Likewise, recorded music was featured on the station. J. M. Rosene states that "when the band was unavailable, the engineers would select a record and fire up the studio phonograph."[115]

The 1928 junior prom dance program may provide the best documented evidence of a large and enthusiastic audience for the station's music programming. The broadcast of the dance from the alumni gym on campus prompted many letters thanking the station for the music and wishing the dance participants luck.[116] One such letter from a listener in Idaho noted, "[T]he enthusiasm was marked, the applause, the laughter and conversation could be heard, together with an occasional 'whoopee' from some happy male. In fact I almost felt as 'among those present.'"[117]

The station featured other popular and entertaining programming with a distinctive southern flavor. The most noteworthy of the weekly programs dealt with reports on the yearlong Alabama egg-laying contests. Also, a local Auburn woman known as "Aunt Sammy" gave a weekly feature on household tips, discussing favorite southern recipes and dispensing home economics advice. The most unique entertainment program aired by WAPI may have been the broadcasting of a hog-calling contest held by the agricultural club.[118] WAPI awarded a five-dollar prize to "Uncle Timothy" Gowder as the champion hog caller, after the station aired eight members of the agricultural club and their best calls.[119] This particular broadcast may have been one of a kind, as it was reported that a man from nearby Columbus, Georgia, had a "loud speaker . . . close to the window, and that all of his neighbor's hogs broke out" during the contest.[120]

THE NOTABLE EDUCATIONAL PROGRAMMING OF WAPI

WAPI also provided limited educational programming. The station's weekly programs included speeches by faculty members, elected politicians, and other important persons on topics as varied as taxes, crop management, and religion. Weather and market reports continued to be broadcast at the beginning of each program whenever the station came on the air. Some of the programs turned out to be successful. For instance, the Wilsonian Literary Society aired a successful broadcast that featured a reading of "The Deceit-

ful Man," by W. B. Hare.[121] Perhaps the most successful educational programming aired by the station was the current events lectures given by
Dr. George Petrie every Thursday night. Dr. Petrie, dean of the Auburn
Graduate School and tenured professor of history at Auburn for at least forty
years, was a true Renaissance man on the campus of API. Petrie was an
accomplished pastor, a published author, and the coach of Auburn's first
football team in 1892.[122]

WAPI MOVES TO BIRMINGHAM

Ultimately, despite some increase in state funds to API, the station "continued to struggle along, doing a better job than . . . WMAV but not good
enough."[123] Although WAPI had attempted to acquire programming from
NBC, its small market was a serious detriment, and the "NBC people in
New York smiled negatively when [Davis] presented [WAPI's] case for becoming an NBC network affiliate."[124] Therefore, with the approval of the
college, Davis and the extension service entered into an agreement with the
city of Birmingham to share in the costs of running a more powerful WAPI
station in Birmingham. The allure of the large populace of the big city, the
necessities of funding for maintenance and other improvements, and the potential of garnering lucrative network programming to make the station
more self-sufficient for the extension service sealed the fate of WAPI at Auburn and ensured its move to Birmingham.

Despite the move, the student press at Auburn seemed excited about the
news, announcing to the student body that the move would aid in the improvement of talent and programming and increase the range of the station.
The new station continued to maintain its studio in Auburn and planned to
add an additional studio in Montgomery as well as one in Birmingham at
the Tutwiler Hotel. The station also continued plans to operate as both an
entertaining and informative broadcasting station.[125] In fact, Davis stated in
an address given at the Tutwiler Hotel that WAPI would feature "entertainment program artists unequaled anywhere in the country, [and] much valuable information relative to agriculture, [and] industry . . . in the nature of
market reports, [and] information on cattle and hog prices."[126] Yet, the agricultural business focus of these reports was informational, not educational,
in nature.

Eventually, the station was placed on Red Mountain, a few miles outside of Birmingham's city limits,[127] with two modern studios housed in the brand-new Protective Life Building in downtown Birmingham.[128] This site was chosen by Auburn for a studio instead of the more prestigious and older Tutwiler site, because API trustee Hanson had significant stock in the Protective Life Insurance Company and was able to pressure the new president of API, Dr. Bradford Knapp, into locating the studios in the new building.[129]

Auburn's station shipped its towers,[130] and sold its old transmitter and other equipment to a station operating in Wisconsin,[131] as WAPI planned an opening program to air from Birmingham on January 1, 1929.[132] This was to be the third formal opening program for the radio station in less than five years. The new Birmingham version of WAPI had a very successful opening as it received more than three thousand responses to its first program wishing the station success.[133] Several prominent speakers, including the governor of Alabama, were supplemented by musical artists as the opening program went on the air at 8:00 P.M. and lasted until 4:00 A.M. the next morning while ringing in the 1929 new year. Now known as "The Voice of Alabama," WAPI aired daytime and nighttime programs as an affiliate of the National Broadcasting Company. Davis had attempted to garner network programming in Auburn but failed "because [originally WAPI was] far from any city of size, meaning that [WAPI] had a very small listener audience" according to NBC experts. WAPI's move to Birmingham demonstrated to network executives that WAPI was serious about wanting a network affiliation, and "soon [after the move, WAPI became] affiliated with NBC, being the first network station in Alabama." Although the Great Depression would lead the city of Birmingham to pull out of its agreement to share in the financing of WAPI in 1929, Auburn eventually reached an agreement with the University of Alabama and the Alabama College for Women in Montevallo, Alabama, to share in the ownership, broadcasting time, and expenditures of the station. Davis held out hope that this arrangement "might be a demonstration in teamwork in other things" between the schools. The arrangement did allow for the continuance of sports broadcasting across the state and aided in the revival of athletic competition between Alabama and Auburn in the 1940s, as the station had "attained reasonable success under handicaps." In 1961 the colleges sold the station for a sum of $340,000, "a capital appreciation of $225,000."[134] WAPI has continued to flourish since its sale and still operates in Birmingham.

FINDINGS

Although the station at Alabama Polytechnic Institute was originally intended to benefit the state's farmers and was publicly dedicated on several occasions to educational purposes, radio in Auburn primarily aired entertaining broadcasts led by extensive sports coverage. WMAV and WAPI turned to music and sports because of cultural and economic forces that converged in Alabama at that historical time. WAPI proves to be an important cultural text, because as the first radio station in Alabama, the station at Auburn helped to close some social gaps in Alabama between the white elite and working-class strata and helped to fuel the popularity of sports culture, particularly college football. WAPI's perseverance and ability to adapt to the listeners of the state, despite its poor and inconsistent funding, demonstrates that the station was dedicated to serving the entertainment needs of its listeners, not its mandated agricultural education mission.

The Development of Commercial Radio and Popular Sport

In the 1920s, educational broadcasters across the country were experiencing limited amounts of success in popular and entertaining programming, led by their broadcasting of music and college athletics. However, commercial broadcasters demonstrated significant advantages over their educational rivals due to consistent network programming and advertising revenues. G. R. Gems argues that as radio was developing into a commercial medium, colleges and universities were almost simultaneously beginning to recognize that college athletics, especially football, were emerging as significant commercialized events in their own right and that sports could be sold as a commodity.[135] R. W. McChesney argues that the sporting newspaper press had legitimated this union of commercialism and college athletics since the Civil War as they turned sport, particularly college football, into an important and popular American cultural institution.[136]

The extensive coverage and development of sports in newspapers had an important impact and influence in the development of sports on radio. W. M. Towers contends that from radio's broadcasting beginnings, sports, especially baseball and college football, were clearly intertwined.[137] Towers explains that the immediate popularity of these broadcasts was almost wholly due to the public's understanding of the popular games being broadcast, thus making sports an easy choice for radio.[138] J. Goldlust adds that un-like the relationship between sports and the newspapers, "live radio broad-casts of sporting events signified the beginnings of an important eco-nomic relationship that was to develop between the mass media and sporting bodies."[139]

While the rich and poor whites of Alabama rarely interacted socially, col-lege football became one popular ritual that would bridge this social gap. Southern historians maintain that Alabama's rural culture held sport in high esteem, especially college football, due to the culture's favoring of physical toil over high culture.[140] By the early 1920s, the success of southern college football teams over more-established northern teams became regular occur-rences that resulted in the improved status of southern college football in the national press and in local communities throughout the South, especially Alabama.[141] The University of Alabama's victory in the 1926 Rose Bowl served as a defining rallying point for the South, a culture that had suffered a history of defeat, disgrace, scarcity, and sociopolitical separation from the American cultural mainstream.[142] This single college football victory served to unite the once-defeated South as a rallying point, while also culturally uniting the rich and poor strata of white society in Alabama behind a single popular sports culture.[143]

Political Economy and WAPI

Media scholar Douglas Kellner argues that an analysis of the systems that controlled the production and distribution of a cultural text gives the cultu-ral scholar great insight into a more informed analysis.[144] Several important social, political, and economic issues in this study of Auburn radio are ex-plicated. First, the original donation of the station by Victor Hanson to API was a public and well-hyped event but did not include any substantial input from the school. In fact, the school was ill prepared to handle the gift and was not sure who should be in charge of the station or how it should be operated. As editor of two of the largest newspapers in the state, Hanson was a powerful and influential API trustee who had obvious ties to the grow-ing mass media and who was an avid sports fan. Hanson practiced great control over the radio station's development by making the original dona-tion, aiding in the negotiations for the equipment donation of WSY from Birmingham, contracting the rights to the 1926 World Series broadcasts, and eventually determining that the station should be relocated to the Protective Life Building in Birmingham, a building in which Hanson owned stock. Hanson's overwhelming presence pressured Davis to merge the extension service's educational outreach mission with Hanson's business and media involvement.

Meanwhile, the Auburn Athletic Association continued to demonstrate that it was the school's largest moneymaker. The station recognized the influence of the powerful athletic association and quickly made plans to broadcast their most profitable events, the football games. Although there is little documented proof of financial backing from the Auburn Athletic Association, in 1925 the station gained the public endorsement of Auburn's athletic director, Roy Dimmitt. This informal relationship with the athletic association proved beneficial to both parties, as the association continued to prosper and as WAPI's sports broadcasts became their most popular feature. Once the athletic association began to show a significant interest in the fate of radio at Auburn, entertaining broadcasts became predominant, while the educational and informational broadcasts dwindled. The resulting broadcast schedule featured more sports and music programming. The station even got involved in the attempted renewal of competition between the Auburn and Alabama athletic teams by broadcasting the University of Alabama's football games at a time when there was public concern about the effects of collegiate football on the educational mission of colleges and universities. Although there is a lack of documented proof that the athletic association directly encouraged a shift in programming, the historical evidence of that shift strongly suggests that the rich and powerful athletic association, through indirect means, influenced the production of programming at WAPI.

The success of college football in Alabama influenced the shift to a primarily entertaining format that featured the broadcasts of these games. However, the politically tumultuous environment at Auburn that led to the ousting of the college's president and football coach and resulting debt incurred by the athletic association, combined with faulty equipment, static from interfering signals, the sharing of airtime with other stations, and limited financial resources, finally forced the extension service to consider moving the station to Birmingham. This move was accelerated by the opportunity to obtain the lucrative, commercial network programming that the station needed in order to be competitive with the increasing number of commercial stations in the state.

The economic and sports focus of Hanson and the athletic association helps to explain how the station came to broadcast more entertaining than educational programming despite its clearly stated educational mission. Radio at Auburn during the 1920s was certainly influenced by the athletic association and by the powerful newspaper owner Victor Hanson. This influence led to programming that reflected the dominant values of business, commercial broadcasting, and popular sport.

NOTES

1. "Radio Station Does Its Share of Advertising," *Plainsman,* November 29, 1922, 1, 4.

2. P. O. Davis to R. B. Draughon, Record Group 708, WAPI Folder, November 25, 1961, Auburn University Historical Collection, Miscellaneous File, Auburn University Archives, Ralph Brown Draughon Library.

3. Smith-Lever Act, 38 Stat. 372 (1914).

4. "WAPI Makes Hit Broadcasting World Series," *Plainsman,* October 16, 1926, 1, 6.

5. In this article Gomery is specifically discussing television history; however, the extension to early radio broadcasting in the southern United States makes sense. Douglas Gomery, "Rethinking TV History," *Journalism and Mass Communication Quarterly* 74, no. 3 (Autumn 1997): 502.

6. Since API's home was Auburn, Alabama, the town's name became synonymous with the school, and those familiar with the institution have always commonly referred to it as Auburn. Indeed, in 1960 API's name was officially changed to Auburn University. Referring to the Alabama Polytechnic Institute as Auburn also helped to avoid confusion with API's cross-state rival, the University of Alabama, which is normally called Alabama or 'Bama. Both schools maintain a rich history in sports, and both extol their sporting rituals and heroes, while sharing a sense of southern pride. With over six hundred wins, Auburn has one of the most successful college football programs in the nation and boasts such coaching legends as John Heisman and Ralph "Shug" Jordan. Therefore, the Auburn football team, the Tigers, is a major reason for the university's popularity in the South and plays a large part in its national reputation. The now annual football game between the Auburn Tigers and Alabama's Crimson Tide football teams, known as the Iron Bowl, has become an important sporting event for many in the state of Alabama and an annual mainstay of national network college football broadcasting, often determining important regional and national rankings. However, this was not always the case, as WAPI played a large role in the renewal of this important sporting ritual, which was discontinued for forty-one years, from 1907 to 1948.

7. Gerald R. Gems, *For Pride, Profit, and Patriarchy: Football and the Incorporation of American Cultural Values* (Lanham, MD: Scarecrow Press, 2000).

8. Davis to Draughon, 1961.

9. "Powerful Radio Broadcasting Equipment Given to Auburn by *The Birmingham News,*" *Birmingham News,* March 19, 1922, A1.

10. Davis to Draughon, 1961; "Desperate Situation at Auburn: Shall Its Solvency Be Assured?" *Plainsman,* March 5, 1927, 2; "Powerful Radio," A1.

11. "Powerful Radio," A1.

12. Ibid.

13. Davis to Draughon, 1961.

14. Ibid.

15. Ibid.

16. "B'ham News to Give Auburn High Power Radiophone Broadcasting Station," *Orange & Blue,* March 25, 1922, 1.

17. "Athletic Association's Statement of Expenditures for 1921–22 Season," *Orange and Blue,* April 1, 1922, 1.

18. "Powerful Radio," A1.

19. "Radio at Auburn Opens New Field to Agriculture," *Birmingham News,* March 20, 1922, A1, A2.

20. L. N. Duncan, "Report of extension work in Alabama—July 1, 1921 to June 30, 1922," Record Group 71, Box 71, Director's Report 1922 Folder, Alabama Cooperative Extension Service Records, Auburn University Archives, Ralph Brown Draughon Library.

21. Ibid.

22. Dr. Wayne Flynt, interview by Samuel Brumbeloe, Auburn University, April 12, 2001.

23. "Broadcasting Station to Begin Regular Programs," *Plainsman,* November 27, 1923, 1; "Radio Station Does Its Share," A1.

24. "Broadcasting Station to Begin," 1.

25. "Radio Station Does Its Share," A1.

26. "WMAV Broadcasts Good Programs," *Plainsman,* March 24, 1924, 1.

27. Flynt interview, April 12, 2001.

28. Ibid.

29. "Broadcasting Station to Begin," 1.

30. "Broadcasting Station to Be Dedicated," *Plainsman,* February 22, 1924, 1.

31. For information on these problems and more see S. E. Frost Jr., *Education's Own Stations* (New York: Arno Press, 1971).

32. Ibid., 8.

33. Davis to Draughon, 1961.

34. "WMAV Broadcasts," 1.

35. Ibid.

36. "Auburn Radio Station Doing Great Work," *Plainsman,* May 2, 1924, 1, 4.

37. Ibid., 1.

38. "Big New Athletic Field Assured," *Plainsman,* May 19, 1924, 1.

39. Davis to Draughon, 1961.

40. "Radio Club Meeting," *Plainsman,* September 26, 1924, 2.

41. Davis to Draughon, 1961.

42. "Radio Station Adds Many New Features Broadcaster," *Plainsman,* October 31, 1924, 1.

43. Ibid.

44. Davis to Draughon, 1961.

45. "Alabama Power Co. Makes Big Donation," *Plainsman,* January 10, 1925, 1.

46. "Radio Set Arrives," *Plainsman,* March 27, 1925, 1.

47. "Plans for Broadcasting Station Being Rushed," *Plainsman,* January 31, 1925, 1.

48. "Radio Set Arrives," 1.

49. Davis to Draughon, 1961.

50. L. N. Duncan, "A Summary Report of the Work of the Alabama Extension Service for the Fiscal Year July 1, 1924–June 30, 1925," Record Group 71, Box 71, Director's Report 1925 Folder, p. 6, Alabama Cooperative Extension Service Records, Auburn University Archives, Ralph Brown Draughon Library.

51. Ibid., 6.

52. Davis to Draughon, 1961.

53. Ibid.

54. "New Addition to Radio Station Made by College," *Plainsman,* September 18, 1925, 1.

55. Duncan, "A Summary Report," 6.

56. "New Addition," 1; J. M. Wilder, "Radio Station W.A.P.I.," *Auburn Engineer* 7 (October 1925): 14, 16.

57. "WAPI Goes on Air for First Time Broadcasting," *Plainsman,* October 2, 1925, 1. The play-by-play was accomplished by having one person at the game sending descriptions via telegraph to Auburn. A broadcaster at Auburn then read descriptions over the air to the audience.

58. Ibid.

59. Ibid.

60. "Tiger Record," *Plainsman,* December 4, 1925, 5.

61. "Congratulations 'Bama," *Plainsman,* January 9, 1926, 2.

62. Ibid.

63. "New Radio Station to Be Ready Feb. 1st," *Plainsman,* January 9, 1926, 3.

64. Extension Service of Alabama Polytechnic Institute, Formal opening program of WAPI, February 22, 1926. Record Group 708, WAPI Folder, Auburn University Historical Collection, Miscellaneous File, Auburn University Archives, Ralph Brown Draughon Library.

65. "Station WAPI Installation Is Complete," *Plainsman,* February 12, 1926, 1, 6.

66. Extension Service of Alabama Polytechnic Institute, WAPI opening program, 1.

67. "Opening WAPI Is Great Event for Old Grads," *Plainsman,* February 27, 1926, 1, 6.

68. "Hon. J. M. Moore Talks to Farmers Over the Radio," *Plainsman,* March 5, 1926, 3.

69. "A.T.O. Fraternity to Broadcast at Station Tonight," *Plainsman,* March 5, 1926, 1.

70. "Kappa Deltas Give Program Over WAPI," *Plainsman,* March 19, 1926, 1, 6.

71. "Tigers' Game with Barons Features 'A' Day Program," *Plainsman,* March 19, 1926, 1.

72. Ibid.

73. Ibid.

74. "Crop Reports Are Broadcast 12 Hrs. after Completed," *Plainsman,* March 12, 1926, 1.

75. Davis to Draughon, 1961.

76. "WIOD and WAPI to Cooperate," *Plainsman,* March 26, 1926, 6.

77. Ibid.

78. "Unique Program Given by WAPI for Auburn Men," *Plainsman,* March 26, 1926, 4.

79. Ibid.

80. "WAPI Reopens with Increase in Wavelength," *Plainsman,* September 24, 1926, 1, 6.

81. Ibid., 1.

82. Ibid.

83. Extension Service of Alabama Polytechnic Institute, "Greetings from WAPI" [Brochure], October 1926. Record Group 708, WAPI Folder, Auburn University Historical Collection, Miscellaneous File, Auburn University Archives, Ralph Brown Draughon Library.

84. Ibid.

85. "Ag. Club," *Plainsman,* February 24 1928, 3.

86. Ibid.; "Former Auburn Boys Send Congratulations to WAPI," *Plainsman,* March 2, 1928, 3; "Local Radio Station Receives Praise for Programs That Are Presented," *Plainsman,* February 17, 1928, 3; "WAPI Goes," 1; "WAPI Makes Hit," 1; "WAPI Receives Many Notes on Good Services," *Plainsman,* October 23, 1926, 1, 6; "WAPI Renders Real Service in World Series," *Plainsman,* October 9, 1926, 1.

87. "Auburn 'Bama Game Favored by Lions Club," *Plainsman,* October 2, 1926, 1, 5; "Classes Discuss the Resumption of Athletic Relations with U. of A.," *Plainsman,* September 24, 1926, 3.

88. "Junior Chamber Favors Alabama Auburn Game," *Plainsman,* October 9, 1926, 4; "Kiwanis Favor Alabama Game with Auburn," *Plainsman,* October 9, 1926, 5; "Other Clubs Boost Auburn 'Bama Game," *Plainsman,* October 16, 1926, 1.

89. "World Series Broadcast by Station WAPI," *Plainsman,* October 2, 1926, 6.

90. "WAPI Renders," 1.

91. "Football," *Plainsman,* October 16, 1926, 2.

92. Ibid.

93. "WAPI Receives Many," 1.

94. Ibid.

95. "Risen South," *Plainsman,* December 11, 1926, 5.

96. Ibid.

97. "News of WAPI," *Plainsman,* November 24, 1926, 3.

98. "Ag. Club," 3; "Former Auburn Boys," 3; "Local Radio," 3.

99. "Stadium Plans Are Supported by Blue Key Men," *Plainsman,* February 19, 1927, 1.

100. "Trustees Have Committee to Study Stadium," *Plainsman,* February 26, 1927, 1.

101. "Desperate Situation," 2.

102. "President of U. of A. Sends Hearty Letter," *Plainsman,* February 19, 1927, 1.

103. "Tigers' Game," 1; "WAPI Goes on Air," 1; "WAPI Makes Hit," 1; "WAPI Receives," 1; "WAPI Renders," 1; "WAPI Reopens," 1; "World Series," 6.

104. "Radio Station Broadcasting Game Results," *Plainsman,* September 23, 1927, 3.

105. "WAPI Features Out-of-Town Art," *Plainsman,* February 10, 1928, 3.

106. "Varsity Gridders Given Fountain Pens by Boosters," *Plainsman,* September 30, 1927, 4.

107. "Night Game Held in Montgomery," *Plainsman,* September 30, 1927, 1.

108. "Former Auburn Boys," 3.

109. "Field Reports of Baseball Games Will Be Broadcast," *Plainsman,* April 6, 1928, 3.

110. "Registration Is Largest in Local History," *Plainsman,* November 20, 1926, 1.

111. "News of WAPI," 3.

112. Ibid.

113. "Farmers Will Cut Acreage," *Plainsman,* January 17, 1927, 5.

114. "Auburn Rated Distinguished College Again," *Plainsman,* September 8, 1927, 1.

115. J. M. Rosene, *The History of Radio Broadcasting at Auburn University (1912–1961)* (master's thesis, Auburn University, 1968).

116. "Local Radio Station," 3.

117. Ibid.

118. "Ag Club News," *Plainsman,* October 16, 1926, 3; Agricultural Extension Work Act (Smith-Lever Act), 38 Stat. 372 (1914).

119. "Ag Club News," 3.

120. Ibid.

121. "Society Gives Radio Program," *Plainsman,* November 11, 1926, 1, 6.

122. "Dr. Petrie Is Read in Far Northland," *Plainsman,* December 2, 1927, 1, 6; "Dean Petrie Organized and Coached First Grid Team," *Plainsman,* April 13, 1928, 3.

123. Davis to Draughon, 1961.

124. Ibid.

125. "Station WAPI to Be Moved to Birmingham," *Plainsman,* September 7, 1928, 1, 6.

126. Ibid., 1.

127. "Plans Are Completed for New Radio Station in Birmingham," *Plainsman,* September 28, 1928, 3.

128. "Auburn Will Operate Powerful Radio Station in City of Birmingham," *Auburn Alumnus* 10 (October 1928): 1.

129. Davis to Draughon, 1961.

130. "Towers of Radio Station Shipped," *Plainsman,* October 4, 1928, 1.

131. "WAPI Sells Old Equipment to Big Rubber Co.," *Plainsman,* October 4, 1928, 1.

132. P. O. Davis, "Alabama Poly Unfolds Big Radio Idea," *Auburn Alumnus* 10 (December 1928): 4–5.

133. P. O. Davis, "Thousand Greet WAPI Opening," *Auburn Alumnus* 10 (February 1929): 3–5, 22–24.

134. Davis to Draughon, 1961.

135. See Gems, *Pride, Profit, and Patriarchy.*

136. R. W. McChesney, "Media Made Sport: A History of Sports Coverage in the United States, in L. A. Wenner, ed., *Media, Sports, and Society,* 49–69 (Newbury Park, CA: Sage, 1989).

137. W. M. Towers, "'Gee Whiz!' and 'Aw Nuts!': Radio and Newspaper Coverage of Baseball in the 1920s," unpublished paper presented at the 62nd Annual Meeting of the Association for Education in Journalism (Houston, TX, 1979), (ERIC Document Reproduction Service No. ED 179 957).

138. Ibid.

139. J. Goldlust, *Playing for Keeps: Sport, the Media, and Society* (Melbourne: Longman Cheshire, 1987): 73.

140. W. W. Rogers, R. D. Ward, L. R. Atkins, and Wayne Flynt, *Alabama: The History of a Deep South State* (Tuscaloosa: U of Alabama P, 1994).

141. Z. Newman, *The Impact of Southern Football* (Montgomery, AL: Morros-Bell, 1994); See also Gems, *Pride, Profit, and Patriarchy,* and Rogers et al., *Alabama.*

142. T. Rieland, *Roses of Crimson* (Tuscaloosa: University of Alabama Center for Public Television & Radio, 1997), film.

143. See Newman, *Impact of Southern Football,* and Rieland, *Roses of Crimson.*

144. Douglas Kellner, "Cultural Studies, Multiculturalism, and Media Culture," in G. Dines and J. M. Humez, eds., *Gender, Race, and Class in Media: A Text-Reader* (Thousand Oaks, CA: Sage, 1995), 5–17.

6 / Femmes Boff Program Toppers

Women Break into Prime Time, 1943–1948

MICHELE HILMES

In January 1945 the showbiz bible *Variety* took note of the new prominence of female comics as "program toppers"—leading players—in prime-time radio shows. Acknowledging that "until very recently Kate Smith was the lone femme headlining a nighttime commercial series," *Variety,* with its characteristically deep sociological insight, attributed the former absence of women in headlining roles to "just one of those screwy accidental things that happen" and predicted that even when the war was over, "femmes have carved a place for themselves" and "their place in radio is secure."[1] In this last prediction they were right: the women of the 1940s who broke through the gender barrier into prime-time prominence became leading contributors to television's top-rated programs in the 1950s and 1960s. Lucille Ball, Joan Davis, Martha Rountree, Eve Arden, Ann Sothern, Marie Wilson, Hattie McDaniel, Judy Canova, and others, most of them former supporting actresses from Hollywood, would not only form the backbone of television's prime-time lineup but would also permanently change the nature of televisual comedy.[2]

However, for a broadcast historian, "just one of those screwy accidental things that happen" somehow fails to satisfy as an explanation for the elaborate system of gendered program types and scheduling patterns developed over two and a half decades of radio practice, now finally breaking down. During the 1930s and early 1940s, as radio broadcasting developed into a stable and highly profitable industry, daytime hours became "women's time," filled with soap operas, household information programs, and children's shows. The networks set advertising rates at one-half those of nighttime, an excellent arrangement as far as leading advertisers of household products were concerned.[3] This emphasis on the feminine audience translated into more open doors for female talent, and many women found careers in acting, writing, producing, and otherwise contributing to this lively and provocative sector of the broadcast economy and culture. Nighttime hours, meanwhile, developed as the prime showcase of network and agency talent, dominated by big-budget variety and drama programs. The corollary to women's dominance in the daytime was their virtual exclusion from positions of authority or prominence at night. Kate Smith remained the only female host of a high-budget nighttime show until Joan Davis's crucial breakthrough in 1943. Other popular shows, like *Burns and Allen* and *Fibber McGee and Molly,* featured female comedians in secondary roles or as part of male/female comedy teams, a staple since turn-of-the-century vaudeville. Only Fanny Brice, as *Baby Snooks,* managed to overcome the barrier of secondary status as she teamed with Frank Morgan in her own comedy half hour starting in 1940.[4]

Yet suddenly, from 1943 to 1948 a host of "femmes" burst forth upon the radio scene. Not all of them lasted; the names above represent the successful tip of an iceberg of lesser-known rivals who debuted and faded from view.[5] Obviously, this phenomenon coincides with the disruption of the war years, and an easy explanation—used by *Variety* to explain the correction of the "screwy accident"—is a shortage of male talent, called away by the war. Yet *Variety* is also full of predictions during these years of where the needed new talent would come from—at various moments announcing the imminent arrival of Broadway players, Hollywood stars, "old standbys" who just hadn't gotten their due airtime glory, daytime performers, revamped announcers, and, yes, women.[6] None of these other groups faced the barriers of long-established practices and entrenched social customs that had kept their acknowledged talent from featuring in prime time before. Why then was it that women—particularly women with movie industry background—managed to move in to radio's prime hours during this particular period and stay there, not in their traditional roles as male sidekick or supporting player but as leading names, and often as controlling producers, of their own programs? And what impact did this breakthrough have on radio and, later, television, programming?

THE IMPORTANCE OF BEING JOAN

The answer to the first question begins with a key yet fairly inevitable decision that would lead to later reinforcement and extension: Joan Davis's June 1943 selection as Rudy Vallee's "hand-picked" replacement on the long-running *The Rudy Vallee Show,* now renamed *The Sealtest Village Store* program.[7] However, the groundwork for this decision had been laid in a slow accretion of industry conditions and practices, within a context of the dramatic social changes brought about by the war, that taken all together produced a seemingly "sudden" shift in traditional conditions. It is worthwhile to begin by tracing the trajectory of Davis's career over the next five years, as it highlights most of the key developments that would affect the fortunes of the other women who rose to prominence during this time. More than any other comic, Joan Davis opened the doors for the feminine headliners who would follow in her wake, including the now much more famous Lucille Ball. Though others might have later surpassed Davis's popularity and renown, it is likely that without her breakthrough and subsequent runaway success, other women might not have been given the opportunity to bring their talents to the public that welcomed them so warmly.

Joan Davis started her career on the vaudeville stage as a child comedian, despite her non-showbiz background as the daughter of a St. Paul, Minnesota, train dispatcher and housewife. She married Si Wills in 1931 and soon added him to her act as her "straight man." Their comedy duo was a success, leading them to the pinnacle of vaudeville performance, the Palace Theater in New York, in 1933. Moving to Hollywood in 1934, Davis appeared in films for both Mack Sennett and RKO before being signed by Twentieth Century Fox in 1937. She made twenty-five films for that company over the next four years before beginning her radio career, and she continued to make films under contract to RKO and Universal even as radio began to occupy most of her time. In 1941 she began appearing as a regular on *The Rudy Vallee Show,* which had evolved away from its original variety format closer to a "narrative sketch" comedy routine, the precursor to today's sitcom.[8] Not coincidentally, it is precisely during these years in the 1940s that the term "situation comedy" first begins to find general use, largely due to Davis and other comediennes.

Davis played her characteristic "zany man-chaser" role with Vallee as her object. When Vallee left to join the U.S. Coast Guard in July of 1943, Joan was promoted to "proprietress" of the store with comedian Jack Haley as her "helper" and romantic interest. Despite playing a character that one reviewer described as a "forlorn, frustrated female, as utterly devoid of glamour and allure as a cold fried egg,"[9] Davis was named "radio's top comedienne" by the Scripps-Howard newspaper poll in 1943 and went on to win *Motion Picture Daily's* Fame Poll in 1944. Though it garnered some unfavorable initial reviews, by January 1945 the show, now billed as "Joan Davis with Jack Haley," occupied the number eight spot in the top fifteen radio rankings, with a 22.7 rating. Could it be mere coincidence that *Variety* ran its story about program-topping women in the issue immediately after the one reporting this "click result"? Davis rose even further in the next Hooper survey in March, coming in at number three nationwide, with a 26.5 rating, ahead of even the Jack Benny and Charlie McCarthy shows.[10]

However, the show's sheer success also brought about a chain of events that would eventually lead to its downfall. Riding high in the ratings in spring 1945, the show's contract with its sponsor, Sealtest, was due to expire in June. Intense bidding ensued, with the eventual winner Lever Brothers through their agency, Young and Rubicam. Buoyed by an innovative and intense three-way promotional campaign combining the efforts of the sponsor, the CBS network, and RKO Pictures, hype for the new *Joan Davis Show* ran high. The ads in *Variety* featured Davis as a diapered baby clutching bars of Swan Soap, held aloft in the bill of a swan that floated over CBS headquarters. This ran adjacent to CBS's double-page Miguel Covarrubias sketch of Davis striding through CBS studio doors as the phalanx of CBS radio stars welcome her enthusiastically. As if that weren't enough, RKO weighed in by picturing Davis holding a CBS microphone in its campaign for the fall movie release of *George White's Scandals,* in which she played a role. In return, Davis plugged the movie on her show. And just to take the whole thing over the top, Young and Rubicam saw to it that a "swan-shaped barometer" was shipped not only to all CBS affiliate stations but to radio editors across the country as well. Furthermore, as *Variety* pointed out, with the program moving into a highly coveted space on CBS's Monday night 8:30 niche between Bing Crosby and the *Lux Radio Theatre* (replacing the *Burns and Allen Show*), all of this promotion may have been just icing on the cake. The program debuted September 3, 1945, and initial reviews were favorable. Joan's husband, Si Wills, served as one of the show's main writers, and supporting stars such as Harry Von Zell and Andy Russell contributed to the overall high profile. As *Variety* put it, "This one's in the chips from scratch."[11]

Packaging Independence

Though Davis's comic persona and situation changed only slightly from the old Sealtest program to the new one—the scene shifted from the former village store to the new "Joannie's Tea Room," with Andy Russell as the new target of her unwanted affections—an important change had taken place in the way the show was structured and financed. Davis had joined the wartime trend toward "package shows"—an important innovation that, as I will argue below, played a key role in bringing women into prime time. By this system, rather than the sponsor's owning the program and paying salaries and other expenses through its advertising agency (which took a 15 percent commission on all expenditures off the top), as had been the preferred structure throughout the 1930s and early 1940s, the package show shifted ownership to the star/producer. Usually at the instigation of a talent agency— whose power in the industry had increased since the 1941 FCC Report on Chain Broadcasting that encouraged the networks to divest themselves of their own in-house artists bureaus—a bankable entity such as a fairly well known Hollywood actress or stage comedian could put together a production company around her own talents. By this system, a star such as Davis formed her own company, in this case Joan Davis Productions, hiring her supporting cast, musical talent, writers, and so forth to produce a particular show. Her talent agency marketed the show to an advertising agency, in this case Young and Rubicam, getting a 10 percent commission on the entire deal—not just the 10 percent on the star's fee that it formerly would have gotten. The ad agency in turn sold the show to a sponsor, taking its customary 15 percent, now an even bigger number due to the talent agency cut that added to the show's total price tag. The sponsor paid all, including network time charges (for which the ad agency also received 15 percent commission!), bringing the total bill for big-name programs to new highs— anywhere from ten thousand to twenty-five thousand dollars per weekly show before network charges, more than triple what they had cost.

Why was the sponsor willing to go along with this? The wartime excess-profits tax had made tax shelters attractive, and during the war years the special tax exemption for dollars spent on advertising encouraged companies to funnel money that otherwise would have figured as excess profits into new advertising ventures.[12] High returns enticed commercial radio performers with established reputations who had not found it sufficiently appealing before, providing an instant glamour infusion for the sponsor's product without a lengthy build-up period. For the star, the arrangement provided a tax break, since corporate taxes allowed for more deductions than personal income. It also gave the leading player far more control over the program, including the ability to hire writers at his or her own discretion, select other key personnel, and if necessary take the entire shebang to a new sponsor or network if things didn't work out rather than losing the entire show that he or she had helped to build, as had happened in the past.

By 1945 it was reported that "more than a third of the big shows, from Jack Benny to soap operas, were operating as packages."[13] *The Joan Davis Show* went for seventeen thousand dollars per week; during the bidding wars Davis had been negotiating for as high as twenty-five thousand dollars but settled at the lower figure, with full control as producer. The package system put more power and control over the circumstances and profits of appearing on radio into the hands of those with some prior reputation. By 1943 a growing number of talented women had begun to see the possibilities for intervening in patterns of radio practice that had long shut them out. By arriving at the point of sale—to the ad agency/sponsor—with the ingredients for their program already set and under their control, far fewer tradition-burdened barriers had to be hurdled, far fewer executives with firm convictions about what women could and couldn't do on radio had to be overcome. And the star's own contractual control over writers ensured that the material presented fitted each woman's own particular brand of humor, less trammeled by what network or agency executives found "suitable for a woman." This worked, of course, for all radio stars, male and female, but for women it may have given them the crucial break that they needed.

It is worth mentioning at this point three other figures who would debut during this period in Davis's wake, with slight variations in trajectory. In July 1943 singer/comedian Judy Canova received top billing in *The Judy Canova Show* on CBS, a half-hour comedy/variety program featuring her "hillbilly" music and persona. Canova had started out on the vaudeville stage with her brother Zeke and sister, Annie, in their act "The Three Canovas." She began appearing on radio in 1933 on the *Rudy Vallee Show* and later became a regular on Paul Whiteman's *Musical Varieties* and then on the *Chase and Sanborn Hour* with Edgar Bergen and Charlie McCarthy. By 1943 she had appeared in several Hollywood films, mostly Republic low-budgeters. Her headlining debut came in the wake of Joan Davis's replacement of Vallee; Canova's show was a summer replacement for Al Jolson. Mel Blanc added to the comedy cast, with Ruby Dandridge playing the character Geranium. The show moved to NBC in 1945, where it ran—consistently sponsored by Colgate and consistently causing headaches for the NBC Continuity Acceptance Department (discussed below)—until 1951, moving to television in November 1952. Though few remember Canova—she is the only one out of this group of comics without an entry in *Current Biography,* nor do most reference books include her work—she has one of the longest continuous performance histories of any of these stars. The fact that her work falls within the "hillbilly" rural genre, and that it never moved fully to situation comedy but always retained a musical variety component, makes her something of an anomaly but nonetheless an example of an alternative that ultimately failed as the emphasis shifted to television.

Another woman whose career took a different form, but who still shares certain aspects in common with the others, is producer Martha Rountree. Not an actress, but rather a journalist with credentials as a reporter and sports columnist at the *Tampa Tribune* and a freelancer for the *American Mercury* and other magazines, her main claim to fame is her origination of the still-running public affairs discussion program *Meet the Press,* which Rountree developed for the Mutual Network in 1945. For eight years she acted as packager, coproducer, and cohost of this extremely well received and highly respected roundtable program, along with *American Mercury* editor Lawrence Spivak, to whom she sold the program in 1953. Most people have forgotten that her first venture into radio was something perhaps more interesting: an all-female roundtable discussion program called *Leave It to the Girls.* Rountree and her sister, Ann, had formed a small production company called Radio House in 1939, producing mostly transcribed programs and commercials. *Leave It to the Girls* started out on Mutual as a "serious panel discussion by four career women on problems sent in by listeners," bringing together a panel of "several glamorous, well-known women" and one male guest, who represented "the man's point of view." Though the main tone was humorous, with the battle of the sexes and romantic affairs given much play, the show also addressed political and social questions, though far from seriously. Lucille Ball served as a featured panelist from 1945 to 1948, along with other radio and Hollywood celebrities such as Jinx Falkenberg, Dorothy Kilgallen, Constance Bennett, and Sylvia Sidney.[14] The program went to television on NBC in 1949 until 1951, then came back in 1953 on ABC, where it was hailed enthusiastically by *Variety* for its panel of "quick-witted, oftimes brilliant and only occasionally acidulous babes whose IQ is on a par with their s.a. [sex appeal]." This incarnation, however, lasted only a year,[15] as Rountree turned her attention to several other news shows that she initiated and produced, including *Washington Exclusive, The Big Issue,* and *Press Conference.*

Finally, Ann Sothern must be mentioned as another Hollywood comic star whose route to radio and television took a slightly different turn. Sothern began her career under contract to MGM, where her most notable appearances occurred in the long-running and popular, if not well received critically, series based on her character Maisie, variously described as a "dumb stenographer," a "Honky-tonk [heroine] with a heart of spun sugar," a "Brooklyn beauty and Jane of all trades who usually ended up broke in some remote dive," and "a sassy commoner." She debuted on CBS radio in July of 1945, during the height of the bidding war over Joan Davis's show, and continued popularly if not spectacularly until 1947, when a long bout with hepatitis forced Sothern to take a break from her career. When she returned to health and work in 1949, MGM decided to capitalize on the now well-established woman-centered situation comedy and produced *Maisie* as a syndicated show until 1952; it found a permanent berth on Mutual during its last year. By this time Sothern had become frustrated by the limitations of her Maisie character; she returned to broadcasting with the successful TV series *Private Secretary* in 1953, produced as a package show controlled and produced by Sothern herself, with a far more competent and intelligent Susie as its main character. It ran for four years on CBS, to be followed by the *Ann Sothern Show* from 1958 to 1961.

These three women represent the first wave of the feminine breakthrough brought about by Joan Davis's bellwether success and the simultaneous development of the package system of production. For Davis herself, however, the story continues in a more problematic vein. With the end of the war and the expiration of the special taxes and exemptions, the sums paid for star-centered package programs began to look increasingly prohibitive to sponsors. By February 1947 *Variety* reported that Lever had offered up the Joan Davis program to other sponsor bids, but no one bit. Contractual obligations forced them to renew for another season, but they announced their intentions to drop the show at the end of the spring season. Camel cigarettes showed some interest but wanted Davis to relinquish control of the program, which she refused to do.[16] Instead, she ventured into another innovative practice briefly attempted in the late 1940s: the so-called co-op system. This was an interesting attempt at what we might call network syndication: led by Mutual, but soon adopted by all three other networks, a prime-time show would be sold not to a single sponsor but to a varied number of individual affiliated stations, at a cost calibrated to the size of each radio market. The stations would themselves sell all advertising time locally for as much as the market would bear. The show's producer was guaranteed a certain minimum amount—for Davis, it was ten thousand dollars—plus a percentage of profits over a certain figure. The network kept the balance—or, as it too frequently turned out, absorbed the losses. One immediate problem the co-op system ran into was the American Federation of Musicians, who refused to allow their members to perform on a multiple-sponsored show. For that reason many co-op programs were of the news, discussion, and quiz variety, where music was not necessary. Most comedy programs at this time regarded a musical break or two as an integral part of the show; Davis tried substituting an a capella group for a while, but this was far from satisfactory. Otherwise, the co-op system provided an opportunity for local or regional advertisers, or smaller national companies, to advertise on a prime-time network program at a price they could afford: the total cost to the stations was usually 60 percent of what the networks would charge a sponsor for the same time slot. By 1947 all four networks were participating in the co-op system, with Mutual the leader.

For Joan Davis, the co-op system failed to provide the number of sponsors necessary to sustain such a high-budget show. Starting out with twenty-five sponsors in October 1947 in the various localities where her show was heard, she had dropped to twenty by March 1948.[17] By June 1948 she had been dropped from CBS, having failed to find a sponsor to pick up the contract. A victim of its own success, her program proved too expensive for the co-op system to handle; as a major star interested in guarding her assets, Davis was reluctant to give up the control she had exercised over her material. Into this vacuum of temporarily stalled opportunity one network moved with far-reaching results.

CBS GETS SMART

Yet a third significant phase of program financing and development occurred in the wake of widespread co-op failure, as CBS, preeminently among networks, caught on to the opportunities presented by a reworking of the package system to its own advantage—namely, cutting out the middlemen. Why couldn't a star/producer sell a program directly to the network instead of going through the talent agency/ad agency/sponsor chain of intermediaries? The network could open the program as a sustaining show, then seek out a sponsor, who (through its ad agency, still taking its 15 percent) would purchase the program cum time slot directly from the net. This cut out the talent agency, which returned to its traditional role of placing talent in productions, leaving ultimate ownership in the hands of the network, which would come in handy as television schedules yawned. It provided sponsors with an already tested and approved property, reducing risk, and absolved the ad agency of much of its former trial and tribulation, but with its 15 percent intact.[18]

Along these lines, CBS initiated the next crucial step in opening up the prime-time air to female stars. Between April 1947 and June 1949, CBS debuted four successful and influential series headed by women, all of which would make the transition to television in one form or another. The first was *My Friend Irma,* with Marie Wilson, which premiered in April 1947. Wilson had established her persona as a Maisie-like "dumb blonde" in a series of lightweight films in the 1930s. She moved from Hollywood to Ken Murray's "Blackouts" stage show in 1942, where she performed in a "satiric strip tease" to much acclaim. Radio producer Cy Howard, looking perhaps for a Maisie replacement in Ann Sothern's absence in 1947 (in fact, the show took over *Maisie's* slot on CBS Fridays at 10:30), put together a package that included Wilson in the title role. Kathy Lewis costarred as her acerbic foil, who narrated Irma's escapades each week. The show was greeted by critics as possessing "spontaneity, freshness and humor" and as a "farce of more than passing promise."[19] *My Friend Irma* soon attracted Lever Brothers as a sponsor—in fact, this is where Swan Soap turned after its disenchantment with Joan Davis—with ratings going as high as a 21.5 in its second season. We may also have to credit *My Friend Irma* with a broadcast innovation that has produced decades of catchy theme music for television shows. *Variety's* initial review noted with atypical surprise: "Premier pulled a switch, in an opening singing commercial, not for the sponsor or product, but for the show!" It continued a successful run on CBS until 1954, going to television in 1952 but simulcasting for radio for two years. In 1949 Wilson starred as Irma in a movie made by Hal Wallis Productions that became one of the top-grossing pictures of that year. By 1950 lucky Marie Wilson was being received with such ambiguous accolades as this one from *Coronet* magazine: "[T]he Dumb Blonde is as indigenous to the American scene as baseball or the Fourth of July, and Marie Wilson is the archetype of all Dumb Blondes."[20]

A somewhat different type of ditzy dame would debut on CBS in July of 1948: Lucille Ball starred with Richard Denning in *My Favorite Husband*, a series based on the "Mr. and Mrs. Cugat" novel and magazine series by Isabel Scott Rorick. Once again a CBS sustaining package revolving around a successful but secondary Hollywood star, this program "hit the comedy jackpot" and launched Ball into a career that scarcely needs recapitulation. The *Variety* reviewer noted that one of the show's strengths was that it had borrowed the writing team from the *Ozzie and Harriet* program, on vacation for the summer. It was produced by Jess Oppenheimer, one of Fanny Brice's mainstays, and written by the team of Madelyn Pugh and Bob Carroll Jr., who would continue on with Ball into Desilu Productions. Ball, who had played mainly secondary film roles under RKO contract, with a few larger musical features at MGM from 1935 to 1947, stuck with *My Favorite Husband* until 1951, with generally favorable reviews but only moderate success in the ratings. It was soon picked up by General Foods as a sponsor, for Jell-O. However, by 1950 Ball and her husband, Desi Arnaz, had formed their own production company, Desilu, and were actively engaged in working up a comedy act that they could market to television together. *I Love Lucy* debuted in October 1951 on CBS, and the rest, as they say, is history. Desilu joined the ranks of independent producers, responsible for much of the decade's more popular, though sometimes denigrated, programming.

One of its very first additional ventures hit the airwaves originally as the third CBS sustaining production, Eve Arden's *Our Miss Brooks*. Premiering just two weeks after *My Favorite Husband*, the program took Arden from the Sealtest program, where she had served as "manager" of the store—under Jack Haley as "proprietor," having moved up since Davis left—since 1945. Playing the role for which she would become famous, a sharp-tongued but kindhearted schoolteacher, Arden found a sponsor almost immediately (Colgate) and ran continuously on CBS until 1952, when the show went to television for an additional five years. In 1953 she won an Emmy Award for "Best Female Star of a Regular Series," and in general the program received excellent reviews for the length of its run. *Variety* called its premiere "a happy integration of production, writing, and acting," while Jack Gould predicted: "Eve Arden, who can deliver a line with a decidedly sophisticated and acerbic wallop, finally has won a program of her own . . . which has the makings of a Hooper hit."[21] In October, when Colgate picked up sponsorship, *Variety* saluted the program's "family appeal" and "swift pacing," though later the magazine claimed that the show "studiously avoids subtlety or sophistication." All credited Arden's comedic talent as the main ingredient of the show's success, praising her "cutting edge" delivery, timing, and inflection; a review of the television program interestingly claimed: "Uniquely, too, she is lacking in warmth, humility and sympathy, the cardinal virtues of the successful mine, yet overrides these liabilities as a straight trader in laughs that seem to have caught on."[22] Arden took *Our Miss Brooks* to the Desilu studio in 1952 for its television incarnation. Lucille Ball deflected any attributions of competition between her own and Arden's show by pointing out that since she owned both, she could hardly be put out when both did well.[23]

Arden had a long career on stage, film, and radio before her signature radio role. She had developed the role of Baby Snooks's mother in the Ziegfeld show with Fanny Brice, whom she understudied, then went to Hollywood, where she performed increasingly more significant roles in over twenty-five motion pictures between 1937 and 1944. She was warmly acknowledged and cited by teachers' groups across the country for her depiction of Connie Brooks, who taught at Madison High in a small town in Middle America —*not* Madison, Wisconsin, according to Al Lewis, the show's main writer and later director. After *Our Miss Brooks* finally retired in 1956, Arden starred in her own show, the *Eve Arden Show,* another CBS half hour based on the autobiography of novelist Emily Kimbrough. Producer Jess Oppenheimer (now working for NBC) had tried to interest NBC in a resurrection of the *Baby Snooks* show with Arden as the star in 1956, but Arden's insistence on retaining control through a package arrangement, and CBS's willingness to pay her a handsome sum for exclusivity, led to the demise of that proposal.[24]

Another film actress making her debut on CBS in this period was Hattie McDaniel, who marked the first African American woman to play that role since it had originated as part of the *Fibber McGee and Molly* show in 1943 performed by the white male actor Marlin Hurt. It spun off into the *Marlin Hurt and Beulah Show* in 1945, but Hurt's death in that same year forced a replacement, first by another white man, then finally by McDaniel in 1947.

McDaniel also figures in film history as the first black woman to win an Academy Award, for her role as Mammy in *Gone With the Wind*. She shone in supporting roles in a number of motion pictures in the 1940s and went on to play similar roles in the limited universe of characterizations available to black actresses on radio, as musical performer, mammy, or maid, on the *Maxwell House Show Boat* program and in 1942 performed as a regular on the *Eddie Cantor Show*.

As housekeeper Beulah, McDaniel was the first African American woman to headline a regular network program. Her show was a solid ratings success, attracting many fan letters weekly. McDaniel insisted that her Beulah jettison the minstrel-type dialect that had typified previous incarnations, writing a clause to this effect into her contract, which also mandated final script approval. Even so, McDaniel faced criticism for her portrayal of Beulah as an uneducated, mammy-type figure prone to malapropisms and constantly emphasizing her large size and weight. The Armed Forces Radio Service went so far as to ban her program from their overseas offerings, ostensibly because of objections by black troops—but perhaps more realistically due to the way such a limited range of roles for black performers might play in countries without the race bias of the United States. When the program went to television in 1950 on ABC, Ethel Waters got the role, with McDaniel continuing the radio program. Waters left *Beulah* in 1951, and McDaniel stepped in, filming six segments over the summer. But failing health forced her to drop her commitment to both radio and television. First Lillian then Amanda Randolph stepped into Beulah's shoes on the radio show, which ran until 1954. Louise Beavers assumed the role on television, until it went off the air in 1953. McDaniel died of heart failure in October 1952.[25]

The final female star to debut as a CBS sustainer during this period was the ever-enterprising Joan Davis. Her new property, *Leave It to Joan,* premiered in June 1949, replacing the first half hour of the *Lux Radio Theatre* for the summer. Produced and directed by Dick Mack, who had been with Joan throughout her radio career, it quickly became CBS's number one summer show and was picked up by the American Tobacco Company for the fall season. It ran on CBS until August 1950, then after a hiatus moved to television, now titled *I Married Joan*. It had also switched to NBC, where it was hailed as that network's rival for the *I Love Lucy* audience. Jack Gould went so far as to say that "in theme and execution it is a close copy of Miss Ball's vehicle. It is also just about as amusing." In the role of the wife of a domestic court judge, played by Jim Backus, Gould found Davis "infinitely more diverting than she was in radio," attributing it to her "good intuitive sense of timing for visual make-believe."[26] The show was owned and produced by Joan Davis Productions, filmed in Hollywood using the now standard three-camera method. Davis became another of the 1950s' successful professional women who would not be permitted to play that role on television. *I Married Joan* enjoyed a moderately high-rated run on NBC until 1955, but it never came close to its rival. Only for one season, 1953–1954, did it make it into the top twenty-five shows—as number twenty-five—while *I Love Lucy* occupied one of the top three slots from 1952 to 1957. Davis's career was cut short by a heart attack in 1961, and she seemed for a long time to be forgotten. But her career exemplifies the conditions that broke through the barriers of gendered practice that had kept female talent in the ghetto of women's daytime programming. From her role as the host of a major variety hour, to her move to packaged programming independence, to her depiction of an unruly funny woman on television, Davis led all the significant trends that led to the domestic situation comedy as we know it.

THE RISE OF THE SITUATION COMEDY

Continuing the insightful analysis that it had begun three years earlier, *Variety* noted CBS's trend toward female-centered comedies in August 1948 with a front-page headline shouting, "Radio's Find: Femme Comics." Mentioning Marie Wilson, Eve Arden, and Lucille Ball's recent debuts, *Variety* once again called the whole thing an "accident" and claimed it was "something that just happened, without any deliberate attempt on the part of the network to groom a new school of femme attractions." In fact, the article states that the network's real aim was "to scout around for up-coming male comics" but that the search simply hadn't panned out. With its usual mix of acuteness and myopia, however, *Variety* also pointed out that "All the shows are situation comedies, peculiarly patterned to the talents of the femmes."[27] While the term "situation," used to designate a show oriented not around one-shot "gags" but around a recurring narrative situation, had been heard since roughly 1944, it had not gelled into a standard practice. *Variety* predicted a coming shift in June 1944, opining: "Joke shows on the air next fall will be fewer and fewer and the 'story line' will be the thing. . . . The joke show is on its way out. Not completely, of course, but to be gradually absorbed by running situations."[28] The article takes note of several long-running programs that had made profitable use of the format—*Fibber McGee and Molly, The Aldrich Family, The Great Gildersleeve*—and a number of others that had recently made the switch to a much more situational format—*Burns and Allen* and, notably, the Joan Davis/Jack Haley *Sealtest* show. To the first category could be added other proto-sitcoms such as *Amos 'n' Andy, The Rise of the Goldbergs,* and *Clara, Lu, and Em,* as well as some other shows more commonly classified as serials; in the latter category such major hits as *The Jack Benny Program* and the *Fred Allen Show* should also be included. By 1947 veteran radio writer Bob Carroll could lament: "Today radio is suffering from a severe epidemic of S.C. [situation comedy] poisoning," noting that one problem was that these shows were much more difficult to write than the former comedy/variety "gag" show. He went on to give what may be the first official definition of the form: "If . . . the characters are more or less three-dimensional with entrances and exits motivated to a noticeable degree by the necessities of the story, rather than by mechanics as arbitrary as the arrangement of doors and beds in an old A. H. Woods farce, you have Situation Comedy."[29]

The term seems to have its origins in the lingo of comedy writing, which distinguished between the "gag writer" and the "situation man." Writer Sidney Reznick described the "situation man" as someone whose responsibility is "creating funny pegs on which to hang the jokes" and to "constantly dream up situations replete with humorous possibilities while the other hirelings concentrate on gags and funny lines."[30] Jack Gould, by this time the country's preeminent radio critic and soon to be a major television voice, in 1946 refined the distinction into one between "the variety format, employed by the majority of laugh shows," and "the situation comedy in which there is some adherence to dramatic form." Criticizing the variety form on radio for becoming "frozen" and repetitious, Gould praises the situation comedy as "less subject to critical barbs. It avoids the fragility of vaudeville and enables the performer to establish a fictional character which feeds on more than his own personality. It affords entertainment where the accent is keeping the audience relaxed and not hopped up for thirty minutes at a time." He makes no mention of the previous two years' crop of feminine situation leads but does praise two other shows in the genre, *The Life of Riley* and

Ozzie and Harriet, both non-prime-time programs.[31] Though he does not note the gender differential in the two types of comedy—variety or gag comedy being almost exclusively the province of men, situation comedy heavily dominated by women—that interesting schism reveals itself in a pair of corresponding articles in 1953. In "A Primer of TV Comics" from May 1953, Gould restricts his analysis to variety comedy only, praising its television practitioners such as Fred Allen, Jack Benny, Red Buttons, and Arthur Godfrey, reserving his highest praise for Donald O'Connor. The only women mentioned are Tallulah Bankhead (a movie star with a short-lived radio career) and Imogene Coca (Sid Caesar's second banana), both somewhat critically.[32] Perhaps responding to the omission, in December another article, "TV's Top Comediennes," featured all the feminine stars discussed above. In the introduction, Gould delivered himself of this somewhat perplexing analysis: "The rise of the comedienne in TV may be attributed to the nature of the medium itself. Since the TV audience is the family at home, the domestic comedy, revolving about the woman of the house, is a natural formula."[33] One is forced to assume that radio was *not* a domestic medium aimed at the family at home in order to make sense of this account of the new feminine-centered sitcom form—hardly a tenable claim. What else could explain the eclipse of radio's old standby variety format by these upstart women?

FUNNY WOMEN, HEARING VOICES

First of all, gag comedy had never been a hospitable form for female comedians. Fanny Brice struggled for years with network censors before finally coming up with her "Snooks strategy," which allowed the character of a small child to get away with lines that Brice, as a mature adult woman, was not allowed to utter.[34] Judy Canova suffered from similar network censoring in her variety/gag format. A summary of the forced cuts from her show in 1947, along with the NBC Continuity Acceptance executives' wry comments (in italics), gives a clear picture of the problems a female gagster faced.

Man: It's nice and dark in here, beautiful. Here . . . lean against my shoulder . . . hey, where is your head?
Judy: Feel around, it's up there somewhere. Golly, this is nice!!

I'll bet it is.
Judy: What's funny about love?
Pedro: Why should a man want to bite a girl on the neck just because she has pretty legs?
They were referred to Volume Seven, page 345, on sex-inhibitions by Havelock Ellis.
Judy: The health inspector says Judy's got to be vaccinated and he can vaccinate her where it won't show.
Blanc: Well, where are you going to have her vaccinated?
Judy: Do you figure the cellar would be a good place?
We didn't think so.[35]

Situation comedy could surround the female comedian with an innocuous, domestic situation, with jokes arising from the interaction of characters and the resolution of comic narratives rather than the often-risqué double entendres of gag comedy. It could substitute female authority in the sphere of home or private life—a fairly palatable place for women to exert control—for female authority as host in the context of a variety show, a place in the public sphere much less hospitable to feminine power. Plus, situation comedies were less expensive to produce, since they avoided the costs of big-name guest stars—whose fees had skyrocketed during the war—and a full orchestra, plus a full cast of regulars that most shows included. This, especially combined with the package system, allowed a headlining Hollywood star to keep a proportionately greater cut of a budget that still remained under control, adding to the attraction of venturing into radio. Situation comedies could combine the appeal of known comedic talent with the narrative flow and familiarity that the daytime serials used so effectively—particularly important as the feminine audience was "discovered" in the 1940s, as will be discussed below. Plus, as the networks' restrictions on the use of transcriptions (recorded programs) relaxed in the late 1940s, situation comedies could be sold in syndication and rerun more readily than the often-topical variety programs.

Two other factors, besides wartime scarcity and the innovation of the program packaging system, contributed to the rise of the female-centered domestic sitcom and added to the advantages described above. Both involve changes in audience research—one developed by Nielsen that gave a more accurate idea of the size of the audience for particular programs, across an entire day's broadcast schedule; the other developed, far from "accidentally," by CBS's research department.

The Nielsen Company was a market research firm that got into broadcast audience measurement after having spent several years testing a device for the automatic registration of radio listening developed in the 1930s at MIT. Its radio service to networks began in 1942 and rapidly displaced the telephone-based Hooperratings system that had been in use previously. By the mid-1940s, Nielsen was dispensing data to the major networks and stations that used far more sophisticated sampling techniques, tied to the Audimeter method of collection, which avoided the potential for misleading answers that audiences might give to the Hooper surveyors. Though ratings had always been a factor considered in making programming decisions, this new "scientific" method contributed to the legitimacy of research-based decisions and also helped networks conceptualize the activities of individual viewers as they moved from show to show, the precursor to the idea of audience "flow."[36]

At CBS—the second-place network that "tried harder" throughout the 1930s—the presence of Frank Stanton contributed to the centrality of research in network operations. Having graduated with a PhD in psychology from Ohio State University, he was hired by CBS in 1936 and by 1937 had been named codirector of the Princeton Radio Project—created by a grant from the Rockefeller Foundation—along with Hadley Cantril and Paul F. Lazarsfeld.[37] They began to produce some of the first studies of the national broadcast audience, backed by scientific expertise and institutional support, which attracted enormous attention—and, not coincidentally in this period of frequent network criticism and FCC investigation, began to legitimate the networks' position as servants of the public interest. Stanton took these developments back to CBS and produced two breakthrough measurement techniques: the program analyzer, which allowed selected studio audiences to register their likes and dislikes on a minute-by-minute basis, and the diary survey technique, which for the first time allowed a breakdown of audience composition by age and gender and also, for the first time, included homes without telephones.

In May of 1943 CBS unveiled the results of its initial diary survey, after much anticipation in the trade press. For the first time it became obvious, beyond much doubt, that women composed the bulk of the listening audience at almost all times of the day and night. Children and adolescents were placed in a separate category, which would also have far-ranging effects on programming. *Variety* grasped the implications immediately when it wrote: "As the network sees it, a program manager for the first time doesn't have to deal in hunches or guesses and is now able to read on a chart exactly what happens to the station's audience—when it leaves the station, where it goes, when it comes back, etc."[38]

The reduction of "guesswork" also recommended the program analyzer. Program directors could now see precisely where their opinion of the quality of a show departed from those of the audience. A study commissioned by the National Association of Broadcasters (NAB) in 1946 published a graph of one episode of the *Arthur Godfrey's Talent Scouts* program, charting the minute-by-minute reaction of "a cross-section of listeners" against a group of "program managers." At several points in the program, the audience's re-action differed diametrically from that of the managers, showing an increase in "liking" where the managers showed a decrease, and so forth.[39] Thus, "accurate" or not, these new measurement methods provided a way to break through the accretion of preferred practice, with its attendant assumptions and prejudices, for those with a mind to do so.

CBS began to apply program analyzer findings to its program selection and development practices. As the *New Yorker* reported in a profile of Stanton done in 1947: "The Analyzer is now used in the preparation of the most important CBS sustaining programs, by advertising agencies handling programs broadcast by CBS, and by the seven stations the network owns." It further reports one so far tentative finding: "The machine has lately suggested that gag comedy, in particular—the backbone of most funny programs—has grown rusty."[40] One key variable in the analysis of reactions was that of gender; men and women often reacted differently to aspects of a show's offerings, and the analyzer allowed program managers to consider this.

By providing a means to bring audience opinion, readily distinguishable by gender, into the process of developing and nurturing radio and TV programs—thus replacing the system of decision making by male executives buttressed by long-standing and often discriminatory practices—these developments helped to break down barriers to women's full participation in the broadcast economy and culture. Though imperfect and subject to many distortions and interpretations throughout their use, these systems gave *actual* audiences, always heavily female, more of a say as to what they liked and wanted to hear and see on national networks. The use of this information may also have been affected by another wartime trend that continued into peacetime: an increasing number of women filling the function of agency time-buyer, the person who made the decision as to which programs advertisers would support.[41] Audiences responded by making the situation comedy the premiere form of television comedy—often, though not always, centered on female characters.

THE TELEVISION FAMILY

This account of the rise of the female-centered situation comedy may help to cut through some of the more naive, "reflection" theories of television representation, which make facile and largely unexamined connections between the rise of domestic comedy and the real-life conditions of American families in the 1950s and 1960s. If domestic sitcoms such as *My Favorite Husband, Leave It to Joan, Beulah, The Baby Snooks Show, Ozzie and Harriet, Burns and Allen, Fibber McGee and Molly, The Aldrich Family, The Goldbergs,* and many others existed on radio in the 1940s and even the 1930s, can extravagant claims about their special relevance to television in the 1950s— along the lines of Jack Gould's rationale above—really be supported? If industry practices such as the package system, changes in audience measurement, and FCC-influenced shifts in control of production can be shown to have contributed significantly to shifts in dominant representational systems, can studies that explain the shift by looking only at a highly generalized social context really be considered persuasive? At the same time, links to other large social forces should not be overlooked. In her article "Sitcoms and Suburbs," for instance, Mary Beth Haralovich makes detailed and persuasive connections between market research strategies, suburban housing planning and financing, and the depiction of families and consumer goods on television.[42] Lynn Spigel examines the overlap between women's magazine discourses about television and representations in TV programs themselves, to produce a more complex picture of the role of television in the 1950s.[43] The kind of focused industry analysis that I have undertaken here can answer some questions, mostly about implementation; it cannot look at the larger forces that positioned some developments close to hand and downplayed others.

Yet without this series of large and small adjustments to industry practice, it is difficult to understand the seemingly "natural" shift to female-centered domestic comedy that dominated television in the 1950s and 1960s. Or perhaps more to the point, it helps us to uncover the seemingly "natural" conditions that led to the exclusion of women from these roles in the past. A final note on the workings of history writing is called for. No scholar looking at significant programming trends in the 1940s and 1950s could miss this shift of women into prime time. There it is, trumpeted in two-inch headlines on the main pages of *Variety;* there are the shows themselves, ranked high in the seasonal ratings. Yet these shows and stars, with the exception of Lucille Ball, are largely absent from standard broadcast histories. While newscasters such as H. V. Kaltenborn and Edward R. Murrow have their papers preserved in prominent archives, these female comedians receive no such historical consideration. Though they warrant the occasional mention by a critic such as Jack Gould, it is minuscule indeed compared to the hundreds of column inches spent on the dramatists of the so-called Golden Age or even the barely more respectable genre of crime/adventure programs, also on the rise during these years. Only the trade press recognizes the centrality of such developments to the evolution of broadcast practices—and then only in its own terms. Such a site of recognition itself speaks volumes for the place that these pioneer situation comedy programs hold in the ranks of "official" or "high culture" history.

Yet it is difficult to think of a cultural form that more millions of people, in this country and now across the globe, are exposed to every day. The situation comedy series is one of the unique and lasting contributions of network broadcasting to global culture, and the women featured in this chapter must be regarded as some of its main contributors. It is not in lived history that their names and lives are obscure, but only in history writing. As long as we accept a model of broadcast history that continues to authorize the same hierarchy of categories—news over entertainment, prime time over daytime, masculine genres over feminine ones, public issues over private— we run the risk of overlooking phenomena that are not only crucial to understanding historical developments but are also especially revealing of larger social practices in their very suppression. We also reinforce and maintain dominant racial, class, and gender categories in our teaching that we would not tolerate in our research. Besides, a lot of very funny work goes unappreciated. Out of all of these Hollywood-based funny women, only Lucille Ball was able, through talent and control over her own production company, to rise above the industrial and historiographical barriers that have obscured Joan Davis, Marie Wilson, Ann Sothern, Judy Canova, Eve Arden, Hattie McDaniel, and Martha Rountree from view. Their work deserves a revaluation in more depth than this quick industrial history has allowed.

NOTES

Most of this essay draws on original research in *Variety* and other trade and general periodicals, and on the NBC and NAB archives housed in the Wisconsin Historical Society in Madison, Wisconsin. I am indebted throughout to the detailed information on schedules, time slots, dates, titles, and casts in John Dunning, *On the Air: The Encyclopedia of Old-Time Radio* (New York: Oxford, 1998), and Harrison B. Summers, ed., *A Thirty-Year History of Programs Carried on National Radio Networks in the United States, 1926–1956* (New York: Arno Press, 1971).

1. "War Gave Femmes Chance to Clinch Place as Boff Program Toppers," *Variety,* January 24, 1945, 34.

2. Of course, many female artists performed on air, in both daytime and nighttime slots. Gertrude Berg, for instance, the creator of *The Goldbergs,* is a pioneer of the series comedy format but found herself primarily relegated to daytime for most of her radio career. Jessica Dragonette starred as lead singer for many years on the *Cities Service Concerts* program and in guest slots on other shows after 1937. Lily Pons was a featured soloist on many programs, as was Grace Moore. Others, like Penny Singleton, who played Blondie on the long-running series of that name based on the famous comic strip, performed as part of a male/female duo, as with Burns and Allen, discussed below.

3. See Michele Hilmes, *Radio Voices: American Broadcasting, 1922–1952* (Minneapolis: U of Minnesota P: 1997), for a full explanation of this practice.

4. See Hilmes, "Fanny Brice and the Schnooks Strategy," in Kristine Brunovska Karnick, ed., *Life of the Party: Comediennes in Hollywood* (New York: New York UP, forthcoming).

5. Other female stars nominated by *Variety* in this category include Dinah Shore, Ginny Simms, Gracie Fields, Arlene Francis, the Andrews Sisters, Charlotte Greenwood, Hildegarde, Mary Small, Beatrice Kay, Cass Daley, and Judy Holliday. See "War Gave Femmes" and "Radio's Find: Femme Comics," *Variety,* August 4, 1948, 1, 53.

6. Thomas B. Luckenbill, "Last Half of '43 Promising, with Flock of New Personalities Scheduled to Be Developed," *Variety,* July 14, 1943, 31; Jack Hellman, "Radio Faces Climactic Era," *Variety,* July 14, 1943, 36; "Radio Spawns New Comics," *Variety,* December 22, 1943, 1, 55.

7. This phrase comes from Dunning's entry on "The Sealtest Village Store" in *On the Air,* 602.

8. This information on Joan Davis's background comes from *Current Biography,* "Joan Davis," 1945; Dunning, *On the Air,* 602; and "Joan Davis, Comedienne, Dead," *New York Times,* May 24, 1961, 41.

9. Dunning, *On the Air,* 603, quoting *Radio Life.*

10. See *Variety,* September 6, 1944, 30; January 17 1945, 26; March 7, 1945, 30.

11. *Variety,* January 31, 1945, 19; March 7, 1945, 30; August 29, 1945, 24, 27–29; review, September 5, 1945, 26.

12. See Hellman, "Radio Faces Climactic Era," 36; "The Package Shows," *Newsweek,* December 17, 1945, 103–04.

13. *Newsweek,* ibid.

14. Sources on Rountree include *Current Biography* 1957; Diana Gibbings, "A Lady Producer," *New York Times,* March 10, 1946, Section 2, pg. 7; Val Adams, "Glamour Girls and Newspaper Men," *New York Times,* September 3, 1950, Section 2, pg. 7; "Know-How Woman," *Time,* July 19, 1946, 54; John Dunning, "Leave It to the Girls," *On the Air,* 390.

15. "Leave It to the Girls," *Variety,* October 7, 1953, 45.

16. *Variety,* February 26, 1947, 33; June 11, 1947, 23.

17. *Variety,* November 12, 1947, 1, 38; March 7, 1948, 31.

18. By 1954 some in the industry were wondering if agencies really deserved their 15 percent cut on direct-to-network package show sales. Agencies responded with a list of "48 Steps Agency Must Take" to accomplish a successful sponsored show, and argued that of course they did. Alfred J. Jaffe, "Are Agencies Earning Their 15% on Net TV Shows?" *Sponsor,* October 18, 1954, 29ff.

19. "My Friend Irma," *Variety,* April 16, 1947, 27; Jack Gould, "Programs in Review," *Variety,* May 4, 1947, II 9:1.

20. Dwight Whitney, "My Friend Irma Is Not So Dumb," *Coronet,* November 1950, 58–62.

21. "Our Miss Brooks," *Variety,* July 21, 1948, 30; *New York Times,* August 11, 1948, 45.

22. *Variety,* October 13, 1948, 27; September 14, 1949, 31; October 8, 1952, 34; and October 7, 1953, 47.

23. "No Competition," *Time,* October 13, 1952, 88–89.

24. Memorandum from Tom Sarnoff to Tom McAvity, July 25, 1956, "Eve Arden," box 387, folder 46, "Wolff-Arden, Eve–1956," NBC.

25. Carlton Jackson, *Hattie: The Life of Hattie McDaniel* (Lanham, MD: Madison Books, 1990). Jackson makes use of many documents pertaining to Hattie McDaniel's career from the Ruby Goodwin papers in North Hollywood, California.

26. Jack Gould, "Radio and Television," *New York Times,* October 20, 1952, 30; Val Adams, "Joan Davis: Physical Comedienne," *New York Times,* November 22, 1953, 11; "I Married Joan," *Variety,* October 6, 1954, 34.

27. "Radio's Find: Femme Comics," *Variety,* 1948, 1, 53.

28. "Joke Shows' Own Tag Line," *Variety,* June 7, 1944, 23.

29. Bob Carroll, "Radio Suffering from 'Situations,'" *Variety,* July 9, 1947, 37.

30. Sidney Reznick, "Quick Look into a Gag Factory," *New York Times,* May 9, 1943, Section 2, pg. 7.

31. Jack Gould, "How Comic Is Radio Comedy?" *New York Times Magazine,* November 21, 1948, 64–68.

32. Jack Gould, "A Primer of TV Comics," *New York Times Magazine,* May 3, 1953, 37–42.

33. Jack Gould, "TV's Top Comediennes," *New York Times Magazine,* December 27, 1953, 16–17.

34. See Hilmes, "Fanny Brice and the Schnooks Strategy," in Karnick, *Life of the Party.*

35. "Judy Canova–Hollywood 11/5/47 cuts," box 151, folder 44, "Continuity Acceptance–Judy Canova Show," NBC.

36. Arthur C. Nielsen Sr., "Statement to the Committee on Interstate and Foreign Commerce of United States Senate," June 26, 1958, A. C. Nielsen Company, Chicago, Illinois.

37. For additional background, see William J. Buxton and Charles R. Acland, "Frank Stanton: Pioneer of Radio Research, An Interview," *Journal of Radio Studies* 7:2 (2000): 474–503.

38. "CBS Unveils 'Diary' Survey," *Variety,* May 12, 1943, 33, 39.

39. National Association of Broadcasters, "It Pays to Know Your Radio Audience," 1946, box 8A, folder 9, "Audience Measurement," NAB.

40. Robert Lewis Taylor, "Profiles: Let's Find Out–I," *New Yorker,* January 18, 1947, 32–36ff.; and "Profiles: Let's Find Out–II," *New Yorker,* January 25, 1947, 28.

41. Kati Cuff, "Femmes' Growing Influence Noted," *Variety,* April 3, 1943, 33, 40.

42. Mary Beth Haralovich, "Sitcoms and Suburbs," in *Private Screenings,* ed. Lynn Spigel and Denise Mann (Chicago: U of Chicago P, 1992): 42–65.

43. Lynn Spigel, *Make Room for Television* (Chicago: U of Chicago P, 1990).

7 / Space and the Speed of Sound
Mobile Media, 1950s Broadcasting, and Suburbia

MATTHEW A. KILLMEIER

Automotive radio and broadcasting emerged in the 1950s as a unique cultural form of radio. Rather than an insignificant change in receiving sets, automotive and portable radio were a unique development in the history of radio—they were forms that reflected and shaped the ways people listened as well as the content of postwar radio and the spaces of listening.

Quantitatively, the emergence and growth of automotive radio in the immediate postwar period was remarkable. While in 1946 the number of automotive radio sets in use was 6 million, by 1950 it was 17 million. In 1955 the number increased to 36 million, and by 1960 the number of automotive radio sets in use numbered 43 million. Approximately 29 percent of all automobiles were outfitted with radio sets in 1947; by 1955 the figure was 60 percent, and almost one-quarter of the radio audience was listening to automotive radio by 1961. Suggesting the scope of change, a 1958 article noted, "there are more radio-equipped autos today than there were radio-equipped homes in 1947."[1]

Invented in 1928 by William Lear, automotive radio was not feasible until the 1950s for several reasons. Technologically, automotive radio was inferior until the civilian application of the transistor in 1947.[2] Earlier automotive radios relied on vacuum tubes, which consumed much electricity, produced a lot of heat, and were fragile and cumbersome in size. They required a separate battery and were unreliable due to high operating temperatures. The practicality of automotive radio was further hindered by disparate types and placement of antennae, which often impeded reception.[3] These early automotive radios were also expensive after-market items in most instances, with few car manufacturers offering them. With the civilian application of the transistor in the late 1940s, integration of the radio into the car was feasible.[4] Reliability, good reception, and the ability to run off of the car's electrical system made transistor models desirable. Automotive radio became an option auto manufacturers could confidently offer.

Automotive radio was also dormant until the 1950s because of the lack of specific programming for increasingly mobile listeners. The radio programming from the 1920s through the 1950s was aimed at a stationary, home-based audience. In contrast, automotive radio was a mobile form of media, which required a different audience, programming, and society. New cultural forms, mobile media, were developed in the postwar period, which were constituted by political-economic changes in industry, social needs, mobility, and reconfigured patterns of everyday life.

Postwar radio is often characterized as declining because of the emergence of television. While the impact of television is a contributing factor in the reconfiguration of postwar radio, particularly regarding its political-economic structure, the argument about the decline of radio's social and cultural relevance does not necessarily follow.[5] Indeed, radio continued to be significant, but in ways yet to be adequately interpreted or accounted for in media historiography.

SOUND, SPACE, AND MOBILITY

Automotive radio, broadcasting content, and 1950s radio were reflective of and interconnected with increasing mobility and social change, and were reflexive or productive of mobility and social change. Susan Douglas insists that in the 1950s "sound redefined public space," as automotive and portable radio brought audio into public places.[6] Concurrently, however, space was also being reconfigured, particularly with automobiles and suburbs, and an overview of the latter is pertinent to understanding how mobile media and programming aided in the redefinition of space in the postwar period.

The growth in suburbs and the entrenchment of car-centered lifestyles were constitutional characteristics of the 1950s. Suburbanization represented an unprecedented migration of people from established cities and towns (places) to new "zones" of living created by a combination of governmental and commercial forces.[7] "Builders constructed 30 million new housing units in the twenty years after WW II, and federal highway-building and home-loan programs helped raise the percentage of homeowners in the United States from below 40 percent in 1940 to above 60 percent by 1960."[8] In 1950 alone, 1.4 million houses were built, the majority of them in the suburbs.[9] The 1950s "saw an average of 3,000 acres of greenland per day bulldozed into suburban submission. Between 1950 and 1960 about 1.5 million persons moved to the suburbs from New York City alone."[10] By 1960 more Americans lived in suburbs than in cities. The suburban shift was not only quantitative. "By 1966 half of all workers and three-fourths of those under the age of forty had taken up residence in suburbs," areas that were almost exclusively white due to exclusionary zoning laws and racist lending practices.[11] Prior to postwar suburbanization, towns and cities rose primarily around clusters of resources and the boundaries of work and agriculture.[12] Historically, towns and cities needed to be in close proximity to such resources as water, in particular, and work environments, as modes of transportation limited the distances people could travel.

Due in large part to the automobile, postwar suburbs were geographically distant from towns and cities. Suburbs were not places in the sense of geographic limits but rather mobile spaces serving as nodal points where mobility ceased, albeit temporarily. For postwar Americans, mobility was an integral part of everyday life. It was reflected in the increased saturation and importance of the automobile, with car registrations increasing in the 1950s by over 21 million. In 1955 seven in ten American families owned cars.[13] The increase in individual automotive transportation led to a decline in established forms of public transportation.[14] Additionally, the 1956 Interstate Highway Act set in motion the largest public works project of the twentieth century and helped accelerate suburbanization, automotive dependency, and mobility. The car was a central component of life, particularly in suburban areas.

Americans in the 1950s were not only mobile on a daily basis but also less likely to live in one place for very long. "By 1958 some 33 million Americans moved each year. The average American pulled up stakes about every five years; for the suburbanite it was more like every three years, and annual moves were not unusual."[15] Frequent moves contributed to a declining sense of rootedness and place, which historically shaped identity and community.

Socially and culturally, suburbs represented a different lifeworld, in particular their geographic separation and consumptive focus. Reflecting a reigning ethos of leisure and consumption promoted and reinforced by the state and advertising, the suburb represented a concretization of U.S. ideology.[16] In such a fragmented existential lifeworld, media served as increasingly important connections.

For new suburbanites with few ties to the suburbs, automotive and portable radio helped bind them to a new world. Without established ties of place, mobile media fostered an often absent sense of community identity, as they became situated in the everyday lives of many Americans, complementing and competing with established forms of media. With changing patterns of living and the concomitant shifts in commuting—the decline of walking and mass transportation between home and work—automotive radio became a staple of morning and evening commutes. Programming specifically aimed at mobile audiences emerged in this period. Peter Fornatale and Joshua Mills note that "the automobile gave radio its new prime time: the commuting hours of 6:00 a.m. and 4:00–7:00 p.m. They came to be known as 'drive time,' a term coined in 1957 by Gerald Bartell, who owned a group of Midwest radio stations."[17] Like afternoon editions of major papers aimed at people commuting by streetcar, train, or bus, automotive radio connected people in cars.[18]

Distinctions between prewar and postwar radio can be categorized into two broad interpretive typifications: prewar radio functioned as foreground, and postwar radio increasingly became background. Foreground encapsulates the sociocultural role of radio as a home-centered medium with generally linear programming forms. Linear programming has distinct, quasi-autonomous demarcations and established narrative flows, is structured so listeners generally have to take in an entire program to understand and enjoy, and develops within lengthy temporal segments (15, 30, or 60 minutes).[19] In contrast, background summarizes mobile programming where radio is subservient accompaniment to other nonstationary and out-of-home activities. Such programming is disjunctive, as temporal segmentation (i.e., the three-minute pop song) and narrative are structured for listeners entering and exiting the soundscape frequently.[20]

This was an important aggregate shift in the cultural form of radio from a home-centered (spatial), relatively group-oriented (social) medium, where broadcasting served a foreground function, toward an individualized and atomized medium that was increasingly mobile, or linked to an individual's room (or other rooms), where radio served as background accompaniment to other activities. Automotive radio in the 1950s functioned as a form of psychic mobility, connecting physically mobile Americans and providing a sense of community that the contours of everyday life increasingly lacked; however, the underlying commercial values and intention of radio remained relatively unchanged.

POLITICAL ECONOMY OF 1950s RADIO

The changing contours of regulation, economics, and ownership of 1950s radio contributed to the environment into which automotive radio emerged and flourished. Radio's structure began changing in the 1940s, in particular as the FCC ceased licensing stations from 1940 to 1945 because of World War II. The net impact was to largely ossify the industry until after the war. Following the war the number of stations increased dramatically. While in 1942 there were approximately 800 AM stations, in 1945 there were 950, and by 1949 the number had reached 2,100. By 1956 there were approximately 3,000 AM stations. In a little over ten years the number of stations more than tripled.

Another factor was the decline of networks.[21] Hastening the networks' declining involvement in radio was the new medium of television. While in 1947 over 97 percent of radio stations were network affiliates, by 1955 it was 30 percent. By 1955 the radio landscape comprised a greater number of stations, the majority with no network affiliation. Susan Douglas notes, "between 1946 and 1951, the number of small stations, between 200 and 1,000 watts, increased by 500 percent."[22] These stations, licensed at lower power than many existing stations, were encouraged to program recorded music due in part to the class of licenses issued. As high-power, clear channel licenses had long been distributed, the postwar licenses were for lower power and allowed for programming of phonograph records.[23] This was shaped by earlier actions by the U.S. Department of Commerce, which institutionalized a bias toward live music on radio and against recorded music.[24] Postwar radio became more competitive and local in orientation as the average station's audience "dropped from 60,000 to 30,000, and thus there were more stations vying to sell smaller audiences to local advertisers."[25] Due to dynamic changes, radio stations no longer enjoyed monopolistic status.

Partly because of the decline of networks, broadcasting to a mass audience fell out of favor in the 1950s. That programming should appeal to the greatest number, an established radio industry practice since the late 1920s, was gradually abandoned in favor of what became known as "modern radio," "segmentation of audiences," or "narrowcasting."[26] Rather than having a mass audience, radio now interpolated different audiences. The differences recognized were not only those of taste or preference but also those of places and circumstances that framed listening. Population segments formerly ignored became desirable audiences.[27] Thus, while the national network audience declined in the 1950s, radio's local audiences increased. These structural changes influenced the established political economy of radio.

While advertiser-supported radio remained the norm in the 1950s, sources of revenues and their relationship to programming changed. With the decline in network programming, attached national advertising revenues decreased. Most network programming was produced under the auspices of advertising agencies for sponsors. The sponsors produced the programming, and radio networks and affiliated stations served as carriers.[28] In place of network programming with attached sponsorship, 1950s radio produced its own programming and sold "spots" to local and national advertisers.[29]

Shifting radio revenues reflected changing advertising practices at individual stations. Radio stations had to more aggressively sell to advertisers and listeners, and the station as programmed product necessitated constant publicity. The structure of the political economy of 1950s radio pushed stations to concentrate on creating and maintaining a unique identity. Structural changes in postwar radio "made the radio audience more than ever a station audience."[30] Postwar radio remained a profitable industry, albeit in altered configurations.

THEORETICAL FRAMEWORK

Although the historical context of 1950s radio—including the mutual impact of mobile media and programming on space, as well as the reconfigured political economy of the radio industry—is necessary to understanding the significance of automotive and portable radio, it is also necessary to engage pertinent theory to interpret these phenomena. This section offers theoretical support for the interpretation made about automotive and portable radio —that postwar radio developed new cultural forms, mobile media, that were constituted by political-economic changes in industry, social needs, mobility, and reconfigured patterns of everyday life. The relationship is one of mutual constitution.

In connoting automotive radio as a unique *cultural form*,[31] I draw attention to a nexus of social, political-economic, and cultural formations that constitute a salient form of mediated communication. While cultural form encompasses a particular medium with attendant technological and operational features (i.e., radio), it extends beyond the medium and its political-economic context (i.e., commercial broadcasting) to encompass and privilege social practice and signification. This conceptualization broadens the limitations of the concept of media and moves toward historical practice, processes, and social formations that shape and are drawn upon in the creation of new forms of mediated communication and signification.

In refining *cultural form* further as *mobile media,* I am highlighting spatial and temporal qualities. Mobile media are cultural forms that are not stationary and that enhance or encourage physical and "psychic mobility."[32] Mobile media influence and shape both horizontal forms of mobility, that is physical, material, or spatial mobility, and vertical forms of mobility—psychic or ideational mobility—which determine, to a certain extent, social being and consciousness.[33] In short, they contribute to a social repertoire where the everyday possibility of mobility is a routine cultural practice.

U.S. broadcasting developed in the early twentieth century not only out of the constellation of science, technology, inventors, existing cultural forms, and entrepreneurs but also in response to social needs and pressures. Raymond Williams contends that broadcasting developed in response to social needs in capitalist societies where increased change and mobility are lived experiences.[34] Social needs can be interpreted along two distinct but interrelated axes. First, social needs are driven by significant pressure from social groups for cultural forms with which they can communicate and build community vis-à-vis change and increasing mobility. Automotive radio can be read as a response to an increasingly atomized and mobile society, where cultural distinctions between public and private communication and space are in flux and influenced in part by new media. Second, social needs can be linked to political-economic pressures to influence and control spatially dispersed individuals and groups, which are less subject to established forms of authority predicated upon relatively stable, stationary forms of living. The increased circulation of commodities, money, capital, and workers can be interpreted as partially constitutive of the increased mobility of people in the late nineteenth century and throughout the twentieth century—part of the cultural analogue of capitalism in this period.

A key linkage between mobility, automotive radio, and 1950s broadcasting is Williams's conceptualization of "mobile privatisation," which is

> characterised by . . . two apparently paradoxical yet deeply connected tendencies of modern urban industrial living: on the one hand mobility, on the other hand the more apparently self-sufficient family home. The earlier period of public technology, best exemplified by the railways and city lighting, was being replaced by a kind of technology for which no satisfactory name has yet to be found: that which served an at once mobile home-centered way of living: a form of *mobile privatisation*. Broadcasting in its applied form was a social product of this distinctive tendency.[35]

Along with the bourgeois private home, broadcasting is a relatively new and powerful form of social integration and control in capitalist societies. Similarly attentive to the linkages between private space, notions of the private, and media, Lynn Spigel notes, "[T]he domestic architecture of the period mediated the twin goals of separation from and integration into the outside world," which complemented the developing cultural forms of broadcasting and media content.[36] Importantly, she also emphasizes the power of media content to augment the separation and integration, and control, in the postwar period:

> [M]ore than simply supplying a tonic for displaced suburbanites, television promised something better: it promised modes of spectator pleasure premised on the sense of an illusory rather than real community of friends. It held out a new possibility for being alone in the home, away from the troublesome busybody neighbors in the next house. But it also maintained ideals of community togetherness and social interconnection by placing the community at a fictional distance. Television allowed people to enter into an imaginary social life, one that was shared not in the neighborhood networks of bridge clubs and mahjong gatherings but on the national networks of CBS, NBC, and ABC.[37]

Cultural forms bridged the seeming contradictions between the private home and mobility, allowing for psychic mobility from the home, in the case of early radio and TV, and accompanying physical mobility outside the home.[38]

The significance of mobile programming as a homologous development of social needs, increasing mobility, and changing patterns of living is also important as a flow of signification. Williams argues that one unique characteristic of broadcasting is flow, which is more important than seemingly discrete segments of programming. Williams insists that we "go beyond the static concept of 'distribution' to the mobile concept of 'flow'" in order to read the organizing values of broadcasting.[39] Rather than examining popular songs, weather reports, or jingles as forms of content alone, we can read them more richly as segments of flow or a soundscape. The planned flow of commercial broadcasting, Williams asserts, is its defining characteristic, "simultaneously as a technology and as a cultural form."[40] Williams challenges the predominant consideration of programming solely as discrete forms: "[T]he apparently disjointed 'sequence' of items is in effect guided by a remarkably consistent set of cultural relationships: a flow of consumable reports and products in which the elements of speed, variety and miscellaneity can be seen as organising: the real bearers of value."[41] Mindful of this theoretical understanding of mobile media and broadcasting, and the context of postwar suburbanization, the mobile content of 1950s broadcasting will be examined.

Fundamental changes in programming flow in 1950s radio exemplify mobile content—a homologous form suited to quotidian mobility and mobile media. Specifically, music, news and information, and other forms of mobile content underscore the evolution of radio in the postwar period.

Music

One of the most successful and widely emulated formats in the 1950s was "music and news," which spawned Top 40 and similar derivations. Historically, recorded music as broadcast content represents a fundamental shift in commercial radio broadcast practice in the United States. It was the first concerted instance where the main content was both content and product, presaging infomercials, product placement, and the commercial resale of content (i.e., recorded series or individual shows). Since the late 1920s, radio industry profits were basically predicated upon the sale of commercial time to advertisers that would hawk their products and services between programming. While derivations existed, they did not fundamentally break with this practice.[42] With the increased intertwining of the radio and recording industries in the 1950s, however, the content was an advertised product the audience could sample. That it was represented simply as content obfuscated the developing role of radio as a record delivery device, making the persuasive efforts of disc jockeys, programmers, and the charts in publications such as *Billboard* seem neutral if not natural. Such practices attempted to present recorded music as content that was democratically driven by the tastes, interests, and desires of listeners; however, the popularity of "hits" was inseparable from their concerted mobilization by the radio and recording industries.

Recorded music became a staple of radio flow by the end of the decade, as "radio and pop records in the years after 1948 became practically synonymous."[43] Although music was by no means absent on radio in earlier periods, its quantity in aggregate programming flows and the distinct forms it took represented a departure from the Golden Age of radio broadcasting. This was especially characteristic of the emerging independent, lower-power radio stations integral to postwar radio growth (see appendix 1 for aggregate programming breakdown). The local orientation of stations shaped the music formats and genres chosen, particularly through the mid-1950s.[44] By 1954 more than half of the programming flow of the average station consisted of record shows, and music far outpaced other forms of content.[45] Indeed, in a 1957 station management poll, record shows constituted 69.1 percent of the programming, while the next greatest programming form, news and weather, totaled a mere 6.1 percent of weekly programming.[46]

The common characteristics of most American popular music made it ideally suited to the structuring characteristics and ideological impetus of U.S. commercial radio.[47] The commercial popular music in the United States acceptable for radio airplay is relatively interchangeable, reflecting the determination of the flow to the structure of commercial radio. As a suitable form of content—not overtly undermining the commercial logic of the industry, relatively inoffensive, and meeting the time and production standards—commercial popular music was interchangeable. A station could program rock 'n' roll, country, old favorites, and other musical formats as part of a general flow without qualitatively changing the underlying foundations of commercial broadcasting.[48] Max Horkheimer and Theodor Adorno note that "the assembly-line character of the culture industry, the synthetic planned method of turning out its products . . . is very suited to advertising: the important individual points, by becoming detachable, interchangeable, and even technically alienated from any connected meaning, lend themselves to ends external to the work."[49]

Two aggregate characteristics of the popular music of broadcast flow during the 1950s—temporality and narrative elements—underscore how music complemented the underlying commercial foundation of radio and the disjunctive flow of mobile content during this period. The temporal span of a popular song during this period ranged from two to four minutes, with the bulk of songs falling in between. This was predicated in part upon earlier, structural limitations of recording technology—the lateral disc record was able to accommodate a maximum of only four minutes per side. Although the advent of magnetic tape recording and the introduction of the long-playing record format in the late 1940s raised this temporal limitation greatly, the standard three-minute popular song was ossified as a cultural industry convention that reflected back upon the industry and musicians. That this standard remains salient testifies to its strength.[50] The relatively short length of most popular songs is complementary to the mobility of everyday life and provides temporal regularity for segments of radio flow— the disjunctive narrative structure homologous to quotidian mobility. It also allows for a large quantity of programming units to be compressed into a relatively short time period.

The aggregate narrative characteristics of popular songs can be read overall as "pseudo-individual" in nature.[51] While interpolating listeners as individual subjects—the use of first-person address, peppering of generic details, and so forth—they had to be universal enough to appeal to and hail a broad range of listeners. For example, a *Billboard* columnist noted that "Wemar music is conducting a gold key charm contest in conjunction with jocks across the country to plug Betty Ann Grove's new Jubilee disc, 'Your High School Key,'" suggesting successful popular music needed adequate plugging, and generic pseudo-individualized narrative elements as well.[52] Their polysemic qualities were determined by commercial flow and were structured to complement—albeit in somewhat diverse ways—not contradict it. The qualities of lyrics and music were relatively standard as well, with most songs offering a derivation of conventional time signatures, verse-chorus-verse structures, and keys. The "new" was always valued in a cycle marked by the turnover of hits and old favorites, but the "new" was tempered by,

and subject to, the familiarity of established patterns. The seemingly obliga-
tory themes of heterosexual love and melodramatic despair were relatively
detachable as well and nicely dovetailed with dominant representations of
youth. As a scholar of the time suggested, "[O]ne role of popular music in
socializing the young may be to create, in combination with other mass media, a picture of childhood and adolescence in America as a happy-go-lucky
time of haphazard clothes and haphazard behavior, jitterbug parlance, coke-
bar sprees, and 'blues' that are not really blue."[53] Thus, narrative elements
may have worked to help construct a mythology of youth in part by articu-
lating elements of lifestyles or identities, which often clearly complemented,
or at least didn't overtly challenge, the foundational elements of the radio
and music industries.

While radio music retained its interchangeability, as well as aggregate
temporality and narrative characteristics, there were salient changes. One
important shift in popular music in the 1950s was the recognition and targeting of teenagers or youth by radio and the recording industry.[54] Renewed
economic prosperity and a concomitant focus on the emergent postwar teen-
ager shifted the attention of the broadcasting and music industries to the
tastes of youth.[55] The emergent teenage subject position was recognized as a
distinct sociocultural and economic entity, and teenagers became a focus for
audience study.[56] The increasing disposable incomes of teenagers made them
desirable for the radio and music industries.[57]

While musical preferences of adults and youth were ostensibly different,
prior to the 1950s the recording industry and the radio industry treated
them as relatively similar in their aggregate genres, marketing, and programming.[58] This changed in the 1950s, where record shows were explicitly targeted at teenagers. The youth market was also a boom for the record industry. Indeed, "by the late 1950s teenagers were buying more records than
adults," and the overall market skyrocketed throughout the decade.[59] According to Andre Millard, "[I]n 1955 there was a 23 percent increase in
constant dollar sales over 1954. In 1956 sales went up another 25 percent
and continued to rise every year until 1960."[60] By 1959 record sales totaled
approximately $613 million.[61] Although the postwar period was character-
ized by a historic expansion of consumer expenditures in nearly all categories, the expansion of record sales was meteoric in comparison to aggregate
totals; "between 1955 and 1966, while consumer expenditures for all goods
and services rose by 81 percent, record sales jumped 224 percent."[62] The

recording industry targeted inexpensive phonographs to play the "unbreakable" 45 rpm single and songs that hailed youth.[63] The disaggregation of the mass audience and the emergence of the youth or teen audience were partly reflected in and constituted by implementation of new types of records in the postwar period. In June 1948, Columbia (owned by CBS) introduced the vinyl, twelve-inch, 33 1/3 rpm microgroove long-playing record (LP); six months later RCA-Victor's vinyl, seven-inch, 45 rpm record premiered. The existing 78 rpm record was relegated to the older, and oftentimes less affluent, market; the LP was aimed at classical and jazz listeners, as it could accommodate lengthier pieces and complete recordings; and the 45 was tailored toward youth.

News and Information

Changes in news and information provide insights into mobile content and the cultural form of automotive radio, particularly its local emphasis, atomistic discourse, immediacy, mobility, and on-the-spot reporting. The increase in news as a component of radio flow and the audio soundscape partially reflected the reorientation of the stations to the local as opposed to the national focus of the networks, the impact of new technologies (magnetic tape and portable tape recorders), and attempts to develop latent potentials of the medium in journalistic practice. It represented a new form of mobile programming that attempted to provide "live" mobile coverage of news events with a high degree of immediacy and reflected a recognition that people were listening in various spatial and temporal configurations.

One practice to emerge was to make news a more regular part of the soundscape and flow. Stations were trying to craft a unique identity with news and establishing a regular temporal rhythm. While a feature in earlier periods, 1950s radio news often became a part of each hour's flow. An ad from the K-JOE, in Shreveport, Louisiana, notes: "The old-fashioned newscasts have been replaced by the 'running account' concept with MICRO-NEWS bulletins anytime . . . KWICKIE headlines on the half hour . . . WEATHER-CHECK on the quarter hour . . . MARK '55' news five minutes before the hour . . . plus a continual flow of reports, on land, in the air."[64] News was part of the rhythmic tapestry of the postwar audio soundscape, with a patterned organization that conveyed urgency, novelty, and connection.

News programming in the 1950s reflected radio's local emphasis in a number of ways. Industry reports noted the role of local news in crafting identity and stressed "the importance of a station concentrating its coverage on its own community."[65] Local events, issues, sounds/voices, and advertisers exemplify this orientation. For example, two stations implemented a program called "*Speak Up Neighbor,* which permits a mutual exchange of ideas on current happenings by listeners."[66] The local dynamic was also crafted through sounds and voices.

Stations in the 1950s stressed local voices, particularly the voices of "ordinary" people. Stations often meshed newsgathering activities with promotions or gimmicks, providing cash, prizes, or other material incentives to get listeners to phone in news tips. The Bartell Group, a successful chain of independents, combined the practice of recruiting news tipsters with the use of local voices: "Whenever possible, telephoned news stories are tape-recorded and broadcast in the voice of the actual tipster, who is paid for his tips and gets a Voice of the News reporter card (honorary) and a 'thank you' note besides."[67] Stations also used the voices of people involved in news events or issues, such as WTTM, Trenton, New Jersey, which crafted the local through "involving the actual voices of the people making the news."[68] In addition to using local voices, stations attempted to project a unique identity by having news personnel adopt informal modes of address.

In a shift away from what Susan Douglas terms "announcer speak"—the formal, third-person voice that was the norm in radio from the 1920s through the early 1950s—news announcers adopted the first-person voice, which I term *atomistic discourse.*[69] Interpolating increasingly isolated individuals who often listened alone in bedrooms, kitchens, and automobiles, the atomistic voice conveyed a sense that the listener was being directly addressed and was privy to events as they unfolded, giving the news a novel, personal quality. *U.S. Radio* noted: "[M]ore and more the present tense and the first person singular are finding their way into newscasts bringing with them the value of projecting the listener into the atmosphere of the event being reported."[70] Effective news copy for radio was viewed as fresh, with atomistic discourse seen as an important component, and stations were admonished to incorporate the "exciting use of the first person singular" into news broadcasts.[71] To the listener, atomistic discourse projected an absent ontological presence, conveying aural presence to the increasingly solitary, atomized listener, and it dovetailed with segmentation, helping to hail individual listeners. Interpolating the listener as an individual and projecting a sense of participatory listening were tied in with the attempt of broadcast news to project immediacy.

Stations tried to inject a strong sense of immediacy into news content, primarily reflected in the speed of reporting. One developing practice, widely used and still a staple of broadcasting, was the "on-the-spot" coverage, a practice partly enabled by new technologies like magnetic tape recorders. Stations in the 1950s purchased or created mobile units for on-the-spot reporting, which afforded mobility to the medium's listeners and enabled programming suited to this constellation.[72] Indeed, a 1958 report in *U.S. Radio* argued that mobile news strongly drew advertisers, as such units were effective mobile bulletin boards and public relations tools combined.[73] Another form of mobile news took the form of stringers, particularly cab drivers.[74]

Mobile units helped stations cover the increasing number of outlying suburban areas. For example, WBAB, New York, which targeted audiences in Long Island, offered silver dollars for news tips. As Long Island grew into a bedroom community, a suburb like thousands in postwar America, the stations that reached the suburbs often localized their content accordingly. Such practices were partly determined by suburban advertisers hoping to hail so-called out-of-city consumers.

On-the-spot reportage in radio news can be interpreted in a number of ways. Inheriting the empiricist epistemology of U.S. journalism, radio news stressed seamless communion between event and listener—objectivity was bolstered by on-the-spot reporting, which conveyed transparency. The competitive ethos of commercial news boosted on-the-spot reporting as stations competed with one another, newspapers, and TV to be first to report an event. And on-the-spot reporting can be read as bound with the social needs of an increasingly atomized and mobile society, the immediacy and intimacy of on-the-spot pieces providing a form of communication that offered a connection with particular places and communities. Geographic and social distances were seemingly overcome by on-the-spot pieces, which promised to take the listener "there" via a mobile medium and mobile news units.

Other Mobile Content

In addition to music and news there were other pertinent forms of mobile content in 1950s radio, including traffic reports, mobile shows, and remotes, which suggests a homologous relationship between an increasingly mobile society and media flow. Such distinct mobile content was developed in the late 1940s and early 1950s and was directed at so-called out-of-home listeners by structuring the content to complement the mobile audience. It was characterized by catering to the on-the-go listener, often traveling by automobile, projecting a dynamic rhythm in their flow, and interpolating a mobile audience likely predisposed toward disjunctive audio flow.

Traffic reports epitomized the regularity of the postwar news flow as part of the rhythm of the new flow of "drive-time"—a term coined to reflect the symbiosis of driver, automotive radio, and morning and evening commuting. Traffic reports bridged news, information, public service, and publicity. Such programming suggests strong social needs determined by the increasing everyday mobility of people, and the role of the automobile and automotive radio as central cultural forms. With Cold War tensions peaking during the decade, and exploitative politicians and cultural mandarins on the home front, Americans understood automotive transportation to have deeper significance—specifically as a conduit for evacuation in the event of nuclear attack.[75] The automobile was the norm for transportation, and traffic reports fulfilled a social need for information about an increasingly "natural" feature of the human environment.[76]

Similarly, mobile shows reflected the intersection between listener and automobile in distinct audio flows. According to an advertising executive, NBC, which in 1955 created "Monitor"—a mobile show broadcast on weekends—claimed "in the summer 45 percent of its audience is car-borne and in the winter 30 percent of its listeners are on wheels."[77] American Motors' advertising agent elaborated on the show's ability to deliver automotive listeners: "Car radio listeners not only make up a sizeable audience but also a most receptive, psychologically conditioned audience. What better time could you approach a prospect about a new car than when he is driving his old one?"[78] Key to success with mobile audiences was the show's flow—"its format forsook the idea of fixed time slots of 15, 30 or 60 minutes. It came up with a kaleidoscope of three to five-minute segments" (see appendix 1 for examples of programming for "Monitor" in 1955).[79]

Likewise, remote broadcasts interjected a strong sense of physical and psychic mobility to radio. For example, WRAL, in Raleigh, North Carolina, which built a roadside studio featuring both stationary and mobile elements, crafted an intriguing derivation of the mobile studio aimed directly at automotive listeners. "Believing that radio should come out of the studio and meet the people face to face, the station has built a special little 'house by the side of the road,' one which turns about on its pedestal to face the in-coming morning traffic and outgoing evening traffic and from which corres-ponding morning and evening remotes are broadcast to the car-borne lis-tener."[80] Derivations of business-based remotes could take advantage of the sizable automotive audience; for example, drive-in theaters served as the site of mobile broadcasts.[81] Shows broadcast from the premises of advertisers were quite prevalent during the 1950s and stimulated station and sponsor identification.

Traffic reports, remote broadcasts, and mobile shows were forms of pro-gramming that complemented listeners' quotidian mobility, exemplifying distinct types of homologous flow. They also were reflexive, providing a physical and psychic impetus to everyday mobility, and were productive of the increased mobility of everyday life. These forms of programming helped colonize temporal segments with mobile programming, providing listeners with late-night and weekend flows. Similarly, they aided the settling of the relatively new spaces of suburbia, marking new residents' (un)familiar sur-roundings with media discourse and audio flow.

CONCLUSION

Automotive and portable radio epitomized the way radio was changing from a stationary to a mobile medium in the 1950s. Mobile media were new cul-tural forms that, along with developing mobile programming flows, comple-mented an increasingly mobile society in a reflective, homologous manner. They were also reflexive and productive of mobility, as they served to shape both horizontal and vertical forms of mobility, which determined, to a cer-tain extent, social being, consciousness, and characteristics of American sub-urbs. There is a mutually constitutive relationship between mobile media and space—sound helped redefine space, while space influenced media. As integral media of postwar suburbia, automotive and portable radio helped shape the representation of suburban space, influencing the ways listeners thought about, discussed, and interacted within developing communities. Radio was no longer largely limited to the confines of the private sphere and was increasingly a fixture of public space, as studies in the late 1940s and throughout the 1950s noted the increase in "out of home listening" and "listeners on wheels."[82]

Social needs inscribed the development of mobile media as cultural forms; in the case of automotive radio, increasing mobility and suburban expansion created pressures for new forms of mobile media. Complementary media were needed for new social suburban formations as increasing numbers of Americans disaggregated into suburban enclaves and sought new media that would provide a sense of connection and aid in the construction of community. Likewise, the pecuniary interests supporting radio needed means of influencing increasing numbers of so-called out-of-city consumers and found in mobile media new cultural forms well suited to established purposes.

This essay suggests that an overlooked component of media studies and mass communication research is space, a key constitutional element of modern society that directly bears upon media. It also suggests that rich interpretative insights are afforded by considering communication and transportation as indelibly linked.[83] In addition, an acknowledgment and accounting of the impact of increased mobility in American society is tantamount to understanding the values, intentions, and significances of modern media forms, particularly broadcasting. Critical perspectives are further bolstered by interrogating the impact of media forms on individuals and society, particularly with regard to their bias toward atomization—the situating of the individualized subject as the ideal listener—thus pointing toward the role of cultural forms in undercutting considerations of the public, citizens, and democracy in favor of audiences, consumers, and markets.

In hindsight, the history of automotive radio is instructive with regard to mobile media that follow in its wake. Newer media, such as the portable TV, Walkman, portable stereos, pagers, mobile phones, and laptop computers suggest that as quotidian mobility and suburbanization continue to increase, and as surveillance technologies allow for unprecedented demographic detail and concomitant narrowcasting, media atomization continues to be the norm. And the human need for communication continues to be subordinated to the machinations of commerce in American society.

NOTES

1. "81 Per Cent More Radio Sets in Use Than in 1948," *RadioActive!* 3, no. 5 (1958): 4.
2. The transistor was instrumental in the technological innovations shaping automotive and portable radio, as Michael Brian Schiffer details; however, their development

into salient cultural forms was contingent upon a host of cultural and social changes that this essay privileges. While the transistor partially enabled the development of these cultural forms, their cultural resonance was neither dependent on nor determined by technological improvements. Rather, the transistor contributed to the material forms of automotive and portable radio, while their cultural forms emerged from a constellation of pressures and needs. The civilian application of the transistor in automotive and portable radio was more a specific innovative response to an increasingly mobile society (Michael Brian Schiffer, *The Portable Radio in American Life* [Tucson: U of Arizona P, 1991]).

3. As Donald Matteson explains, the abundant number of automotive radio manufacturers and suppliers and the evolving structural design of the American automobile contributed to a variety of antennae configurations, including wires rigged under the car; wires strung under the headliner; and running board, cowl-mounted, and rooftop antennae. These limited the reception of automotive radio, placing the onus on set manufacturers to improve receivers. "Because of the antenna limitation imposed by the design of the car, it was important for good reception to have a stage of radio-frequency amplification 'up front' and most receivers on the market had that circuit feature" (Donald W. Matteson, *The Auto Radio: A Romantic Genealogy* [Jackson, MI: Thornridge, 1987], 184). Until auto manufacturers began to earnestly manufacture and incorporate automotive radio into automotive design in the 1940s and 1950s, adopting the rooftop or cowl-mounted antennae as the eventual standard (with some derivations), early automotive radio quality and reception was often limited.

4. According to Schiffer, mass production of transistors did not take place until late 1952 in the United States, thus their earlier circulation was limited in part by higher initial costs.

5. Of course the impact of television on radio broadcasting was by no means uniform; its implementation varied with major urban centers and markets receiving the new medium in advance of rural areas and small towns.

6. Susan J. Douglas, "The Kids Take Over: Transistors, DJs, and Rock 'n' Roll," in *Listening In: Radio and the American Imagination: From Amos 'n' Andy and Edward R. Murrow to Wolfman Jack and Howard Stern,* ed. Susan J. Douglas (New York: Times Books, 1999), 221.

7. Tom Lewis notes that "changes in the Federal Housing Act of 1949 offered builders profit incentives to construct large developments, usually single-family homes in suburban areas" (Tom Lewis, *Divided Highways: Building the Interstate Highways, Transforming American Life* [New York: Viking, 1997], 74). Similarly, the postwar GI Bill of Rights guaranteed veterans housing loans, and the Federal Housing Administration and the VA aided veterans' purchases of homes with low down payments and long-term loans. See also George Lipsitz, *Rainbow at Midnight: Labor and Culture in the 1940s* (Urbana: U of Illinois P, 1994), 257.

8. Lipsitz, *Rainbow at Midnight,* 257.

9. Douglas T. Miller and Marion Nowak, *The Fifties: The Way We Really Were* (Garden City, NY: Doubleday, 1977).

10. Ibid., 134.

11. Lipsitz, *Rainbow at Midnight,* 257.

12. There were, of course, exceptions. Los Angeles in particular grew despite its lack of water, which must be transported from the Colorado River through an extensive network of aqueducts. Mike Davis posits that Los Angeles is the vanguard American city where the automobile is the ur-form of transportation (Mike Davis, *City of Quartz: Excavating the Future of Los Angeles* [New York: Vintage, 1990]). The streetcar suburbs of the late nineteenth and early twentieth century are also an exception, as well as precedent (Kenneth T. Jackson, *The Crabgrass Frontier: The Suburbanization of the United States* [New York: Oxford UP, 1985]).

13. As Miller and Nowak note (*The Fifties,* 139), "by 1958 over 67.4 million cars and trucks were in use, more than one for every household. (Nearly 12 million families, mostly in suburbia, had two or more cars.) Vehicle miles traveled jumped from about 458 billion in 1950 to nearly 800 billion by the early 1960s. In 1960 the census reported that 65 percent of the working population drove to work; a mere ten percent walked." Furthermore, "consumer spending on private automobiles had averaged $7.5 billion per year in the 1930s and 1940s, but by 1950 it had reached $22 billion, and by 1955 the figure had approached $30 billion" (Lipsitz, *Rainbow at Midnight,* 257).

14. Urban streetcars became practically extinct during the 1950s, and "the number of railway passenger cars declined from 37,359 to 25,746" (Lewis, *Divided Highways,* 81).

15. Miller and Nowak, *The Fifties,* 136.

16. This ideology can be defined as a conflation between freedom/democracy and consumption/capitalism, or what Warren Susman terms the culture of abundance (Warren I. Susman, *Culture as History: The Transformation of American Society in the Twentieth Century* [New York: Pantheon, 1984]). A curious manifestation of this can be evidenced in the so-called kitchen debate that occurred in the late 1950s. In 1959 the USSR and the U.S. exchanged exhibitions featuring, among other things, model homes. This debate took place in the U.S. exhibition, located in a model suburban home on Long Island where Vice President Nixon extolled the superiority of American living standards and household appliances. See Thomas Hine, *Populuxe* (New York: Knopf, 1987), 129–30.

17. Peter Fornatale and Joshua E. Mills, *Radio in the Television Age* (Woodstock, NY: Overlook Press, 1980), 20.

18. See Peter Fritzsche, *Reading Berlin, 1900* (Cambridge: Harvard UP, 1996), for an earlier historic example of media and mobility—the intertwining of newspapers and public transportation in metropolitan Berlin.

19. For example, *One Man's Family,* a serialized, dramatic show revolving around a

fictional extended family, was linear as it assumed a degree of familiarity with the numerous characters and past shows to completely comprehend and appreciate. This is not to suggest all listeners met these criteria, but rather it was presented in this manner. Foreground also encompasses so-called old-line radio, an industry term, which described this general content, and a station's present or former relationship with one of the networks. Foreground, linear programming, and old-line radio are synonymous in this respect.

20. Background also describes so-called modern radio, an industry term used during the late 1940s and 1950s to describe new stations or stations with new formats where recorded popular music, news, and sports were the dominant forms of programming. Background, disjunctive, and modern radio are synonyms for the emergent mobile programming of the postwar period. See "A Spirited Defense of Modern Radio: Adam Young Testifies That It Works," *Broadcasting-Telecasting Yearbook* (Washington, DC: Broadcast Publications, 1958), 77.

21. In the early 1940s, governmental discourse and actions suggested major networks were under scrutiny. The FCC released the *Report on Chain Broadcasting* in 1941, ostensibly an attack on monopoly tendencies in the industry. The report called upon RCA, which operated the two NBC networks, Red and Blue, to sell one of them. Following an unsuccessful legal challenge, RCA sold NBC Blue in 1943. See Douglas, "Kids Take Over," 187. As newspapers were known to be unfriendly toward the FDR administration, Lucas Powe posits that FCC chairman Lawrence Fly's actions were influenced by Roosevelt's "specific desire to rid broadcasting of newspaper owners" (Lucas A. Powe Jr., *American Broadcasting and the First Amendment* [Berkeley: U of California P, 1987], 72). Douglas posits that Fly opposed the monopolistic structure of radio, where ownership of approximately one-third of stations in the early 1940s rested with newspapers, the end result of the protracted radio-press war of the 1930s.

22. Douglas, "Kids Take Over," 224.

23. Philip Ennis notes, "after 1946 the small, independent station, the type empowered and encouraged to program current phonograph records, became the fastest growing entity in radio and by 1948 was the most numerous kind of station broadcasting to American audiences" (Philip H. Ennis, *The Seventh Stream: The Emergence of Rocknroll in American Popular Music* [Hanover, NH: Wesleyan UP, 1992], 136).

24. According to Susan Smulyan, "The U.S. Department of Commerce institutionalized the prejudice against records in 1922 by relegating stations transmitting recordings to less desirable frequencies. Even when improved technology permitted the electrical broadcast of recordings, regulations still favored live programming and thus the wealthier stations that could afford to pay performers" (Susan Smulyan, *Selling Radio: The Commercialization of American Broadcasting, 1920–1934* [Washington, DC: Smithsonian Institution Press, 1994], 95). Additionally, until the 1940s the radio and music publishing industry lacked a stable, mutually agreeable arrangement for broadcast royal-

ties of recorded music. See Ennis, *Seventh Stream,* and Eric Rothenbuhler and Tom McCourt, "Radio Redefines Itself, 1947–1962," in *The Radio Reader: Essays in the Cultural History of Radio,* ed. Michele Hilmes and Jason Loviglio, 367–87 (London: Routledge, 2002), 369.

25. Douglas, "Kids Take Over," 233.

26. The segmented nature of soap operas, children's programming, and country music prior to this period indicates that the viability of narrowcasting was recognized prior to the 1950s. However, the political economy of 1950s radio made narrowcasting practically a necessity.

27. The first black-oriented radio formats emerged after World War II. Prior to this, African Americans were rarely targeted as audiences, and African American performers were infrequently represented on radio. Brian Ward cites the "white-owned WDIA in Memphis and WOOK in Washington, D.C." as having "the first all-black programming formats" in the late 1940s (Brian Ward, *Just My Soul Responding: Rhythm and Blues, Black Consciousness, and Race Relations* [Berkeley: U of California P, 1998], 30).

28. During the summer, network affiliates were responsible for programming, as the network shows were not broadcast. This may have contributed to, or provided precedent for, the development of station-specific programming vis-à-vis the decline of the networks in the 1950s.

29. Spot and local revenues increased throughout the 1950s. In 1951, for the first time, spot billings outran network business—$134.2 million for spot to $116.6 million for national networks (*Broadcasting-Telecasting Yearbook,* 13). "Between 1946 and 1958 advertising on radio by local businesses quadrupled" (Douglas, "Kids Take Over," 225).

30. Sherman P. Lawton, *The Modern Broadcaster: The Station Book* (New York: Harper & Bros., 1961), 43.

31. Raymond Williams, *Culture* (London: Fontana, 1981).

32. Hanno Hardt and Matthew Killmeier, "Wireless Pleasure: Locating Radio in the American Home," in *In the Company of Media: Cultural Constructions of Communication, 1920s–1930s* (Boulder, CO: Westview Press, 2000), 137.

33. "Determining," or "determine" and "determination," are used herein to encapsulate the setting of limits and exerting of pressures, thus acknowledging human agency within structural barriers. See Raymond Williams, *Marxism and Literature* (London: Oxford UP, 1977), 84.

34. See Raymond Williams, *Television: Technology and Cultural Form* (New York: Shocken, 1974).

35. Ibid., 26.

36. Lynn Spigel, *Welcome to the Dreamhouse: Popular Media and Postwar Suburbs* (Durham, NC: Duke UP, 2001), 32.

37. Ibid., 45.

38. See Lynn Spigel, *Make Room for TV: Television and the Family Ideal in Postwar*

America (Chicago: U of Chicago P, 1992), on the relationships between media, broadcasting, gender, the bourgeois home, and community. Spigel also argues that portable television, which promised to bring the interior of the bourgeois home to the outside world, inverts Williams's mobile privatization to privatized mobility (Spigel, *Welcome,* 71).

39. Williams, *Television,* 78.

40. Ibid., 86.

41. Ibid., 87.

42. For example, Golden Age programming such as *The Jack Benny Show* might incorporate advertisements into the beginning of the program, but separation between the narrative flow of the show and the advertisement was generally distinct. Similarly, advertisers created, produced, and often owned programs, epitomized by soap operas, thus cultivating a flow conducive to the explicit appeals of the ads.

43. Ennis, *Seventh Stream,* 136.

44. Successful disc jockeys often retained a good deal of influence on programming in many markets, although their impact waned with the rise of Top 40 and similar programming predicated on the charts. See Matthew A. Killmeier, "Voices between the Tracks: Disc Jockeys, Radio, and Popular Music, 1955–60," *Journal of Communication Inquiry* 25, no. 4 (October 2001): 353–74. See Brian Ward on music choices being bound up with the social mores and cultural politics of particular regions, with many Southern stations reflecting, and contributing to, the predominant pressures of segregation.

45. Philip K. Eberly, *Music in the Air: America's Changing Tastes in Popular Music, 1920–1980* (New York: Hastings House, 1982), 174.

46. "1957 Disc Jockey Poll," Station Management Section, *Billboard,* November 11, 1957, 58.

47. Without dismissing the creativity, expressiveness, and social resonance of popular music, I nevertheless privilege aggregate characteristics of popular music as determined by commercial radio flow. However, it is useful to distinguish between the pecuniary interests and attendant characteristics of the cultural industries and the individual and collective creative endeavors constituting music. "The production of popular music can be called 'industrial' only in its promotion and distribution, whereas the act of producing a song-hit still remains in a handicraft stage. The production of popular music is highly centralized in its economic production, but still 'individualistic' in its social mode of production" (Theodor W. Adorno, "On Popular Music," in *On Record: Rock, Pop, and the Written Word,* ed. Simon Firth and Andrew Goodwin [New York: Pantheon, 1990], 306).

48. For example, if a station played rock 'n' roll and R&B in the early 1950s, it sometimes came under attack by religious groups, racial segregationists, right-wing groups like the John Birch society, and quasi-Puritanical sexual prudes. Some stations changed to another type of popular music when the pressures threatened the underlying

foundations of their practices—the advertising revenues. On the contrary, other stations that received strong listener support for rock 'n' roll and R&B, and advertising revenues, continued to play these types of popular music. It is in this regard that commercial popular music is interchangeable.

49. Max Horkheimer and Theodor W. Adorno, *The Dialectic of Enlightenment*, trans. John Cumming (New York: Continuum, 1972), 163.

50. As Adorno argues, the standards of today originated in a creative, competitive process that has since become an industrial standard.

51. See Adorno, "On Popular Music."

52. June Bundy, "Vox Jox," *Billboard* 15, September 1956, 58.

53. Davis Riesman, "Listening to Popular Music," in *Mass Culture: The Popular Arts in America,* eds. Bernard Rosenberg and David Manning White (Glencoe, IL: Free Press, 1950), 410.

54. The Top 40 format exemplifies the targeting of youth, the use of the charts, and the impact of R&B and rock 'n' roll on the radio and recording industries during the 1950s. The format is predicated on playing the top 40 popular singles as determined by industry publications, primarily *Billboard,* assuming listeners enjoy, or least stay tuned to, hearing the most popular songs repeatedly. The rise of R&B, and particularly rock 'n' roll—new, primarily youth genres—dovetails with the emergence of Top 40 and suggests how it contributed to the youth as a distinct target audience. During 1954 and 1955, several popular artists had hits that defied the established boundaries of the charts. For example, Elvis Presley, initially considered to be a country artist, simultaneously had hit songs listed on the R&B, pop, and country charts in *Billboard.* Their heavy rotation on Top 40 stations contributed to his success as a popular artist, and the widespread, mainstream dissemination of rock 'n' roll on commercial radio.

55. The concept of adolescence (or the teenage years) as a distinct period between childhood and adulthood became firmly embedded among experts and in popular consciousness in the 1950s, the social construction of which could be read in psychology, child-rearing practices, and sociopolitical anxieties about juvenile delinquency. See Beth A. Bailey, *From Front Porch to Back Seat: Courtship in Twentieth-Century America* (Baltimore: Johns Hopkins UP, 1988), on the origins of youth culture in the 1920s, and Roland Marchand, "Visions of Classlessness, Quests for Dominion: American Popular Culture 1945–1960," in *Reshaping America: Society and Institutions 1945–1960,* ed. Robert H. Brenner and Gary W. Reichard (Columbus: Ohio State UP, 1982), 165–70.

56. For example, NBC surveyed teenagers about their listening habits. "More on the Teen Age Audience," *Radio-Active!* 2, no. 7 (July 5, 1957).

57. By 1960, approximately $10 billion a year was spent by America's 18 million teenagers. See Bailey, *From Front Porch to Back Seat,* 10.

58. Genres of music such as jazz and forms of dance music were tied to youth;

however, youth was not a distinct segmented hailed by advertising and marketing, but rendered as part of the mass audience.

59. Douglas, "Kids Take Over," 227.

60. Andre Millard, *America on Record: A History of Recorded Sound* (Cambridge: Cambridge UP, 1995), 233–34.

61. Douglas, "Kids Take Over," 107.

62. Paul Hirsch, *The Structure of the Popular Music Industry: The Filtering Process by Which Records Are Preselected for Public Consumption* (Ann Arbor: University of Michigan Institute for Social Research, 1969), 10.

63. Ennis details how in 1948 RCA produced and marketed a specific phonograph for youth: "the small, plastic, $12.95 record player that could only play 45 rpm records" (Ennis, *Seventh Stream,* 133).

64. "K-Joe Shreveport," *U.S. Radio.* (February 2, 1958).

65. "Report from Representatives: Future Adam Young Report, The Katz Estimator, NBC Spot P.M. Study," *U.S. Radio,* January 1958, 47.

66. "Radio Formats: What Is Radio Today?" *U.S. Radio,* May 1958, 25.

67. Seymour Freedgood, Seymour. "The Money-Makers of 'New Radio,'" *Fortune,* February 1958, 222.

68. "Radio Formats," 25.

69. Douglas, "Kids Take Over," 236. Disc jockeys of the 1950s also used this type of discourse.

70. "Selling the 'Sound,'" *U.S. Radio,* December 1958, 37.

71. Ibid., 38.

72. Indeed, the trappings of certain technologies and apparatus often conveyed these characteristics through implementation alone. For example, the sounds of a teletype, beeping required by the FCC on recorded telephone interviews, and hollow shadings evident on tape-recordings or remotes tapped into established cultural representations of machines and technology, which projected an ethos of speed, immediacy, efficiency, and progress.

73. "Mobile News Units Attract Advertiser Support," *U.S. Radio,* November 1958, 53.

74. "KFSD (San Diego) has an arrangement with the Yellow Cabs in the city so that the 200 cabs in the area can be directly connected to the station's news center" ("Report from Representatives," 26). KXOK, St. Louis, also used this practice and had over three hundred stringers, who were paid five dollars per news tip and competed for a twenty-five-dollar best-tip-of-the-week award.

75. In signing the 1956 Interstate Highway Act, Eisenhower made this explicit with the rationale that "in case of atomic attack on our key cities, the road net must permit quick evacuation of target areas" (Jackson, *Crabgrass Frontier,* 249).

76. Jackson cites a 1941 survey by the Bureau of Public Roads, which "found that

2,100 communities, with populations ranging from 2,500 to 50,000, did not have public transportation systems of any kind and were completely dependent upon the private automobile for personal travel" (Jackson, *Crabgrass Frontier,* 189).

77. "Rambler Buys Radio's Economy," *U.S. Radio,* March 1958, 19.

78. "Radio Helps Trigger Start for '59 Cars," *U.S. Radio,* November 1958, 38.

79. Ibid.

80. "Equipment Changes Tone Up Station Sound," *U.S. Radio,* April 1959, 46.

81. Bundy, "Vox Jox," 28, 58.

82. For example, a "Pulse 1952 Out-of-Home Listening Survey" is cited repeatedly in the *Broadcasting-Telecasting Yearbook* 1953, and the Broadcast Advertising Bureau compiled and issued a report in 1953, "Listeners on Wheels," which detailed the characteristics of this new audience.

83. See Harold Innis, *The Bias of Communication* (Toronto: U of Toronto P, 1951), James W. Carey, *Communication and Culture: Essays on Media and Society* (Boston: Unwin Hyman, 1989), and Armans Mattelart, *The Invention of Communication,* trans. Susan Emanuel (Minneapolis: U of Minnesota P, 1996).

8 / *Cop Rock* Reconsidered

Formula, Fragments, Failure,
and Foreshadowing in Genre Evolution

GEORGE PLASKETES

On the June 10, 2001, edition of CBS's cultural magazine show *Sunday Morning,* critic John Leonard invoked the television title *Cop Rock* in the lead to his review of the film *Moulin Rouge.* The citation was a curious connection, or resurrection, considering that the Steven Bochco–produced police drama/musical lasted a mere half season, eleven one-hour episodes on ABC in 1990 (September 26–December 26). In contrast, director Baz Luhrman's anachronistic romantic musical spectacle—a three-ring Cirque du Soleil, rock popera, garage collage of farce and folly—would receive considerable recognition, including an Academy Award nomination for Best Film.

Bochco's experimental *Fame*-meets-*Hill-Street-Blues* medley was a formula for failure. The fusion was better suited for stage than for the small screen. Television audiences were not ready for crooning cops, suspect serenades, junkies jammin', and judge-and-jury jingles from week to week in a dramatic series. The responses from audiences, ABC affiliates, advertisers, and critics to Bochco's police project ranged from "ambitious, innovative, risky, and audacious to baffling, off-putting and irritatingly odd."[1]

Hindsight and context reveal that despite its critical and commercial failure, *Cop Rock* represents a plausible progression for the police genre during the inaugural MTV era of the 1980s into the 1990s and beyond. Bochco borrowed, blended, and blew up formulaic fragments from the genre, including conventions from two of the decade's touchstone series—his own *Hill Street Blues* and Michael Mann's stylish *Miami Vice.* At the same time,

Bochco also paid homage to Dennis Potter's farcical British television productions, *Pennies from Heaven* (1978), and more specifically, *The Singing Detective* (1986).

Cop Rock might also be viewed as a musical muse and martyr that foreshadowed the further integration of music into dramatic and comic narratives. Thus, it may not be critical hyperbole to suggest, as Leonard does, that *Cop Rock's* lyrical legacy can be linked to the Napster (free music-sharing software and Web site) approach to postmodern pop/rock period pieces in film such as *Moulin Rouge* and *A Knight's Tale.* In television, Bochco's series served as a stepping-stone or hinge between Potter's *The Singing Detective* and comedies and musical dramedies, particularly *Ally McBeal,* and other musical episodes of series, including *The Drew Carey Show, Chicago Hope,* and *Buffy the Vampire Slayer.* Retrospection reveals that *Cop Rock* quietly cultivated creativity and contributed dramatic musical license to various productions and cross-genre formal and aesthetic advances.

STEVEN BOCHCO: BEGINNING A BLUE STREAK

> I think what is amazing about my career is that I've never had any specific goals and ambitions. I like the *process.* I like the work. I have no idea what I'll do next.
>
> —Steven Bochco

Television series, like any cultural product, are subject to numerous individual, collaborative, organizational, sociocultural, and economic conditions and circumstances that collectively foster or hinder their inception, development, distribution, and success or failure. Production ethnographies, authorship studies, and literature on innovation suggest that within television the development of an unconventional form, such as *Cop Rock,* may be determined by variables such as a producer's or production company's track record and relationship with a network; a producer's ability to operate "outside" the normal organizational channels; the competitive environment between networks and their positions in the ratings; and programming executives willing to take risks and allow a show time to cultivate an audience.[2]

In 1987 Steven Bochco left NBC, the network that had nurtured much of his success as a writer-producer. After turning down an offer to be president of CBS Entertainment, Bochco signed an unprecedented ten-year, ten-series, $50-million-guaranteed contract with the ABC network. The arrangement was ideal, and unusual by any creator's standards, as it represented both financial and artistic freedom. If one of Bochco's ideas was rejected or a show ran fewer than the standard thirteen-episode run before renewal, Bochco was paid, and paid well. Cancellation compensation was $1.5 million. More staggering to industry observers was the stipulation that Bochco would own the rights to his shows.

To ABC, whose prime-time schedule at the time lacked prestigious and successful programs, Bochco was an investment in hits and respectability. Bocho was proven product, a producer with an impressive track record, particularly for police and detective series. His creative cop credits date back to the 1960s as a writer for NBC series *The Bold Ones* and *The Name of the Game.* His 1970s work includes *Columbo, McMillan and Wife, Richie Brockelman–Private Eye,* and the CBS series *Delvecchio,* starring Judd Hirsch, and *Paris,* featuring James Earl Jones. In the 1980s Bochco established himself as one of television's top creators of drama with two groundbreaking shows for NBC, *Hill Street Blues* (1981–1987) and *L.A. Law* (1986–1994). Both series introduced a new candor to prime-time drama and pioneered what would become central elements of Bochco's stylistic signature: large ensemble casts featuring ten to fifteen relatively unknown actors and actresses playing complex characters; serial storytelling with multiple plotlines that weave in and out of an episode and take weeks to resolve; absurdist humor; fast-paced scene changes; and a gritty cinematic realism.

Collaborator David Milch was among many who characterized Bocho as a "Wunderkind," adding that the adulation from his acclaimed shows (*Hill Street* and *L.A. Law*) perhaps tempted Bochco "to think that he could do anything."[3] Some of Bochco's post–*Hill Street* projects and his inaugural ABC endeavors reinforce Milch's notions of Bochco's indulgence in creative whimsy. For example, *Bay City Blues* (1983, NBC), a minor-league baseball drama with a big-league budget, rivaled Fred Silverman's *Supertrain* (1979, ABC) as one of the biggest financial fiascos in broadcast television history. Production costs included set design consisting of building a stadium exclusively for the show and hiring crowds at eighty-five dollars per person per day. The investment did not pay off, as the series lasted only four episodes.

One of the notable programming trends that emerged in the 1987–1988 prime-time schedule was the comedy/drama hybrid labeled "dramedies," represented in series such as the one-hour *Moonlighting* (ABC), and half-hour series *The Days and Nights of Molly Dodd* (NBC), *Frank's Place* (CBS), *The Wonder Years* (ABC), and *The "Slap" Maxwell Story* (ABC). Bochco's contribution to this subgenre, *Hooperman* (ABC), featured John Ritter as a San Francisco detective. According to Bochco, the show "just popped out of my face . . . the whole thing came to me in five minutes."[4] In 1989, when *Hooperman* ended its two-season run, Bochco paid tribute to his father, a child prodigy violinist, with *Doogie Howser, M.D.,* another half-hour dramedy series about a sixteen-year-old physician.

THE SOAP COPERA:
HILL STREET BLUEPRINT, BROADWAY, AND THE BBC

[It would not make sense to invite comparisons with a breakthrough program like *Hill Street*] unless you find a compellingly different way to reach people. And music reaches people; it reaches them underneath their flak jackets.
—Steven Bochco

During the 1980s, conventions of the police/crime genre on network television were largely redefined by the cluttered, gritty realism of Bochco's *Hill Street Blues* (1981–1987, NBC) and the pulsating pastels of Mann's *Miami Vice* (1984–1989, NBC). According to broadcast programming lore, the idea for *Cop Rock* originated from a note—"MTV Cops"—scribbled by NBC entertainment president Brandon Tartikoff. Mann used Jan Hammer's theme and score, along with popular songs performed by original artists, to create a striking soundtrack that linked music to story the same way composer Henri Mancini did in the 1950s with *Peter Gunn.*[5]

Bochco and Mann took somewhat divergent paths of progress with the sequels to their successes. Mann chose the retro route with *Crime Story* (1986–1988, NBC), a cop-and-mobster *Untouchables* update set in Chicago in 1963. The only hint of *Miami Vice* in the show was in the opening theme, featuring a revamped version of Del Shannon's 1961 hit "Runaway." With his next project, Bochco looked beyond the commercial viability and creative convenience of duplicating *Hill Street Blues* in its entirety.[6] He was particularly interested in advancing the use of music beyond the norms of soundtrack. Bochco's vision was vaudevillian; he was inspired by both Broadway and British productions, specifically the work and vision of Dennis Potter, whose characters frequently break into song, miming the words from old recordings. "I think [*The*] *Singing Detective* is possibly the best seven hours of television I've ever seen. Period; without qualification," states Bochco. "It gave us permission, at least internally. Creatively, it gave me permission to do *Cop Rock*."[7]

In addition to Bochco's admiration for Potter's productions, he considered a suggestion to adapt *Hill Street Blues* to Broadway as a musical. Though the theatrical project did not materialize, the seeds of song for a small screen "soap copera" had been sown. "Why not reverse it [the idea of a police musical], I thought; bring it to this medium [television]," said Bochco.[8] Mike Post, one of television's busiest and best music composer-arrangers, cautioned Bochco about the costs and creative risks of producing a weekly television musical. Despite the words of discouragement from his friend and collaborator, Bochco proceeded, and even convinced Post to be the show's musical producer despite his reservations.

Post's concerns about the elaborate nature of such a production appeared well founded. Every stage of the process, from preproduction to postproduction, presented unusual problems that required special planning and puzzle solving. Casting weekly guest roles had to be based on performers' abilities not only to act but to sing and dance as well. Complicated rehearsals required an eight-day-per-episode shooting schedule, one more than standard for an hour-long show. The editing process was also demanding, as it required mixing music and dialogue tracks. The cumulative result was a budget for *Cop Rock* that exceeded the average cost for a one-hour show by nearly 40 percent, translating into approximately $1.3 million a week to produce.

The fragmented formula for the series required two creative staffs, one for the script and one for the songwriting, music, and choreography. Bochco envisioned five original songs per episode, with no cover versions and no lip-syncing. Projected over a season of twenty-two episodes, that meant 110 songs would have to be to be composed, performed, and choreographed within conventional dramatic scenes. The songs were central to the narrative, serving essential dialogue purposes of providing information, advancing the plot, and revealing character and emotion. Popular singer-songwriter Randy Newman composed and performed *Cop Rock*'s main title theme, "Under the Gun," and wrote the pilot episode's five songs. However, the cost of keeping a company of songwriters of Newman's caliber on a weekly song-on-demand basis was not feasible. In subsequent weeks, six to eight lesser-known songwriters were assembled under Post's musical direction. The group included Amanda McBroom, who wrote the song "The Rose," and Donnie Markowitz, who won an Oscar for the song "I Had the Time of My Life" from the film *Dirty Dancing*. Bochco hoped to eventually enlist other popular artists such as Paul Simon and Billy Joel as special guest composers for episodes. Another long-term musical goal was to compile the show's best songs into a *Cop Rock* soundtrack. "My anxiety with *Cop Rock* wasn't whether it would be a hit, but whether we could actually do the damn thing and get it on the air every week," said Bochco of the production process.[9]

The "*Hill Street Blues* on Broadway via the BBC" blueprint became *Cop Rock* on September 26, 1990, at 10 P.M. (EDT) on ABC. True to its novel design, and framed by Bochco's signature style of storytelling, characterization, and production values, *Cop Rock*'s premiere fused familiar conventions of the police/detective genre with traditional elements of the musical. From the opening scene—a cluttered, nocturnal collage of hovering helicopter searchlights, plainclothes officers, and swarming SWAT teams in a frenzied, break-the-door-down descent upon a crack house—the nervous camera, gritty realism, and urban setting is vintage Bochco, with a hint of the reality camcorder cop series *Cops* (FOX).

Cop Rock's unflinching violence, unsettling plot twists, frank dialogue, realism, and intensity rise above the levels of other television dramas. A car chase involving cops and a red-light-running van squealing and swerving through streets and alleys appears like standard stock from cop formulas seen in *C.H.I.P.S* or *T. J. Hooker* until the pursuit climaxes with a graphic shoot-out near a playground and a slain officer, which establishes the "cop killer revenge" theme. During an interrogation in "the box," a determined detective tortures a suspect by forcing him to drink hot coffee after each question until he urinates in his pants. As the storyline develops, the same renegade detective shoots a bound suspect point-blank and becomes a heroic avenger to the squad. The lone dissenter is the captain, who, like *Hill Street*'s head, Frank Furillo, represents the busy precinct's moral center.

In addition to Bochco's usual masterful exploration of the gray areas of the law through cops who often resemble criminals, there is characteristic contrast in partners: male/female, young/old, black/white, clean/corrupt. Sprinkled in for comic relief are a few offbeat characters such as a pistol-packing police chief who duels with a mechanical gunslinger in his office closet for spontaneous rounds of target practice.

The familiar dramatic narratives shift into diverse song-and-dance intervals that substitute for action and dialogue. Following a drug bust, a group of apprehended suspects who are being escorted into squad cars begin rapping a response in a handcuffed chorus taunting the arresting officers, "In these streets, *we* got the power." A junkie mother croons a lullaby on a bus stop bench before selling her baby. A police lineup becomes a threatening chorus line. A cop's eulogy is a spiritual. Some of the production numbers border on spectacle: homeless people emerge from under a bridge into the streets to perform an extensively choreographed musical number reminiscent of the "Be a Pepper" long-form television commercials for Dr. Pepper or the pop star Pepsi ads showcased during the Grammy Awards during the 1980s. The mayor does her best Helen Reddy roar about graft and corruption from atop her office desk. A jury delivers its verdict in a rousing gospel choir fashion, with the entire courtroom swaying and clapping to the beat. Other performances seem better suited for animated Disney tales. A forensics specialist sings a forlorn love ballad in his dimly lit den. The good captain listens to his wife's lyrical lament about "watching my dreams and wishes drown in dirty dishes." Still others are farcical. An agitated yuppie, watching his BMW being impounded after being busted for buying cocaine in a seedy parking lot, wails a pseudo-soulful, "I want my Beemer back."

SINGIN' THE BLUES:
"FLOP ROCK," "COP WRECK," AND DE-FAME-ING THE FORCE

Despite a heavy promotional campaign, which included trailers in movie theaters (an uncommon marketing strategy for television series at the time), *Cop Rock* could not sustain sufficient audience numbers beyond the initial episode's curious crowd. Nor was there a groundswell of support from critics. Though many commended Bochco for his creative courage, they also got carried away with cute in their columns, using playful pity in paraphrased epithets pronouncing the police project "Flop Rock" and "Cop Wreck." The critical consensus concluded that the show needed to be de-Famed; the shotgun marriage of musical fantasy and inner-city mayhem just did not work. Though programming executives at ABC pledged patience, they were not encouraged by the initial ratings response to the series. "When you try something as different as *Cop Rock,* you have to be prepared as a programmer for the fact that it is just not going to work," said ABC entertainment president Robert Iger.[10] The struggling third-place network was committed to developing shows that "created different experiences" for viewers. From 1989 to 1990, in addition to *Cop Rock,* ABC boldly introduced *Twin Peaks,* the David Lynch/Mark Frost surreal "sap opera" set in a timber town in the Pacific Northwest; *Elvis,* a bio-drama of Elvis Presley's early years; *The Young Riders,* a revisionist Western about Pony Express recruits; and *America's Funniest Home Videos,* a contemporary *Candid Camera* and programming precursor to the current reality show trend.

Cop Rock exceeded ABC's ambitious agenda for "different" programming in excessive—not to mention expensive—form and fashion. However, in this case, deviant distinction meant demise. "Viewers do seek a comfort level in programs and the music can create some discomfort and probably has," said Iger of *Cop Rock,* sounding like a programming doctor diagnosing an ailment, or perhaps more appropriately, a coroner at an autopsy.[11] *Cop Rock* went from an off-Broadway audition to off television, as the series was canceled in December after a mere six episodes.[12]

Iger's assessment of the audience's discomfort may be understated. Bochco himself was likely aware from the show's conception stage that he might be committing "telecide" with his small-screen "soap copera." Fusing fragments of Tin Pan Alley, Disney, Broadway, and MTV with a realistic police drama was a drastically different, if not discomforting, experience for viewers. The musical medley both challenged and violated standard expectations inherent in the genre. The singing was incompatible with character and continuity and too often interrupted the narrative flow. Minus the music, *Cop Rock's* storylines and characters combined to create a quality drama comparable to any on television, including Bochco's best. Yet, the musical interludes became intrusions that fostered apprehension and misplaced anticipation of the next song rather than plot twists or character arcs. The singing sequences demanded that viewers suspend disbelief and balance intense emotionalism with farce and absurdity of characters who appeared to have trained with Debbie Allen at a dance academy rather than at a police academy. *Cop Rock's* colliding conventions were so incongruous that the show could not even manage "acquired taste" status beyond the initial curiosity attraction of the pilot episode. In subsequent weeks, when viewers were presumably better prepared for the show's musical elements, the distraction did not diminish; the show's ratings dwindled. In the end, Bochco's creative vision was undermined as much as anything by the venue itself. Even with music video established for nearly a decade by MTV in the American cultural experience by the time *Cop Rock* premiered in 1990, the musical in its more traditional form did not translate well to the confines of television sets in living rooms. *Cop Rock* was better suited for a theatrical stage and setting where audiences *expect* characters to sing their lines, a point that Bochco himself concedes: "In retrospect, I think the show embarrassed viewers—it made them uncomfortable to see characters bursting into song in a TV drama. When we tested the pilot for groups of people, it always went over great. Now I realize it was because we had a group of people together, as you would in a Broadway theater. But watching it in your living room, it came off more like Uncle Joe, loaded at Thanksgiving, with a lamp shade on his head and singing 'Sweet Sue.'"[13]

MUSICAL INTERLUDES:
SCENES, SOUNDTRACKS, AND SMALL-SCREEN SPECTACLE

In the early 1990s creators of crime-time television series did not take a musical cue from Bochco's chorus of cops. Instead, producers preferred camcorder cops. Low-budget, reality-based dramatic crime re-creations and missing-person crusades emerged as a programming trend in *Cop Rock*'s immediate wake. The video vérité variations included *Unsolved Mysteries* (NBC) —hosted by a trio of ex-television cops, Robert Stack, Raymond Burr, and Karl Malden— *Top Cops* (CBS), *Cops* (FOX), *FBI: The Untold Stories* (ABC), *Secret Service* (NBC), *True Detectives* (CBS), and *Stories of the Highway Patrol* (Syndicated).

Music continued to become widely integrated into other comic and dramatic presentations during the same period, though not on the scale of *Cop Rock*. *Northern Exposure*'s (1990–1995, CBS) use of music was arguably the most eclectic, captivating, reflective synthesis of soundtrack and storyline on television, particularly during the show's closing three minutes. A scene depicting a coffin catapulting through the sky toward its final resting place in a lake as Procol Harum's "A Whiter Shade of Pale" plays ("We skipped the light fandango") is emblematic of the meditative codas to the narratives involving fictional Cicely, Alaska's colorful characters, their relationships and rural rituals.

Pop-star cameos also became commonplace, especially during competitive ratings sweeps periods. Soundtrack synergy also emerged, just as Bochco had envisioned with *Cop Rock*. One-hour dramatic series, particularly those with key teen demographic appeal such as *Melrose Place* (FOX) and *Party of Five* (FOX), spawned accompanying music collections of songs featured in the shows. By the late 1990s television soundtracks were established as a standard across genres on networks and cable. Shows ranging from *Dawson's Creek* (WB), *Gilmore Girls* (WB) and *Providence* (NBC), to *Friends* (NBC) and *Scrubs* (NBC), to *The X-Files* (FOX) and *The Sopranos* (HBO) were among those contributing to the expanding catalog of television music.

An increasing number of series began to devote at least one of their twenty-two episodes in a season to a special musical production, often presented in some fantasy form or dream narrative. Recent examples include *That 70s Show* (FOX), which marked its one-hundredth show in 2001 with a musical episode featuring The Who. On *Scrubs* (NBC), a comedy that utilizes numerous unconventional production techniques, including *Wonder Years*–style voice-over commentary, a group of young interns transforms Sacred Heart Hospital into song-and-dance scenes from *West Side Story*. Perhaps the most stunning stagelike presentation is *Buffy the Vampire Slayer*'s (UPN) musical episode, "Once More with Feeling," a surreal, small-screen spectacle featuring original singing performances by the cast. Promoted as a "special television event," the episode was nominated for an Emmy Award, and complete versions of all the songs are compiled in an original soundtrack recording.

Elaborate mini–production numbers have become a distinguishing trait of *The Drew Carey Show* (ABC). The blue-collar comedy's opening title tunes—the Vogues' "Five O'Clock World," and in subsequent seasons, a cover version of Ian Hunter's "Cleveland Rocks"—have been accompanied by large-cast choreography. Flamboyant productions over a number of seasons include a *Full Monty* strip routine, a rowdy dance-off outside a midnight showing of *The Rocky Horror Picture Show*, and a musical fantasy sequence with Carey explaining his escape from an institution to Leo Sayer's "Long Tall Glasses." In 1999 the series commemorated its one-hundredth episode with an ambitious "Brotherhood of Man" production adapted from *How to Succeed in Business without Really Trying*. Its 2001 season premiere, "Drew Carey's Back to School Rock and Roll Comedy Hour," features Sugar Ray, Uncle Kracker, Motorhead, Joe Walsh, Peter Frampton, SheDAISY, and Smash Mouth at the Cleveland cast's watering hole, the Warsaw Tavern.

COP ROCK CROSSOVERS:
MUSIC AND MEDICINE, LYRICS AND LAWYERS

I'm singing because it's easier than talking. It's like a mask; it's one step from reality.
——Dr. Jeffrey Geiger, *Chicago Hope* (1997)

Every time she speaks it sounds like a song to me.
——Client to Ally McBeal, *Ally McBeal* (2002)

A 1997 musical episode of the medical drama *Chicago Hope* (CBS), created by Bochco protégé David E. Kelley, simultaneously mirrors *Cop Rock* and magnifies some of its generic miscalculations.[14] Elements such as setting, soundtrack, and the subconscious combine to make the presentation more accessible as a musical.

The storyline centers on neurosurgeon Dr. Aaron Shutt (played by Adam Arkin), who is stricken with a life-threatening brain aneurysm. The script establishes music as the central narrative thread when the cantankerous Shutt collapses in pain to the floor of a convenience store while trying to unplug an annoying old-timey, tin-roll piano locked in an unrelenting "Red Red Robin" loop.

Shutt's perilous condition not only grounds the story with an inner logic that was lacking in *Cop Rock*'s episodes, but it also provides permission for a surreal, soul-searching sing-along involving friends, family, and colleagues. As Shutt is gurneyed down the halls of the emergency room, the disabled doctor is in delirious drift. His cloudy colleagues hovering over him appear as lounge lizards lip-syncing Dean Martin's "Ain't That a Kick in the Head." The setting smoothly shifts from emergency room into a nightclub with the singing doctors dressed in tuxedos, leaning against a bar. Various medical personnel check charts and push morphine drips in crisscross choreography through the scene. The visual transition is one of several seamless segues. In another, as the anesthetized Shutt drifts off into oblivion, the camera pans from the operating room into a recording studio where the staff rehearses, once again with lyrical tongue-in-cheek, "Well I think I'm going out of my head / Over you."

Melody and movement mix well with all things medical. The set, props, and iconography supply a more natural backdrop for a musical production than the streets, tenements, alleys, guns, speeding cars, and low-watt inter-rogation rooms of a police drama. A hospital's interiors intrinsically resemble a stage set, from the emergency room entrance, to the colorful checkered floors of linoleum, to the long hallways leading to luminous operating rooms. Studio-like props abound: carts and charts, tubes and operating tables, X-rays and exit signs, monitors and machines. Characters appear in costume wearing scrubs, gowns, lab coats, and masks, accented with acces-sories such as stethoscopes and syringes.

Within this setting the singing is less intrusive; music is a staple of sur-gery, recovery, and bedside manner. Diverse production numbers become an ethereal narrative for Shutt as he confronts his mid-career crisis, clashes with colleagues, and life choices and changes. The performances are playful, among them a roller-skating nurse's flirtatious Melanie classic, "Brand New Key"; the hard-line chief surgeon's soft and supportive gender reversal of Helen Reddy's "You and Me Against the World"; and the surgical staff in a coordinated Elvisian coif-and-costume chorus of Frankie Valli and the Four Seasons' "Walk Like a Man." An elaborate, full-cast song-and-dance routine to Frank Sinatra's "Luck Be a Lady" fuses fear and fate into benediction moments before Shutt's delicate surgery. When a complication suddenly arises during the procedure, a multiple monitor montage chronicles Shutt's life in music video fashion with Jimi Hendrix's electric version of "All Along the Watchtower" playing. The song-and-dance details delightfully and faith-fully mirror Dennis Potter's *The Singing Detective* and, to a lesser degree, elements of *Cop Rock*. The homage is undeniable, as the brain surgeon brought in to operate on Shutt is named "Denise Potter."

The episode illustrates subtleties between singing and soundtrack. Whereas *Cop Rock* opts exclusively for authenticity, with the cast performing original compositions, *Chicago Hope* goes the safer route, with its medical staff lip-syncing familiar songs. Other than Shutt's off-key Sinatra, the only character who actually sings is Dr. Jeffrey Geiger, played by Broadway's Mandy Patin-kin, whose numbers include a shivering falsetto cover of the Jackson Five's "I'll Be There" and a vaudevillian "Red Red Robin" that echoes Shutt's con-venience store collapse. The production and casting nuance is that Patinkin, in addition to being a Tony Award–winning actor, is an established recording artist who specializes in show tunes.[15] Though both dramas deal with life-and-death situations, *Chicago Hope*'s costume karaoke approach signals a more fanciful presentation. *Cop Rock*'s characters' singing original, unfamiliar tunes may be a slight contrast to lip-sync and cover versions. Yet the method amplifies the incongruity between the music and narrative's dramatic realism. As always, there are exceptions. In the *Buffy the Vampire Slayer* musical, the characters sing original songs. The disparity again lies in the setting. The horror/fantasy realm of *Buffy's* dark underworld is theatrical, thus conducive to creepy choruses, singing spirits, and dancing demons. For television series, especially those merging music with narratives, location may not be everything, but it does make a difference.

Incorporating musical elements into a storyline of a single episode is obviously less complicated than sustaining singing from week to week as the basis for an entire series. *Cop Rock* clearly demonstrates that the pitfalls of a weekly musical outweigh the possibilities. Such special productions contain novel appeal for audiences, creators, and casts. Audiences are willing to tolerate, if not welcome, a refreshing diversion from the weekly, and often weak, formulaic storylines. Likewise, writers, producers, and performers have a rare opportunity to temporarily deviate from the norm and construct a creatively convenient "anything goes" atmosphere, often in the form of flashbacks, fantasies, or dream sequences, for their characters and storylines. In addition, the special episodes usually benefit from extensive promotion as "viewing events," which better prepares the audience and modifies conventional expectations.

Cop Rock's telecidal mission magnifies the "one-episode musical" as the safe standard, the genre and audience allotment for a series. It is highly unlikely that *Chicago Hope* would have succeeded had it been designed as a musical series. Conversely, it is safe to speculate that *Cop Rock* might have lasted longer minus the music. And Bochco likely could have arranged a musical extravaganza with *Hill Street Blues*, *L.A. Law*, or *NYPD Blue*, as long as it was limited to a single episode.

There is one network program that provides a series, rather than single episode, frame of reference. The same season the *Chicago Hope* musical aired, its creator, Kelley, expanded elements of the experimental episode into *Ally McBeal* (FOX), a flighty, one-hour legal dramedy that closely approximates *Cop Rock's* musical ambitions. Obscure singer Vonda Shepard is cast as an accompanist on the show. She not only performs the opening theme, "Searchin' My Soul," which became a hit single, but is also cast in dual roles, as a maestro and meandering muse. Shepard's piano-driven, bluesy cover-song serenades thread scenes with moods and motifs; provide glimpses of leading lady Ally's (Calista Flockhart) thoughts and emotions; and serve as nightclub karaoke classics for lawyers looking for love and libation at the local lounge.

Beyond Shepard, music is manifest in many variations throughout the show. "You get the feeling sometimes the song comes first, and David [Kelley] writes the story and script around it," says producer Steve Robin.[16] Swinging stall door song-and-dance numbers are common in the law firm's unisex bathroom. Ally's therapist, played by Tracey Ullman, encourages clients to have a personal "theme song." The cavalcade of musical cameos includes Sting, Elton John, Mariah Carey, Tina Turner, Al Green, Gladys Knight, Gloria Gaynor, the Barrys—White and Manilow, and teen baritone Josh Groban. Jon Bon Jovi's appearance led to a nine-episode acting stint.

Conversely, Robert Downey Jr.'s acting role resulted in several musical moments for him, including an "Every Breath You Take" duet with Sting and an impressive rendition of Joni Mitchell's "River." Other cast members' rock-star and neon-Broadway fantasies routinely surface in minor, self-indulgent subplots that evolve no farther than the nightclub stage with Shepard's piano accompaniment in scenes that often conclude episodes.

In its five seasons (1997–2002), *Ally McBeal* generated more than 400 songs or musical performances. On the surface, that total is striking, especially for a show not billed exclusively as a musical presentation. Yet, projections of Bochco's aims with *Cop Rock* (five or six songs per episode, multiplied by the standard twenty-two-episode block for a series, meaning 100 to 120 songs per season) would have exceeded 400 and set a precedent for music and drama. *Ally McBeal* also fulfills Bochco's vision for musical guests, composers, and soundtrack synergy. The series' songs were compiled into four soundtracks featuring Vonda Shepard: *Songs from Ally McBeal* (1998), *Heart and Soul: New Songs from Ally McBeal* (1999), *A Very Ally Christmas* (2001), and *Ally McBeal: For Once in My Life* (2001).

Ally McBeal may lose a hypothetical hindsight battle of the bands by the numbers, but its five seasons certainly surpass *Cop Rock*'s mere six episodes. The reasons are obvious. Whether single episode or series, producer Kelley places music in a different dramatic context than Bochco. (Kelley also benefited from having another legal series in prime time on another night, *The Practice* [ABC], where he could use serious storylines.) The settings and situations on *Ally McBeal* were safer, often surreal, and sometimes silly. Places make musical performances both permissible and plausible. This primary distinction is deftly demonstrated in the opening musical montage of *Ally McBeal's* series finale in May 2002. As episode fragments frantically flash before a wistful Ally in Wonderland—an urban Dorothy swirling in her inner tornado—she cries out, "But what about the music?" The record-scratch sound effect interrupts, and a voice-over clarifies, "It's a fantasy!" For punctuation, the law firm's familiar bathroom stall door opens, and Barry Manilow appears, singing "Even now. . . . "

PERMISSION AND POSSIBILITY: HOMAGE AND HINGE

When we first did *Hill Street,* people didn't get it at all. Then they kind of accepted what we were doing. And once they accepted it, it really did kind of change the rules of dramatic television. I think we can potentially do the same [with *Cop Rock*]; I think we can expand what's possible.

—Steven Bochco

Twelve years after its final episode, *Cop Rock* lingers in obscurity as a tele-version of the B-film, albeit without a B-movie budget. Its scant eleven episodes are barely enough to block a "cult classic" court, cop, or comedy mock marathon in cable's kitschy late-night landscape. In July 2002 one of those rare *Cop Rock* citations materialized from the files of failure. This one was predictably less complimentary than John Leonard's insightful linking of *Cop Rock* with *Moulin Rouge* on *Sunday Morning.* In an article in its July 20–26 issue, *TV Guide* presented a list of "The 50 Worst Shows of All Time." *Cop Rock* ranked number eight.

The deriding distinction is typical of *Cop Rock's* legacy in the twelve years following its final episode. Predictably, the predominant view is that *Cop Rock* is more laughable than legitimate. Attributing some sense of impact, influence, or inspiration to such a critical and commercial failure is a premise likely to be regarded as ridiculous and easily rejected on any level. Even minuscule mentions such as those by John Leonard should not be misconstrued as literate lobbying for *Cop Rock's* lofty place in broadcast programming history. Any acclaim for the show from critical corners risks revealing one of the potential perils of the auteur approach—that is, emphasizing the creator over the work itself, an evaluative blind spot that can elevate an undeserving production to a level of aesthetic quality.

Likewise, it is a comparable critical convenience to emphasize only successful texts—those leading in the ratings, charts, box-office sales, and critical kudos—and neglect or ignore the failures, overlooking any value they may contain. *Cop Rock* demonstrates how fragments of failure are capable of floating and finding themselves in other forms and fashions. Just as the short-lived series' significance should not—and likely never will—be overstated, its value should not be dismissed, especially when placing the production within the context of genre evolution and cross-genre contributions.

The individual works that compose any genre represent stepping-stones or links in its evolution. Whether the steps are big, small, or stumbling, the series of inventions and conventions embodied in narratives unfold and develop, defining and redefining a genre over a period of time. Following *Hill Street*'s and *Miami Vice*'s important advances within the police/crime genre's evolution in the 1980s, *Cop Rock*'s inventive steps further explored and expanded the parameters of the genre's familiar conventions. "If you look at a 30-year curve, television has gotten much better, and you can't stop its progress," says Bochco. "We're moving forward, like it or not. Take a long look at television and you realize it just continually becomes smarter, broader in its appeal, more sophisticated."[17]

More markedly, *Cop Rock* signals a subtle shift on the television time line that extends beyond its own genre. By importing *The Singing Detective* and integrating its elements within the police/crime programming progression via *Cop Rock,* Bochco accomplished more than mere homage to Dennis Potter. *Cop Rock* represents a hinge, a pivotal point on the door of possibility. Just as *The Singing Detective* gave Bochco "permission" to create *Cop Rock,* Bochco in turn passed along similar lyrical license to other producers to explore the further variations of music and narratives, whether situation comedy, dramedy, police, law, hospital, horror, or family dramas.

By the 2002 television season, the police/crime genre was so prevalent that the network prime-time schedule appeared to be wrapped in the yellow "Police Line" tape that outlines a crime scene. From Dick Wolf's *Law and Order* franchise on NBC, which includes *Special Victims* and *Criminal Intent* units; to Jerry Bruckheimer's highly rated *CSI* series (CBS), its clone in Miami, and its Thursday night companion show *Without a Trace;* and to *Boomtown* (NBC) and all precincts and points in between, prime time has become a place crawling with cops, corpses, coroners, and forensics experts. None of the characters in television's nightly police lineup sing or dance.

While there may be little evidence of *Cop Rock* at the scenes of the current crime wave in television's dramas, its remnants continue to reveal themselves in other popular prime-time productions. The season premiere of *Scrubs* in NBC's prestigious Thursday night lineup featured singer Colin Hay as an omnipresent street musician turned serenading stalker. Hay, the former front man for the popular 1980s group Men at Work, strums an acoustic rendition of their hit "Overkill" while shadowing rumpled medical intern J. D. Dorian (Zach Braff) from his home to the hospital.

In an episode of the family drama *7th Heaven* (WB), the father, Eric Camden (played by Stephen Collins), undergoes heart bypass surgery. While under anesthesia, Camden hallucinates that he is Elvis Presley. Costumed variously in black leather, gold lamé, and a spangled Vegas jumpsuit, Camden delivers Elversions of "All Shook Up," "Don't Be Cruel," "Teddy Bear," and "Rock-a-Hula Baby."

These musical moments are déjà view; they are distant duets that nod to Ally McBeal, her karaoke cast and queen Vonda Shepard, and Buffy's singing spirits. Hay's unplugged cameo is Warsaw Tavern–worthy of the Drew (Carey) crew. Eric Camden is Aaron Shutt in *Chicago Hope*'s operating room. The evolution of these musical interludes can be traced to 1990 with *Cop Rock*. Then, a few homage(nous) steps farther to 1986 with *The Singing Detective*.

Though *Cop Rock* will routinely be recognized among the "Worst Shows of All Time," it nonetheless remains an unsung series. *Cop Rock*'s consequence is as a hinge, a preface of permission and possibility for music and narrative in television. *Cop Rock*'s fusion, fragments, and false notes may not resonate; rather, its residue and relevance ripple as a reminder beneath the surface of scenes and soundtracks. It is there that *Cop Rock* whispers; it winks; it whistles a faintly familiar television tune.

NOTES

1. Bill Carter, "Why Bochco's Cops Say It with Music," *New York Times,* September 23, 1990, 25.

2. James S. Ettema and D. Charles Whitney, eds., *Individuals in Mass Media Organizations: Creativity and Constraint* (Beverly Hills, CA: Sage, 1982).

3. Mark Christensen, "Bochco's Law," *Rolling Stone,* April 21, 1988, 81.

4. Ibid., 76.

5. Because the songs were performed by the original artists, *Miami Vice's* producers spent an average of $50,000 per episode for music licensing rights.

6. Perhaps the closest Bochco comes to producing a *Hill Street Blues* sequel is with *NYPD Blue,* which premiered on ABC in 1993, complete with content controversy. Conservative groups targeted the show, objecting to its sex, nudity, profanity, and violence. Initially, 57 of 225 ABC affiliates did not air the show. As *NYPD Blue's* ratings, critical acclaim, and advertising revenues increased, so did the number of station programmers who abandoned Reverend Donald Wildmon's conservative cause for Bochco's bandwagon.

7. Bill Shebar (Producer), Steven Weinstock, Michael Jackson (Executive Producers), "Bochco/Potter," on *Edge,* Thirteen WNET/BBC-TV PBS, October 9, 1992.

8. Carter, "Bochco's Cops," 33.

9. Ken Tucker, "A Blue Streak," *Entertainment Weekly,* October 11, 1996, 65.

10. Matt Roush, "Should Programs Court the Cutting Edge? Bold Moves Are Rewarding," *USA Today,* October 15, 1990, 3D.

11. Ibid.

12. *Cop Rock's* swift demise did not deter Bochco from his risk-taking approach as a creator of television drama. His ensuing project in 1992 was *Capitol Critters,* an animated series set at the White House, featuring vermin—rats, mice, and roaches—as its central characters. The series' run was shorter than *Cop Rock's,* lasting a mere four episodes. In 1995 Bochco's *Murder One* (ABC) deviated from conventional law dramas by following one case for the entire twenty-two-episode season. The timing of the series suggests the concept may have been inspired, in part, by the exhaustive coverage of the O. J. Simpson case.

13. Tucker, "Blue Streak," 65.

14. Bochco mentored Kelley as a writer on *L.A. Law.* The two also worked closely together on *Doogie Howser, M.D.*

15. When Shutt confronts his long-time colleague Geiger—"Hey, why is that your real voice? Stop with the singing! I have never liked your singing. Never!"—it becomes subtext, a reference to critical reviews that have widely characterized Patinkin's voice as an "acquired taste."

16. Chelsea J. Carter, "Performers Still Flock to Music-happy 'Ally,'" *Atlanta Journal-Constitution,* February 1, 2002, E2.

17. Tucker, "Blue Streak," 65.

9 / Sex, Society, and Double Standards in *Cheers*

HEATHER HUNDLEY

Although television rarely depicts any negative consequences from sexual encounters,[1] the AIDS epidemic revitalized public concern over sexual practices in the 1980s. "According to the study from the Center for Media and Public Affairs the battle against AIDS received four times the TV coverage of any health care issue between November 1, 1991, and May 1, 1992."[2] Furthermore, a report compiled by the Global AIDS Policy Coalition predicted that "more than 25 million people will have the disease by the end of the decade and as many as 120 million will be infected with HIV, the AIDS virus."[3]

Before NBA star Magic Johnson's announcement that he was HIV positive, many members of the American public held the common misconception that only homosexuals and drug users were vulnerable to this deadly virus. However, in the aftermath of the media coverage of Magic's disclosure, people came to realize that heterosexuals are just as susceptible.[4] Still, Caroline Bradbeer explains that while "the gay community is well informed and homosexual lifestyle has already changed," now "education needs to be aimed at highly sexual active heterosexuals."[5]

In examining AIDS information and sexual practices, Masako Ishii-Kuntz, Les Whitbeck, and Ronald Simmons (1990) indicate that "certainty about AIDS sexual transmission was found to have little impact on condom use."[6] They concluded that sexual behavior is more likely to change when the threat of AIDS is great and not just with knowledge of the disease. The

Centers for Disease Control reported there were 200,000 confirmed cases of AIDS in the United States in January 1992[7] and that the AIDS rate in women was rapidly rising.[8] Further, "the World Health Organization estimated that between 11 million and 13 million people worldwide were infected with HIV, the virus that causes AIDS."[9]

Social concerns about sexual practice in the 1980s were not limited to AIDS but also included the problems of sexually transmitted diseases and unwanted pregnancies. "Sexually transmitted diseases (STDs) are one of the most important public health problems in the United States. An estimated twelve million persons acquire a sexually transmitted infection each year."[10] Combined, these health-related concerns made sexual practices a salient issue on the national public agenda during the 1980s and on into the 1990s.

CHEERS' POPULARITY AND SEXUAL BEHAVIOR

As sexual practices piqued the national agenda during the 1980s, the televised situation comedy Cheers rose in popularity as well. In fact, from 1982 to 1987 Cheers was watched by millions of viewers weekly. The primary storyline revolved around the on-again, off-again sexual relationship between waitress/graduate student/writer Diane Chambers (Shelley Long) and bar owner Sam Malone (Ted Danson). After 1988, when Long left the sitcom, the show's primary storyline followed the love-hate, on-again, off-again romantic relationship between Sam Malone and bar manager Rebecca Howe (Kirstie Alley). From their first encounter, Sam unceasingly propositioned Rebecca, actions that clearly could be considered sexual harassment—another issue brought to the public's consciousness with the 1991 Hill/Thomas debate.[11] During the first few years Rebecca appeared on the show, she was portrayed as a hard-working businesswoman whose only interests were working for the good of the company and marrying the company's president, Evan Drake. When Evan, who barely acknowledged her existence, left Boston to open a branch office in Japan, Rebecca's focus switched to multi-millionaire Robin Colcord. After several years of courtship, Robin eventually proposed to Rebecca. However, soon thereafter he was convicted of insider trading. When he was released from prison, Rebecca no longer wanted to marry the now-poverty-stricken Colcord.

The series' heterosexual relationships begin to reveal the myriad examples of sexual innuendos displayed in this program.[12] Of the seven regularly recurring characters, two (Woody and Norm) were married; however, that did not impede them from making sexually explicit and suggestive comments. The main protagonist, Sam Malone, was known and revered for his sexist and sexual exhibits. At one point, in fact, he participated in a sexual therapy group for oversexed people, only to make sexual advances to its female members. During the show's eleven seasons, sex was a central characteristic in *Cheers.*

Perhaps the mantra "sex sells" is no more evident than in *Cheers,* for during the 1989–1990 season it was among the top ten most-watched shows, and for the 1990–1991 season it was "the top-rated show of the year."[13] Now in syndication, *Cheers* initially aired on September 30, 1982, and its finale was May 20, 1993, with a total of 275 episodes.[14] Earning the title of one of the longest-running prime-time situation comedies, *Cheers* received 111 Emmy nominations—more than any other series—and received 28 Emmys altogether, just behind the number one Emmy Award winner, the *Mary Tyler Moore Show,* with 29 awarded Emmys.[15] *Cheers* was one of a select few television series to keep the interest of a diverse audience with few character and setting changes for over a decade.[16] Indeed, because of the show's popularity, the Bull and Finch (the real bar in Boston after which *Cheers* was modeled) made at least $7 million a year selling *Cheers* T-shirts, ashtrays, and Bloody Mary mix.[17]

Indeed, regardless of the AIDS epidemic, the transference of sexually transmitted diseases, and a number of unwanted pregnancies, *Cheers* remained a popular program that contradicted the day's social health concerns. In fact, the dominant ideological message perpetuated in *Cheers* was that casual, unprotected, promiscuous, heterosexual sex was sport for men. Moreover, the juxtaposition of class and gender reveals that *Cheers* advanced double standards, in that upper-middle-class white men may enjoy the pleasures of sex without guilt, remorse, or health concerns, while working-class women suffer serious consequences for the same actions. Thus, within *Cheers,* Sam represented the male hero figure constructed through his sexual conquests, while bar server and main character Carla Tortelli-LeBec (Rhea Perlman) portrayed a nymphomaniac who reveled in her self-condemnation as a slut and "paid the price" for her loose morals.[18]

TELEVISION AND SEXUAL PRACTICES

There is an abundance of content analyses regarding the number of sexual acts seen on television,[19] the types of sexual behaviors (e.g., kissing, touching, intercourse) seen on television,[20] and the subject of contraception on television.[21] In addition, a plethora of studies examine television's depiction of sex-related topics such as sex roles, stereotyping, gender, body image, and intimacy.[22] However, there are few close textual analyses of the portrayal of sex on popular television sitcoms.

E. J. Roberts reviewed, synthesized, and assessed published literature from 1972 to 1980 that examined sex on television and concluded that "contraceptive responsibility seems to be a 'non-issue' on most television programs, and pregnancy or venereal disease is often used as the punishment for sexual activity by the 'wrong people'—people who are too young, too old, too poor, too ugly, etc."[23] Dennis Lowry and David Towles's study agreed that the subject of contraception has been almost ignored in television.[24] Their examination of afternoon soap operas broadcast from May 1 through August 1, 1987, found that sexual intercourse, innuendos, and verbal references to intercourse steadily increased over that period.

Other studies examine the effects of showing sexual behavior on television. John Courtright and Stanley Baran, for example, conclude that "peers and the mass media are powerful agents in the acquisition of sexual information of young people."[25] Christine Nystrom argues that "the moral majority" should be concerned with the long-term effects of television's treatment of such topics given that "the teachings of the television curriculum work themselves ever more deeply into the fabric of social values, attitudes, and behavior."[26] Jane Brown and Susan Newcomer identify a statistically significant correlation between the sexual activity status of their subjects and the programming they watch.[27] Although a direct connection between viewers' sexual activity and the effects of television's content cannot be determined, the study did find a correlation between viewers' sexual activity and their viewing choices.

Thus, it is clear from this review that many dimensions of sex and sexual behavior on television have been examined. Few of these studies, however, used methods other than survey research or content analysis. Indeed, only a handful of critical analyses have attempted to identify the sexual values affirmed in the narrative actions, dialogue, and plots of television programs. Further, the cross-section of class and gender has not been qualitatively applied to the discourse of sex. This study addresses this gap in research by analyzing sexual discourse in the ever-popular prime-time television program *Cheers*.

Although *Cheers* may be a place "where everybody knows your name," it is not the subject of much academic study.[28] Bradley Greenberg's hypothesis suggests that an important line of inquiry is the particular representation of a topic, such as sex, in a popular prime-time television program. Considering *Cheers'* longevity, continuance in syndication, and the sexual discourse centrally inscribed in its premise, combined with the salience of sexual issues in the public's agenda, an examination of the show's handling of the discourse of sex is warranted. Greenberg's drench hypothesis argues that one very long-running series may "be so forceful as to account for a significant portion of the role images we maintain"[29] because it "drenches" viewers with its portrayals. Thus, since sex was a central feature on the popular television series and was a salient social concern during *Cheers'* heyday, this study examines the discourse of sex during the eleventh and final season of the show. Even though the program continues in syndication, the final season of any series is the last opportunity for the producers to change the characters or topics presented. Essentially, the final season leaves the audience with a sense of closure regarding the characters' behaviors, traits, and motives as well as the program's ideology.[30]

CODING *CHEERS'* PORTRAYAL OF SEX

"A discourse is both a topic and a coded set of signs through which that topic is organized, understood, and made expressible."[31] In *Cheers* the discourse or topic of sex is understood through examining three dimensions. These dimensions are expressed by the characters' (1) self-reported sexual activity level and fidelity, (2) sexual practices, including protected and unprotected sex expressed verbally and behaviorally, and (3) narrative outcomes. Thus, the discourse of sex in *Cheers* is organized, understood, and made expressible in examining these coded sets of signs.

I investigate the discourse of sex as portrayed by the seven recurring characters in the final season of *Cheers.*[32] The findings reveal that a distinct gender bias was explicitly evident. For instance, Sam and Carla engaged in similar sexual behaviors; nevertheless, he was praised while she was condemned for their exploits. Sam Malone and Carla Tortelli-LeBec expose the epitome of sexual double standards. Thus, this examination specifically explores these two characters' ideological positions (attitudes and values) toward sex.

Sam's and Carla's heterosexuality provides an accessible entry of investigation by establishing a common sexual orientation. Both characters are clearly heterosexual, as Sam boasted of his sexual conquests with women and Carla disclosed her encounters with men. The departure of sexual double standards occurs in the characters' class and gender. In discussing the discourse of sex and identifying the double standards, the characters' sexual activity levels are first examined, and then their sexual practices are identified. Finally, their overall narrative outcomes are revealed. As a result, readers can understand how Carla was condemned for the same sexual behaviors for which Sam was valorized. As a working-class woman, Carla was not afforded the same praise as her male employer, who was lauded as a retired professional athlete.

Sexual Activity Level and Fidelity

One dimension of sexual discourse in the 1992–1993 *Cheers* season concerns Sam's and Carla's reported sexual activity level in relation to their level of monogamy as indicated in their words and actions toward themselves and others. Identifying this dimension helps determine their behaviors and attitudes toward sex. Both Carla and Sam were the most sexually active characters in the final season. Indeed, they were presented as self-indulgent nymphomaniacs compared to the other main characters.

During the 1992–1993 season, Carla made sexual advances toward Rebecca's father in the episode titled "Daddy's Middle-Aged Girl" (see appendix 3 for a complete list of episodes from *Cheers'* final season), John Hill,[33] Don the beer tap repairman,[34] and "the toll booth guy."[35] Not only did she make sexual advances toward these men, but also on at least one occasion Carla could not even remember with whom she slept the previous night.[36] By the end of that episode, when Carla finally learned she had sex with Paul, a *Cheers* patron, Sam consoled her with the reminder, "You've gone to bed with a lot of guys before."[37] Even strangers knew of her promiscuous sexual activity. Indeed, Don, the beer tap repairman, whom she just met, refused her advances by saying, "Look, Carla, I don't think I could satisfy you. I don't think the men of Desert Storm could satisfy you."[38] These examples illustrate Carla's reputation as a sexually active person. She demonstrated her lust repeatedly, and friends as well as strangers were privy to her sexually aggressive nature.

Moreover, Carla often self-reported her ample sexual indulgence. For example, in "Daddy's Middle-Aged Girl" an older man in a U.S. Navy uniform walked into the bar looking for his daughter, Rebecca. When Rebecca introduced him to the *Cheers* regulars and employees, she informed them that they call him Brig because he puts so many sailors in jail. Carla responded, "Then why don't they call *me* Brig?" This statement implies that her sexual exploits warrants sailors' arrest as well. Furthermore, Carla displayed sexual aggressiveness in her conversations about sex. For example in "Feelings . . . Whoa, Whoa, Whoa," Carla explained what happened when her sexual partner, Hill, had his heart attack: "Last night started out as an average date—Hill and I getting it on hot and heavy. I'm cursing at him, he's cursing at me. A real beauty. The headboard was begging for mercy." Thus, Carla's reputation preceded her and she bragged about it as well. Obviously she did not extol a puritan Victorian demure, but rather she proudly embraced her sexual pleasures.

Furthermore, a *Cheers* regular, Cliff, verified Carla's sexual excesses. In "Woody Gets an Election," Frasier Crane bet Sam that Woody would get at least 10 percent of the votes if he ran for public office. According to Frasier's calculations, to get 10 percent he merely had to display three hundred campaign posters of Woody. Cliff then suggested to Frasier, "Well, in that case why don't you just put them up on Carla's headboard?" The implication is that the men Carla encountered in her bedroom would account for at least 10 percent of the eligible votes in Boston and clearly indicates that the other characters and the audience were invited to see her as a sexually permissive character.

Sam was just as promiscuous and sexually aggressive as Carla was, if not more. In "The Magnificent Six," Henri, a friend of Woody's wife who rarely appeared in the show, called Sam "a babe hound," and in "Daddy's Middle-Aged Girl" Rebecca's father called him "sex boy." In "The Guy Can't Help It," when Frasier indicated that he thought Sam had a sexual addiction, Sam refused to believe Frasier and hypothetically asked Carla to marry him. Carla refused, citing Sam's sexually indulgent behavior: "Sammy, nobody loves you as much as I do, but I know you. You know we'd be taking our wedding vows and you'd be checking out the bridesmaid. You're a hound. I can't marry a hound." Even though Carla and Sam might be made for each other, at least in terms of their sexual behavior, Carla's statement implies that she knows he would be unfaithful. In fact, Sam's reputation is well known by the regular characters on the show and by casual viewers of the sitcom as well.

Like Carla, Sam also self-reported his sexually indulgent lifestyle. For example, in "Bar Wars VII: The Naked Prey" he said, "Never have I been naked and not had fun." In another episode, Sam attempted to console Cliff about not having sex with his ex-girlfriend Maggie. In this attempt, Sam said, "I've dated lots of women and not had sex with them." When Cliff responded, "That's kind of hard to believe," a frustrated Sam retorted, "You're not working with me here, Cliff."[39] Sam's comment implied that his first statement had been a falsehood uttered merely to help Cliff feel better for not having had sex with his date. Perhaps the most direct admission of Sam's nymphomania occurred when he took Frasier's advice and attended a therapy group for sexual compulsives. At the session Sam confessed, "I've had a lot of sex in my life."[40] Like Carla, Sam is just as eagerly boastful of his sexual aggressiveness and tawdry reputation.

Sam's nymphomania was also narcissistic. His words and behaviors reflected his conceit and self-admiration. Sam kept with him behind the bar a mirror, a comb, and cologne to prep himself for beautiful women who entered the bar. Sam frequently commented favorably on his appearance, especially his hair. For example, in the therapy group for sexual compulsives that he attended, Sam stated, "Granted, it's a big part of my life. When I'm not having sex, I'm thinking about it. I don't want you to think I'm shallow, 'cause I have other interests too. Like my hair. The babes really love my hair." Additionally, in the "Sunday Dinner" episode, Sam encouraged Frasier to go on a date by reminding him, "This is not a test. You're not expected to perform at my level." Despite Sam's egotistical statements, he consistently sought confirmation. For instance, in "The Bar Manager, The Shrink, His Wife, and Her Lover," when Sam thought Rebecca had slept with Frasier, he asked, "So who's better? Me or Frasier?" Disclosing that sex is a major component to his life, Sam sees himself as a highly desirable sexual demigod; however, he simultaneously seeks reinforcement of his machismo to ensure that others view him as he views himself.

A very obvious double standard exists in that, ironically, Sam's self-reported sexual activity, his narcissistic attitude, and others' acknowledgment of his sexual behaviors were not acceptable actions for his friends and customers in the bar. He often flaunted his sexual exploits to the others; however, as he explained to Paul, other people should not behave in this manner. Specifically, during a conversation with Paul in "It's Lonely on the Top," Sam requested that Paul not reveal his sexual exploits with Carla to everyone in the bar, reminding Paul that "a gentleman does not kiss and tell." Paul pointed out the contradiction and responded, "You do, Sam." To which Sam replied, "I'm Sam Malone—by definition, everything I do is cool." Sam's contradictory messages imply that for those with power and status (being a small business owner and ex-professional athlete), it is acceptable to act the part of the "babe hound."

As the bar's owner, Sam set the rules and everyone obeyed. This is true for Carla as well—that is, as his employee and as a woman, she must follow Sam's policies. Further, even though she had a sexual encounter with Paul, she was embarrassed and ashamed. This not only contradicts the earlier examples of her boastful nature but also presents a double standard that Sam can create rules of sexual conduct that he may break. Another observation is that Sam never displayed regret or remorse after engaging in sexual pleasure; however, Carla was not pleased to learn that Paul had been her partner the previous night. Viewers can easily interpret the message that oversexed working-class women, such as Carla, lose control of their sexual desires, bedding down with whoever is convenient. Male hero figures such as Sam, on the other hand, are always in control of their accelerated libido, selectively choosing the most attractive women, and gleam with pride for their sexual conquests and deserve respect and admiration.

While both Sam and Carla were the most sexually active characters, their relational commitments were lacking. Understanding their fidelity provides additional insight and clarification in terms of their sexual portrayal, embodiment, and values. Even though Carla had an ongoing sexual relationship with John Hill during the final season, it was not monogamous. When she refused to visit Hill in the hospital after his heart attack, Frasier asked, "You've been seeing this man for over a year now. Don't you have feelings for him?" Carla's response—"I can't get attached to some guy just because I split the sheets with him"[41]—indicated that she did not value commitment with her sexual mates. When she did finally visit him in the hospital, Hill formally stated, "Frankly, Ms. Tortelli, I don't know why you're here. My doctor informs me I have to remain celibate for the next eight weeks." Carla said, "Don't insult me, Hill. You think that sex is all I have on my mind? I have other facets to my personality." Then she questioned, "Eight weeks?" After the couple attempted a conversation and failed, Carla said, "See you in eight weeks." Hill rejoined, "Make it four." Carla asserted, "Make it two," to which Hill responded, "Pull the curtains," indicating that they would risk his health and have sex immediately. Later in the season viewers were reminded that Carla was seeing Hill when she commented that it would be easy to get Melville's Restaurant as a reception hall for her daughter's wedding because she was "boinking the owner."[42] This illustrates that she did not particularly value the sanctity of intimacy but rather could use sex for material gain and favors.

Carla also had several other sexual relationships while she dated Hill. She admitted in "It's Lonely on the Top," after a night of heavy drinking, that she could not remember whom she had slept with—"I think I went home with a guy. A *Cheers* guy. Oh, Sammy, Sammy, please tell me it was you"— and concluded, "I'm now officially a slut." Additionally, Carla informed the audience of her promiscuous tendencies in "The Guy Can't Help It" when Carla rejected Sam for a hypothetical marriage. Disgruntled, Sam questioned, "I thought we had something special going on between us." Carla's response was, "Definitely we do. I just always thought that I'd be the woman you cheated on your wife with." Carla's willingness to engage in sex with a married man lets the audience view her as a promiscuous slut who uses men for her own selfish reasons.

Sam was even more promiscuous than Carla. He was not selective in the women he dated except that his only criterion was their physical attractiveness. At times he dated women he was not interested in just to prove a point or make someone jealous. For example, Sam once dated Hill's daughter only because he knew that Mr. Hill would not approve. In "Love Me, Love My Car" Sam dated Susan a couple times because her late husband had bought Sam's Corvette and Sam was plotting to buy it back from her. As he discussed his intent to the *Cheers* patrons, he said, "That lady right there, that's the widow. So I figure what, you know, I just take her out to dinner a few times, let her get to know me, you know, pour on the charm and then boom! I lowball her." After Sam and Susan dated for two weeks, Sam informed the *Cheers* regulars, "The funny thing about it is the more we talk, the more she likes me. The more she likes me, the more she trusts me. The more she trusts me, the closer I get to snaggin' that car." When she realized his intentions, she angrily gave him the car for nothing and walked out of the bar. Like

Carla, Sam is equally willing to use his sexuality to acquire material possessions. This example clearly shows that sex is a means to an end for these characters and suggests that sex is commodified. Certainly, this view of sex contradicts the serious public health messages concerning safe sex. Furthermore, *Cheers'* portrayal of sexual attitudes challenges religious and cultural values inherent in American society.

Sam's sexual activity dominated his life. For example, in "The Last Picture Show" a gentleman walked into the bar and asked Sam, "Do you know me?" Sam responded, "No, but I never touched your daughter." After they chatted for a bit, they realized that Sam had indeed gone out with the man's daughter. Sam's promiscuity was also affirmed in "The Guy Can't Help It" episode. After Rebecca sarcastically told Sam, "All you want is sex and you think you'll make some woman feel special," Sam joined a therapy group for sexual compulsives. However, his incorruptibility was affirmed when he asked a woman for a date after she disclosed her unusual sexual desires to the group. In this example, obviously Sam was not concerned about how others perceived his problem; Rebecca, Carla, and Frasier have all suggested that he ought to reduce his sexual prowess. He ultimately ignored their criticism. Indeed, he found a way to use their perception of his sexual addiction to obtain more sexual gratification via his sex therapy group.

The discourse of sex in the final season of *Cheers* illustrates two sexually active characters who use sex to feed their egos, gratify their desires, and gain material possessions. However, an initial examination of sexual activity level and relational fidelity as one coded set of signs reveals that a discrepancy exists between the characters' class and gender. While class and gender do not discriminate between the quantity of sexual encounters and lack of monogamy, Sam, the bar's owner, sets the rules of conduct and clearly creates a different set of standards for himself. The double standards emerge as their exploits are coded: Carla negatively and Sam positively. Both characters boast of their sexual exploits, to a point. That is, Carla becomes embarrassed one time when she cannot remember with whom she had spent the evening. Upon learning it was a *Cheers* patron, she is embarrassed it was Paul rather than Sam. Sam, on the other hand, never regrets his sexual liaisons. In fact, others laud his sexual conquests based on the women's appearance, thus reinforcing the view of sex as male sport. Sam is honored for his sexual reputation, while Carla is ridiculed for her sexual encounters.

Sexual Practices

A second dimension of the discourse of sex in *Cheers* concerns the characters' casual sexual practices. This encompasses any reference to safe sex, including the use of condoms, birth control, or abstinence. Although the mention of safe sex occurred during the 1992–1993 season, safe sex was not seriously addressed by any of the characters. Clearly neither Sam nor Carla was abstinent. Thus, with the serious health messages prevalent throughout the 1980s and 1990s, their practices are inconsistent with the news, public service announcements, and other vital public messages concerning healthy and safe sexual activity.

During the last season, Sam did not make any personal references concerning the use of condoms. Further, his nonchalant attitudes concerning sex could lead viewers to believe that safe sex was not his concern. Moreover, Sam did not follow any religious beliefs or marital vows to dictate his sexual choices and practices.

Carla clearly did not engage in protected sex. When Diane returned during the season finale and discovered Carla had birthed children since her departure, she exclaimed, "Good God! You breed like a fly!"[43] Over the course of *Cheers'* eleven seasons, Carla had eight children. This serves as evidence that she did not regularly engage in protected sex. Since Carla was a practicing Catholic, her religious beliefs prohibited her from using any form of birth control. Although Carla observed the Catholic doctrine of shunning birth control, she conveniently neglected the Catholic Church's appeal to engage in monogamous sex within the bounds of marriage. She also encouraged this behavior in her daughter Sarafina. In the "Loathe and Marriage" episode, when Sarafina disclosed that she was pregnant with an unplanned child, Carla responded, "So do you know who the father is?" Sarafina answered, "Yes," to which Carla exclaimed, "Oh, I'm so proud of you!" This light-hearted response serves as an example of how *Cheers* encouraged casual sexual activity. This message directly contradicts the serious health-related messages prevalent in the 1980s and 1990s. By displaying a sense of pride in knowing the father of a child that is the result of casual sex, the sitcom explicitly made light of the issues of unprotected sex and abstinence. The characters might as well have also rejoiced over Sarafina's not contracting STDs or AIDS despite unprotected casual sex.

Identifying the two characters' attitudes about safe sex is an additional step in understanding *Cheers'* discourse of sex. It further illustrates the class and gender differences in this popular television series. Specifically, although neither Carla nor Sam engaged in protected sex, Carla had to deal with the consequences of pregnancy. Sam, on the other hand, never fathered any children. As a woman, Carla endured sixty-three months of pregnancy (she had twins once). This represents 48 percent of the eleven years the series originally aired. Further, as a working-class person, Carla had to work continually to support her children and provide the basic necessities for living. Sam, however, never appeared concerned with the possibility of impregnating anyone and thus maintained his financial status and independence. Consequently, double standards were prevalent in *Cheers*. While the two characters both engaged in promiscuous sexual activity, the blue-collar woman was penalized, while the somewhat higher-class man was valorized. The consequence of virtually the same action varied and therefore perpetuated the dominant patriarchal and classist hegemony. As Carla was punished (by bearing more children, adding to her financial burden and responsibilities), Sam was hailed as a champion of sexual sport and allowed to continue his quest to "bag as many babes" as possible.

Narrative Outcomes

A third dimension of the discourse of sex in *Cheers* entails the characters' narrative outcomes. Thus, to better understand how the comedy series presented this topic, it is important to examine the positive or negative consequences of the characters' actions. In light of the potentially detrimental results derived from the serious action of one's sexual activity, the narrative outcomes uphold or contradict societal messages about this topic.

In *Cheers,* Sam's overall narrative outcome was depicted positively by being applauded by his friends for his sexual conquests. He never contracted sexual transmitted diseases or fathered children. Although he was talked into going to the therapy group for sexual compulsives, he inappropriately used the encounter to meet women who were sexual compulsives. Some may argue that Sam's loneliness (never settling down with one woman) is considered a negative outcome; however, viewers learned in "One for the Road" that his one true love was the bar. Therefore, as long as he kept the bar he would never be lonely. Ultimately the character was depicted as the show's hero, and only positive outcomes prevailed.

Carla, on the other hand, was the character with the most negative outcome regarding her sexual behaviors. She was repeatedly pregnant through-out the series. The relationships she engaged ended negatively by contempo-rary standards and values. She and her first husband divorced, her second husband died, and other fathers of her children either abandoned the family or she refused their offers of marriage. Even her ongoing relationship with restaurateur John Hill was not portrayed positively. During sex in "Feelings . . . Whoa, Whoa, Whoa" he had a heart attack, and although he later re-covered, Carla explained to Sam that it was bad for her to show that she cared for John. This disclosure reveals that Carla did not want to become emotionally involved with her partner. Instead, she attempted to be more like Sam in a "love 'em and leave 'em" fashion. However, by denying her feelings, Carla continued to suffer sexual double standards. That is, by at-tempting to be like her counterpart, Sam, she was affirming his actions and empowering him as a role model for sexual behavior. By doing so, she con-tinually placed herself in an inferior position to Sam.

The juxtaposition of Sam's and Carla's narrative outcomes in terms of the discourse of sex parallels the other dimensions examined. It is no surprise that Sam's sexual activity was heroized, while Carla's was demonized. While neither contracted an STD, she gave birth to numerous children. Addition-ally, the terms "babe hound" for Sam versus "slut" for Carla provide a great contrast of perspective for the same actions. Ultimately, the narrative out-comes are very telling in understanding the discourse of sex in *Cheers*.

CONCLUSIONS

The dominant ideological message affirmed in the television series *Cheers* is that casual, unprotected, promiscuous, heterosexual sex is male sport. De-spite 1980s social concerns spurred from the onslaught of AIDS, sexually transmitted diseases, and unwanted pregnancies, this analysis finds that the text presents a different approach to sex. The discourse of sex on *Cheers* af-firmed attitudes, values, and practices directly contradictory to other health-related messages that permeated the 1980s and 1990s. The dominant official societal message during the 1980s was "just say no" to premarital and all nonmonogamous unprotected sex; however, the dominant discourse of sex on *Cheers* was negative and unhealthy overall.

Two major characters, Sam Malone and Carla Tortelli-LeBec, predomi-nantly portrayed this unhealthy and unsafe message. It is through these characters that the discourse of sex is actualized. That is, through its discourse of sex, including sexual activity level, relational fidelity, sexual practices, and narrative outcomes, millions of viewers witness unsafe sexual behaviors that are reinforced throughout the show's 275 episodes. In addition to the dominant ideological position toward sex that *Cheers* purported, the series depicted double standards in terms of class and gender.

Sam, for instance, was presented as a sleazy, promiscuous, aggressive, exhibitionistic narcissist who never suffered as a result of his unsafe sexual activity. He was presented as the "hero" of the macho sex game and was rewarded for his sexual indulgences. Carla, on the other hand, was repeatedly punished for virtually the same values, behaviors, and attitudes.

Greenberg's drench hypothesis suggests that one very popular, long-running series may have a far greater impact on viewers than many short-term series, because over time the series "drenches" audience members with its portrayals.[44] The potential power of the sexual behaviors endorsed and tolerated on *Cheers* for eleven network broadcast years, plus its continuation in syndication, contradicted serious social public health concerns and messages of the 1980s and early 1990s. The ideological position that *Cheers* affirmed was that white-collar male heterosexuals need not be concerned about their hedonistic practices, while working-class heterosexual women will generate negative associations and repeated pregnancies due to the same actions.

Although its producer, Tim Berry, asserted that *Cheers* was not an issues show,[45] for eleven years the popular series conveyed messages about the social issue of sexual behavior, and Greenberg's drench hypothesis suggests that the impact on viewers may have been substantial. Berry argues both that the production staff was concerned with social concerns and that it was not *Cheers'* place to tackle them. He added that *Cheers* had produced an episode on AIDS, but that when they found it simply was not funny they decided not to air it. This indicated, he claimed, that although the production staff agreed that AIDS was an important social topic, it did not fit within the conventions of the situation comedy.

Despite Berry's claims that situation comedy is no place for serious social concerns, other popular situation comedies have tackled serious topics. For example, in 1992–1993 *Roseanne* featured an episode dealing seriously with birth control, an episode of *Designing Women* debated the issue of sexual harassment in light of the Clarence Thomas Supreme Court nomination hearings, and an episode of *Seinfeld* made light of the socially taboo topic of masturbation. These situation comedies were popular and considered funny; yet, unlike *Cheers*, they managed to address serious sexual topics within their overall comedic frame. Precisely because *Cheers* was a very popular and long-running series, it would have been an ideal forum within which to address serious issues concerning sexual practices.

NOTES

1. E. J. Roberts, "Television and Sexual Learning in Childhood," in *National Institute of Mental Health Television and Behavior: Ten Years of Scientific Progress and Implications for the 80s,* vol. 2, *Technical Reviews,* ed. D. Pearl, L. Bouthilet, and J. Lazar (Washington, DC: U.S. Government Printing Office, 1982), 209–23.

2. "AIDS Getting Bulk of Health Coverage," *Sacramento Bee,* June 17, 1992, Scene section, 5.

3. "Huge Increase in AIDS Feared: Study of 25 Million Cases," *Sacramento Bee,* June 4, 1992, A1.

4. Jane Adams, "The Lie about AIDS: Only Bad People Can Get It," *Sacramento Bee,* October 25, 1992, D4.

5. Caroline Bradbeer, "HIV and Sexual Lifestyle," *British Medical Journal* 294 (1987): 5–6.

6. Masako Ishii-Kuntz, Les B. Whitbeck, and Ronald L. Simmons, "AIDS and Perceived Change in Sexual Practice: An Analysis of a College Student Sample from California to Iowa," *Journal of Applied Social Psychology* 20 (1990): 1301–21.

7. "CDC Reports 200,000 Cases of AIDS in U.S.," *Grass Valley [California] Union,* January 17, 1992, B1.

8. "AIDS Rate in Women Rising Rapidly: Females May Soon Be Primary Victims," *Sacramento Bee,* July 21, 1992, A1, 10.

9. Ibid., A1.

10. Department of Health and Human Services, *Sexually Transmitted Disease Surveillance* (Atlanta, GA: Centers for Disease Control and Prevention, 1990), Appendix.

11. Jane Gross, "Suffering in Silence No More: Fighting Sexual Harassment," *New York Times,* July 13, 1992, A1, D10; Jill Nelson, "Anita Hill: No Regrets," *Essence,* March 1992, 116.

12. Ever since the introduction of television, prime-time network broadcasts increasingly push the envelope regarding acceptable standards of sex, nudity, and innuendo. Indeed, the explicit portrayals of intimacy are a far cry from Rob and Laura Petrie's (*The Dick Van Dyke Show*) separate beds or the concern of whether to show Lucille Ricardo (*I Love Lucy*) pregnant, which implied she had sex with husband, Ricky.

13. *Facts on File* (New York: Facts on File, 1991).

14. Matt Roush, "A Farewell Toast to 'Cheers,'" *USA Today*, May 20, 1993, D1–2.

15. Thomas O'Neil, *The Emmys: Star Wars, Showdowns, and the Supreme Test of TV's Best* (New York: Penguin Books, 1992).

16. S. Galloway, "The Gang at Cheers Toast Their Most Memorable Moments," *TV Guide*, November 3–9, 1990, 20–25.

17. Tom Gliatto, "The Taproom That Inspired Cheers Tries to Change Its Name, Until Barflies Cry, 'Bull—& Finch!'" *People Weekly*, November 12, 1990, 81–82.

18. These relationships are not unique to television sitcoms but also appear in classical and Restoration comedies in television and film.

19. Carlos F. Fernandez-Collado, Bradley S. Greenberg, Filipe Korzenny, and Charles K. Atkin, "Sexual Intimacy and Drug Use in TV Series," *Journal of Communication* 28, no. 3 (1978): 30–37; Bradley S. Greenberg and Dave D'Alessio, "Quantity and Quality of Sex in the Soaps," *Journal of Broadcasting and Electronic Media* 29 (1985): 309–21; Bradley S. Greenberg, Carlos Fernandez-Collado, David Graef, Filipe Korzenny, and Charles K. Atkin, "Trends in Use of Alcohol and Other Substances on Television," in *Life on Television: Content Analyses of U.S. TV Drama,* ed. B. S. Greenberg (Norwood, NJ: Ablex, 1980), 137–46; Dennis T. Lowry, Gail Love, and Malcolm Kirby, "Sex on the Soap Operas: Patterns of Intimacy," *Journal of Communication* 31, no. 3 (1981): 90–96; Barry S. Sapolsky, "Sexual Acts and References on Prime-Time TV: A Two-Year Look," *Southern Speech Communication Journal* 47 (1982): 212–26; Barry S. Sapolsky and Joseph O. Tarbarlet, "Sex in Prime Time Television: 1978 Versus 1989," *Journal of Broadcasting and Electronic Media* 35 (1991): 505–16; Teresa L. Silverman, Joyce N. Sprafkin, and Eli A. Rubinstein, "Physical Contact and Sexual Behavior on Prime-Time TV," *Journal of Communication* 29, no. 1 (1979): 33–43.

20. Susan Franzblau, Joyce Sprafkin, and Eli Rubinstein, "Sex on TV: A Content Analysis," *Journal of Communication* 27, no. 2 (1977): 164–70; Bradley S. Greenberg, Robert Ableman, and Kimberly Neuendorf, "Sex on the Soap Operas: Afternoon Delight," *Journal of Communication* 31, no. 3 (1981): 83–89; Joyce N. Sprafkin and Teresa L. Silverman, "Update: Physically Intimate and Sexual Behavior on Prime-Time Television, 1978–1979," *Journal of Communication* 31, no. 1 (1981): 34–40.

21. Eleanor Blau, "Study Finds Barrage of Sex and TV," *New York Times,* January 27, 1988, C26; Mary Cassata and Thomas Skill, "Exploring Sex on Television: A Qualitative Study of Interpersonal Behaviors," in *Life on Daytime Television: Tuning in American Serial Drama* (Norwood, NJ: Ablex, 1983), 71–82; Dennis T. Lowry and David E. Towles, "Soap Opera Portrayals of Sex, Contraception, and Sexually Transmitted Diseases," *Journal of Communication* 39, no. 2 (1989): 76–83.

22. Daniel C. Bello, Robert E. Pitts, and Michael J. Etzel, "The Communication Effects of Controversial Sexual Content in Television Programs and Commercials," *Journal of Advertising* 12 (1983): 32–42; Jane D. Brown and Susan F. Newcomer, "Television Viewing and Adolescents' Sexual Behavior," *Journal of Homosexuality* 21 (1991): 77–91;

John A. Courtright and Stanley J. Baran, "Acquisition of Sexual Information by Young People," *Journalism Quarterly* 57 (1980): 107–14; Christine L. Nystrom, "What Television Teaches about Sex," *Educational Leadership* 40 (1983): 20–24.

23. E. J. Roberts, "Television," 222.

24. Lowry and Towles, "Soap Opera."

25. Courtright and Baran, "Acquisition," 113.

26. Nystrom, "What Television," 24.

27. Brown and Newcomer, "Television Viewing," 77.

28. Arthur Asa Berger, "'He's Everything You're Not . . .': A Semiological Analysis of *Cheers*," in *Television Studies: Textual Analysis*, ed. Gary Burns and Robert J. Thompson (New York: Praeger, 1982) 89–102; Caren J. Deming and Mercilee M. Jenkins, "Bar Talk: Gender Discourse in *Cheers*," in *Television Criticism: Approaches and Applications*, eds. Leah Vande Berg and Lawrence Wenner (White Plains, NY: Longman, 1991), 47–57; Heather Hundley, "The Naturalization of Beer in *Cheers*," *Journal of Broadcasting and Electronic Media* 39 (1995): 350–59.

29. Bradley S. Greenberg, "Some Uncommon Television Images and the Drench Hypothesis," in *Television as a Social Issue: Applied Social Psychology Annual* 8, ed. Stuart Oscamp (Beverly Hills: Sage, 1988), 88–102.

30. M. S. Piccirillo, "On the Authenticity of Televised Experience: A Critical Exploration of Parasocial Closure," *Critical Studies in Mass Communication* 3 (1986): 337–55.

31. John Fiske, "Popularity and Ideology: A Structuralist Reading of Dr. Who," in *Interpreting Television: Current Research Perspectives*, ed. Willard D. Rowland Jr. and Bruce Watkins (Beverly Hills: Sage, 1984), 165–98.

32. Heather Hundley, "Sex and Suds: The Discourse of Sex and Alcohol in *Cheers*" (master's thesis, California State University, Sacramento, 1992).

33. *Cheers*, "Feelings . . . Whoa, Whoa, Whoa," December 3, 1992.

34. *Cheers*, "The Guy Can't Help It," May 13, 1993.

35. *Cheers*, "Norm's Big Audit," January 14, 1993.

36. *Cheers*, "It's Lonely on the Top," April 29, 1993.

37. Ibid.

38. *Cheers*, "One for the Road," May 20, 1993.

39. *Cheers*, "Do Not Forsake Me, 'O My Postman," October 20, 1992.

40. *Cheers*, "The Guy Can't Help It," May 13, 1993.

41. *Cheers*, "Feelings . . . Whoa, Whoa, Whoa," December 3, 1992.

42. *Cheers*, "Loathe and Marriage," February 4, 1993.

43. *Cheers*, "One for the Road," May 20, 1993.

44. Greenberg, "Some Uncommon Television Images."

45. Tim Berry, interview by author, Burbank, CA, November 17, 1992.

Appendix 1
Monitor's Broadcast Schedule

Aggregate Programming Breakdown, 1955

	Stations 5,000 watts or more	Stations under 5,000 watts
Record shows	42%	53%
Network shows	30%	20%
News, weather	10%	8%
Station shows	6%	5%
Syndicated, transcribed shows	4%	4%
Local sports	3%	3%
All other	5%	7%

(Source: *Billboard* 67, no. 42, October 15, 1955.)

MONITOR'S BROADCAST SCHEDULE, 1955

Saturday, December 17

Highlights include live reports from a children's Christmas party in Milwaukee at 11:30 A.M.; sporting events on the playing fields of Eton at 1:30 P.M.; a look at atomic medicine from San Francisco at 1:30 and 2:30 P.M.; a look at the workings of the FBI in Washington, D.C., at 4 P.M.; a talk on the operations of CARE by Ambassador Clare Booth Luce at 7:30 P.M.; the Grand Ole Opry live from Nashville at 9:30 P.M.; and much more (all times Eastern). Guests include Frank Sinatra, Marlon Brando, Joan Crawford, Katy Randolph, Richard Boone, Dorothy Dandridge, and many others. Bob and Ray provide live comedy routines, and Miss Monitor gives weather forecasts from around the country and the world. Plus news, weather, sports, comedy, music, special features, interviews, and remote pick-ups from all parts of the world throughout the weekend.

Sunday, December 18

Highlights include reports on Vice President Nixon's plea for aid to Europe's needy, through gifts to CARE at 2:30 P.M.; Christmas messages from American servicemen at 3:30, 7:30 and 9:30 P.M.; the International Children's Christmas party in Washington, D.C., at 6:30 P.M.; the story of New Orleans' oldest jazz band at 7 P.M.; a native jam session from Pakistan at 8:30 P.M.; an illustration of life-saving operations from the St. Bernard Hospice in Switzerland at 10 P.M.; and much more (all times Eastern). Guests include Katherine Dunham, Carmen Amaya, Morton Kahn, George Bailey, and many others. Bob and Ray provide live comedy routines, and Miss Monitor gives weather forecasts from around the country and the world. Plus news, weather, sports, comedy, music, special features, interviews, and remote pick-ups from all parts of the world.

(Source: "On Radio," *New York Times,* December 17, 1955, pg. 41; "On Radio," *New York Times,* December 18, 1955, Section 2, pg. 12x. Originally accessed through http://www.monitorbeacon.com/thisweekend.html on December 10, 2001.)

Appendix 2
Cop Rock Episodes

"COP ROCK" (09/26/90)

A crack-house raid yields a young mother, Patricia Spence, who, after being befriended by Officer Vicki Quinn, sells her baby for drug money. Tyrone Weeks, a pusher apprehended at the bust, is released due to overcrowded jails. He kills a cop, leading to an explosive confrontation with maverick detective Vincent LaRusso. Captain Hollander questions LaRusso's tactics. The mayor and chief of police square off over funding for new jails. Quinn's partner, Andy Campo, has a crush on her even though she is married to an older forensics specialist, Ralph Ruskin.

"ILL-GOTTEN GAINES" (10/03/90)

The suspicious death of drug dealer Tyrone Weeks sparks outrage in the black community. Hollander intensifies his investigation, focusing on LaRusso's account of the incident and the forensics report. Several cops are unhappy with their partners. The squad covers a break-in at the home of an affluent couple.

"HAPPY MUDDER'S DAY" (10/10/90)

LaRusso's partner, Detective Donnie Potts, is pressured to come clean on LaRusso's role in Weeks's death. When he and LaRusso are taken off their drug case, LaRusso uses his mud-wrestling girlfriend to set up a bust. Mayor Plank undergoes plastic surgery to improve her political profile.

"A THREE-CORPSE MEAL" (10/17/90)

LaRusso is charged with murder. Officers Quinn and Campo pose as parents to break up the baby-selling ring that bought Patricia Spence's infant. Chief Kendrick takes the mayor on a date.

"THE COCAINE MUTINY" (10/24/90)

Detective McIntyre becomes a fan of an actress seeking protection from an obsessive admirer. Captain Hollander confronts Chief Kendrick when cocaine charges against a councilman's assistant are dropped. LaRusso is attracted to his attorney. Patricia makes an emotional appeal to get her baby back.

"OIL OF OL' LAY" (10/31/90)

Ruskin is jealous of the patrol partnership of his wife, Quinn, and the lovesick Campo. LaRusso's defense attorney plans to make LaRusso into a heroic figure. Gaines helps a homeless man. The romance between the chief and the mayor continues.

"COP-A-FELLIAC" (11/07/90)

Ruskin's jealousy intensifies as he follows Quinn and Campo. Potts receives threats for "betraying" his brothers in blue. A gay journalist threatens to "out" the mayor's assistant. (James Sikking reprises his *Hill Street Blues* SWAT commander character, Lt. Howard Hunter, in an uncredited cameo.)

"POTTS DON'T FAIL ME NOW" (11/21/90)

Rose pushes a bigoted detective to follow up on the shooting of a black youth. Potts has second thoughts about testifying in the LaRusso trial. The chief goes on the offensive against the press. (Jimmy Smits and Michele Greene crossover their *L.A. Law* characters, Victor Sifuentes and Abby Perkins, in uncredited cameos.)

"MARITAL BLITZ" (12/05/90)

LaRusso's trial begins. Quinn and Campo clash with their new partners. Chief Kendrick's conflict with the press continues.

"NO NOOSE IS GOOD NOOSE" (12/12/90)

LaRusso takes the stand as the case goes to jury. Quinn and Ruskin begin marriage counseling. Campo's new partner goes undercover as a prostitute. Chief Kendrick refutes accusations that he is racist.

"BANG THE POTTS SLOWLY" (12/26/90)

A blown bust forces the cops to be creative in catching a serial rapist. LaRusso returns to the squad room to Potts's dismay. Quinn reflects on the end of her marriage to Ruskin. The mayor renews her run for the Senate.

(Synopses written by George Plasketes.)

Appendix 3
Eleventh-Season *Cheers* Episodes

"THE LITTLE MATCH GIRL" (09/24/92)

As the gang migrates back to the bar after Woody and Kelly's wedding, Rebecca is depressed because she is unmarried and unhappy. She starts smoking again but vows to quit smoking and get her life in order. First, however, she must tell Sam that she burned down the bar with her last cigarette.

"THE BEER IS ALWAYS GREENER" (10/01/92)

While Sam is rebuilding Cheers after the fire, the gang heads over to a new watering hole. The guys really like the place, and Carla even gets a temporary job there as a waitress. They like it so much that Sam can't drag them back for Cheers' grand reopening. Meanwhile, it's not quite marital bliss for Woody and Kelly as they discover a religious difference that threatens their marriage.

"THE KING OF BEERS" (10/08/92)

When a marketing analyst for a beer company comes into Cheers, Norm brushes him off until he realizes who he is. Norm is chosen to taste a few beers, and he does so well that he's hired on as the official beer taster. Also, the bar is mistakenly delivered a slot machine and Rebecca plays it until she wins.

"THE MAGNIFICENT SIX" (10/22/92)

Henri is back; this time he's jobless and looking to stay that way in order to keep his unemployment insurance. Unfortunately for him, Sam hires him to sub for the honeymooning Woody. While at Cheers, the young Frenchman shows his expertise with women and the gang encourages Sam to join Henri in a phone-number-getting contest. Meanwhile, Rebecca has fallen off the no-smoking wagon, so Sam enrolls her in an addiction clinic.

"DO NOT FORSAKE ME, 'O MY POSTMAN" (10/29/92)

Cliff's "girlfriend" Margaret O'Keefe is back—but in the family way. As the gang congratulates Cliff on his impending parenthood, Margaret confides in him that the baby isn't his, but Cliff still vows to marry her and raise the child as his own. Meanwhile, Rebecca hires a less-than-competent jingle writer to advertise the bar.

"TEACHING WITH THE ENEMY, PART 1" (11/05/92)

When Rebecca sees Lilith passionately kissing a man outside Cheers, Rebecca assumes it was Frasier. To her surprise, it turns out to be Lilith's coworker, Dr. Louis Pascal. While Rebecca tries to keep from telling the gang, Lilith tells Frasier about her affair. She tells him it was a one-time fling and that it's over between her and Dr. Pascal. Meanwhile, a new type of clientele forces Sam to get a bouncer for the bar.

"THE GIRL IN THE PLASTIC BUBBLE, PART 2" (11/12/92)

Even though Lilith told Frasier that she was ending her affair with Dr. Pascal, she changes her mind and decides to spend a year with him sealed in an underground eco-pod. This doesn't sit well with Frasier, and it sends him to the edge . . . the edge of a window above Cheers from which he intends to throw himself to his death.

"ILL-GOTTEN GAINES" (11/17/92)

Woody, tired of being run over by his father-in-law, decides to tell Mr. Gaines to quit running his life. Woody accidentally sees Mr. Gaines in the middle of "an affair," so Mr. Gaines agrees to all of Woody's requests. Meanwhile, Rebecca decides to cook a Thanksgiving dinner and invites the gang. It turns out to be bigger than planned, so she moves it to the bar.

"FEELINGS . . . WHOA, WHOA, WHOA" (12/03/92)

The gang is surprised to learn that John Allen Hill is in the hospital after suffering from a heart attack. They are even more surprised to learn that Carla hasn't visited Hill, her lover. She tells the gang (and herself) that she doesn't have strong feelings for him, but they all know better. In addition, Cliff believes Adolph Hitler is living in his apartment building.

"DADDY'S MIDDLE-AGED GIRL" (12/10/92)

Rebecca's father comes from San Diego to visit her. He's an admiral with the navy and doesn't approve of the way she's living her life. He is especially critical of her decision to have a baby with Sam. He decides that it would be best for her to come back to California with him, and she agrees. Also, Kelly balks at moving into Woody's Chinatown apartment.

"LOVE ME, LOVE MY CAR" (12/17/92)

Now that the bar has been rebuilt after the fire and is somewhat profitable, Sam thinks about getting his car back. He learns that the guy he sold the car to died, so Sam moves in on the guy's schoolteacher widow. Meanwhile, Woody's mother has sent a pig to him, but his dinner plans are interrupted by Rebecca, who adopts the swine.

"SUNDAY DINNER" (01/07/93)

After his separation from Lilith, the gang tries to get Frasier to cheer up by encouraging him to date. When his new secretary makes it clear that she likes him, he asks her out, despite their age difference. She invites him to dinner at her house, but instead of a quiet, intimate dinner with her, it turns into a family affair with her parents and brother—and her boyfriend. Meanwhile, Cliff has bought a camcorder, and to pay for it he is hired to tape a family reunion.

"NORM'S BIG AUDIT" (01/14/93)

As an accountant, Norm had to help many clients through the terrible trauma of being audited. Now it's his turn. He hopes that he can reason with the IRS person, but it turns out to be a hard-nosed, no-nonsense woman who sees through all of his ploys. As a last resort, he makes a pass at her, which she accepts. Meanwhile, the gang has learned that an old Red Sox game is scheduled to be replayed, and when Sam remembers that he didn't do so well, he schemes to keep them from seeing it.

"IT'S A MAD, MAD, MAD, MAD BAR" (01/21/93)

Robin Colcord is back, but instead of the multibillion-dollar tycoon he once was, he's now a pauper. Rebecca falls for him again, thinking that his miserly appearance is a test of her—to see if she really loves him or his money. While in Cheers, Robin makes a few comments about hiding another money belt somewhere in the bar, sending the gang into a treasure-finding frenzy.

"LOATHE AND MARRIAGE" (02/04/93)

When Carla finds out that her daughter Serafina is pregnant and engaged, she begins busily preparing for the wedding. She wants everything to be perfect, but when her ex-husband Nick Tortelli and his lovely wife, Loretta, show up for the nuptials, Carla fears everything will be ruined.

"IS THERE A DOCTOR IN THE HOWE?" (02/11/93)

Frasier is depressed when he gets a telegram from Lilith asking him to start divorce proceedings. Rebecca decides to throw him a "happy divorce" party to cheer him up. At the party, Woody has a little too much to drink and turns into a mean drunk. After the party, Rebecca drives Frasier home. One thing leads to another, and before long they decide to sleep together. Things don't go as planned, for as soon as they're in bed, they're interrupted—first by the gang, and then by Lilith.

"THE BAR MANAGER, THE SHRINK, HIS WIFE, AND HER LOVER" (02/18/93)

After leaving the eco-pod and her lover, Dr. Louis Pascal, Lilith is back and wants to resurrect her marriage to Frasier. He's not sure if he wants to take her back, but Dr. Pascal is sure *he* wants Lilith back. To prove his point, he pulls a gun.

"THE LAST PICTURE SHOW" (02/25/93)

The gang learns that the Twi-Lite drive-in is closing. It's the spot where Norm proposed to Vera, Carla saw a lot of action (on- and off-screen), and Cliff went to movies with his mother. To bring back the memories one last time, Cliff borrows his mom's convertible, and they're off to the movies. Meanwhile, back at the bar, Sam lets the previous owner, Gus, behind the bar to serve a few up like the old days. Gus takes things a little too seriously, and Sam, Rebecca, and Carla mutiny.

"BAR WARS VII: THE NAKED PREY" (03/18/93)

It's St. Patrick's Day, and that means the yearly contest with Gary's Olde Towne Tavern to see which bar makes more money. Cheers suffers a humiliating defeat, and as a last resort, they look to Harry the Hat to exact revenge on Gary.

"LOOK BEFORE YOU SLEEP" (04/01/93)

Sam's apartment building is scheduled for fumigation, so he plans on spending the night at a "friend's," but when she cancels on him and he accidentally locks himself out of the bar, he finds himself in need of a place to stay. After fending off Shriners, he ends up at Cliff's.

"WOODY GETS AN ELECTION" (04/22/93)

The gang at Cheers is treated to a campaign visit from their city councilman. Frasier, turned off by the man's insincerity, berates all politicians and vows that even Woody could get 10 percent of the vote. The gang doesn't believe him, so to prove his point, he gets Woody on the ballot and starts campaigning. However, when Woody's opponent stumbles, Woody is poised for a win.

"IT'S LONELY ON THE TOP" (04/29/93)

With Woody about to become a Boston city councilman, Sam thinks about hiring his replacement. Carla volunteers, and after she begs Sam, he relents and lets her tend bar for an evening. The next morning, the whole gang has a hangover, especially Carla, who can't remember whom she slept with the night before.

"REBECCA GAINES, REBECCA LOSES" (05/06/93)

Rebecca is pleased to learn that she and Mr. Gaines have similar interests in classical music. She uses this to start up a conversation, and before long he has invited her to his house to hear some Mahler. She looks forward to the occasion, only to find out that he has intended for her to serve his guests. Meanwhile, the gang is convinced that Cliff has finally killed his mother.

"THE GUY CAN'T HELP IT" (05/13/93)

Sam, unhappy and scared that he won't ever find the right woman, decides to go into therapy. He attends a group session devoted to sexual compulsives to try and get a handle on his out-of-control skirt-chasing. Rebecca, tired of chasing rich, powerful men, starts dating a sweet, honest plumber.

"ONE FOR THE ROAD" (05/20/93)

The gang is stunned as they watch Diane receive an award for a screenplay she has written. To congratulate her, Sam sends her a telegram, and she calls back to thank him. They talk about their lives and lie to each other about having spouses and families. In a moment of weakness, however, Sam invites her back to Boston. Meanwhile, Rebecca is ecstatic when Don finally pops the question, but she finds it hard to say "yes," thinking that she can't possibly marry a plumber. Diane does return to Boston, with her alleged "husband," and has dinner with Sam and his "wife," Rebecca. The truth comes out, and it's not long before the passion between Sam and Diane is rekindled. Back at the bar, Sam informs the gang that he is going to California with Diane.

(Source: http://cheers.dhs.org/episodes/episodes.html)

Selected Bibliography

Adorno, Theodor W. "On Popular Music." In *On Record: Rock, Pop and the Written Word,* ed. Simon Frith and Andrew Goodwin. New York: Pantheon, 1990.

Aitken, Hugh. *Syntony and Spark.* New York: John Wiley, 1976.

Allen, Woody, Milos Forman, Sydney Pollack, Ginger Rogers, and Elliot Silverstein. "Colorization: The Arguments For." *Journal of Arts Management and Law* 17 (1987): 79–93.

Appleby, Joyce, Lynn Hunt, and Margaret Jacob. *Telling the Truth about History.* New York: W. W. Norton, 1994.

Bailey, Beth L. *From Front Porch to Back Seat: Courtship in Twentieth-Century America.* Baltimore: Johns Hopkins UP, 1988.

Barnouw, Erik. *A Tower in Babel: A History of Broadcasting in the United States.* Vol. 1 (*to 1933*). New York: Oxford UP, 1966.

———. *The Golden Web: A History of Broadcasting in the United States.* Vol. 2 (*1933 to 1953*). New York: Oxford UP, 1968.

———. *Tube of Plenty: The Evolution of American Television.* Oxford: Oxford UP, 1975.

Barzun, Jacques. *The Culture We Deserve.* Middletown, CT: Wesleyan UP, 1989.

Beard, Charles A. *The American Leviathan: The Republic in the Machine Age.* New York: Oxford UP, 1941.

Bello, Daniel C., Robert E. Pitts, and Michael J. Etzel. "The Communication Effects of Controversial Sexual Content in Television Programs and Commercials." *Journal of Advertising* 12 (1983): 32–42.

Benjamin, Louise. *Freedom of the Air and the Public Interest: First Amendment Rights in Broadcasting to 1935.* Carbondale: Southern Illinois UP, 2001.

Berger, Arthur Asa. "'He's Everything You're Not . . . ': A Semiological Analysis of *Cheers.*" In *Television Studies: Textual Analysis,* ed. Gary Burns and Robert J. Thompson. New York: Praeger, 1989.

Berkhofer, Robert, Jr. *Beyond the Great Story: History as Text and Discourse.* Cambridge, MA: Harvard UP, 1995.

Boddy, William. *Fifties Television: The Industry and Its Critics.* Urbana: Illinois UP, 1990.

Bradbeer, Caroline. "HIV and Sexual Lifestyle." *British Medical Journal* 294 (1987): 5–6.

Brannigan, John. "New Historicism." In *Literary Theories: A Reader and Guide,* ed. Julian Wolfreys. New York: New York UP, 1999.

Brooks, Tim, and Earle Marsh. *The Complete Directory to Prime Time Network TV Shows, 1946–Present,* 7th ed. New York: Ballantine, 1999.

Brown, Jane D., and Susan F. Newcomer. "Television Viewing and Adolescents' Sexual Behavior." *Journal of Homosexuality* 21 (1991): 77–91.

Buxton, William J., and Charles R. Acland. "Frank Stanton: Pioneer of Radio Research, An Interview." *Journal of Radio Studies* 7 (2000): 474–503.

Carey, James W. "The Problem of Journalism History." *Journalism History* 1 (1974): 3–5, 27.

———. *Communication as Culture: Essays on Media and Society.* Boston: Unwin Hyman, 1989.

Cassata, Mary, and Thomas Skill. "Exploring Sex on Television: A Qualitative Study of Interpersonal Behaviors." In *Life on Daytime Television: Tuning in American Serial Drama,* ed. Mary Cassata and Thomas Skill. Norwood, NJ: Ablex, 1983.

Courtright, John A., and Stanley J. Baran. "Acquisition of Sexual Information by Young People." *Journalism Quarterly* 57 (1980): 107–14.

Czitrom, Daniel. *Media and the American Mind: From Morse to McLuhan.* Chapel Hill: U of North Carolina P, 1982.

Dahlgren, Peter, and Colin Sparks. *Journalism and Popular Culture.* Newbury Park, CA: Sage, 1992.

Davis, Mike. *City of Quartz: Excavating the Future in Los Angeles.* New York: Vintage, 1990.

Dell, Chad. "Researching Historical Broadcast Audiences: Female Fandom of Professional Wrestling, 1945–60." PhD diss., U of Wisconsin–Madison, 1997.

Dellinger, J. H. "Analysis of Broadcasting Station Allocation," *Journal of the Institute of Radio Engineers* 16 (November 1928): 1477–85.

Deming, Caren J., and Mercilee M. Jenkins. "Bar Talk: Gender Discourse in *Cheers.*" In *Television Criticism: Approaches and Applications,* ed. Leah Vande Berg and Lawrence Wenner. New York: Longman, 1991.

Douglas, Susan J. *Inventing American Broadcasting, 1899–1922.* Baltimore, MD: Johns Hopkins UP, 1987.

———. "The Kids Take Over: Transistors, DJs, and Rock 'n' Roll." In *Listening In: Radio and the American Imagination: From Amos 'n' Andy and Edward R. Murrow to Wolfman Jack and Howard Stern,* ed. Susan J. Douglas. New York: Times Books, 1999.

Dunning, John. *On the Air: The Encyclopedia of Old-Time Radio.* New York: Oxford, 1998.

Eberly, Philip K. *Music in the Air: America's Changing Tastes in Popular Music, 1920–1980.* New York: Hastings House, 1982.

Edgerton, Gary. "'The Germans Wore Gray, You Wore Blue,' Frank Capra, Casablanca, and the Colorization Controversy of the 1980s." *Journal of Popular Film and Television* 27 (Winter 2000): 24–32.

Ennis, Philip H. *The Seventh Stream: The Emergence of Rocknroll in American Popular Music.* Hanover, NH: Wesleyan UP, 1982.

Ettema, James S., and D. Charles Whitney, eds. *Individuals in Mass Media Organizations: Creativity and Constraint.* Beverly Hills, CA: Sage, 1982.

Fernandez-Collado, Carlos F., Bradley S. Greenberg, Filipe Korzenny, and Charles K. Atkin. "Sexual Intimacy and Drug Use in TV Series." *Journal of Communication* 28 (1978): 30–37.

Fiske, John. "Popularity and Ideology: A Structuralist Reading of *Dr. Who.*" In *Interpreting Television: Current Research Perspectives,* ed. Willard D. Rowland Jr. and Bruce Watkins. Beverly Hills, CA: Sage, 1984.

Fornatale, Peter, and Joshua E. Mills. *Radio in the Television Age.* Woodstock, NY: Overlook Press, 1980.

Franzblau, Susan, Joyce Sprafkin, and Eli Rubinstein. "Sex on TV: A Content Analysis." *Journal of Communication* 27 (1977): 164–70.

Friedman, Sharon, Sharon Dunwoody, and Carol Rogers, eds. *Scientists and Journalists: Reporting Science as News.* New York: Free Press, 1986.

Fritzsche, Peter. *Reading Berlin 1900.* Cambridge: Harvard UP, 1996.

Frost, S. E. *Education's Own Stations: The History of Broadcast Licenses Issued to Educational Institutions.* New York: Arno Press, 1971.

Gallagher, Margaret. "Negotiation of Control in Media Organizations and Occupations." In *Culture, Society, and the Media,* ed. Michael Gurevitch, Tony Bennett, James Curran, and Janet Woollacott. London: Routledge, 1982.

Gems, Gerald R. *For Pride, Profit, and Patriarchy: Football and the Incorporation of American Cultural Values.* Lanham, MD: Scarecrow Press, 2000.

Gilderhaus, Mark T. *History and Historians: A Historiographical Introduction,* 2nd ed. Englewood Cliffs, NJ: Prentice Hall, 1992.

Goldlust, J. *Playing for Keeps: Sport, the Media, and Society.* Melbourne: Longman Cheshire, 1987.

Greenberg, Bradley S. "Some Uncommon Television Images and the Drench Hypothesis." In *Television as a Social Issue: Applied Social Psychology Annual 8,* ed. Stuart Oscamp. Beverly Hills, CA: Sage, 1988.

Greenberg, Bradley S., Robert Ableman, and Kimberly Neuendorf. "Sex on the Soap Operas: Afternoon Delight." *Journal of Communication* 31 (1981): 83–89.

Greenberg, Bradley S., and Dave D'Alessio. "Quantity and Quality of Sex in the Soaps." *Journal of Broadcasting and Electronic Media* 29 (1985): 309–21.

Greenberg, Bradley S., Carlos Fernandez-Collado, David Graef, Filipe Korzenny, and Charles K. Atkin. "Trends in Use of Alcohol and Other Substances on Television." In *Life on Television: Content Analyses of U.S. TV Drama,* ed. Bradley S. Greenberg. Norwood, NJ: Ablex, 1980.

Haralovich, Mary Beth. "Sitcoms and Suburbs." In *Private Screenings: Television and the Female Consumer,* ed. Lynn Spigel and Denise Mann. Minneapolis: U of Minnesota P, 1992.

Hardt, Hanno, and Matthew Killmeier. "Wireless Pleasure: Locating Radio in the American Home." In *In the Company of Media: Cultural Constructions of Communication, 1920s–1930s,* ed. Hanno Hardt. Boulder: Westview Press, 2000.

Hess, Gary N. *An Historical Study of the DuMont Television Network.* New York: Arno Press, 1979.

Hilmes, Michele. "Fanny Brice and the Schnooks Strategy." In *The Life of the Party: Comediennes in Hollywood,* ed. Kristine Brunovska Karnick. New York: New York UP, forthcoming.

———. *Only Connect: A Cultural History of Broadcasting in the United States.* Belmont, CA: Wadsworth, 2002.

———. *Radio Voices: American Broadcasting, 1922–1952.* Minneapolis: U of Minnesota P, 1997.

Hine, Thomas. *Populuxe.* New York: Knopf, 1986.

Hirsch, Paul. *The Structure of the Popular Music Industry: The Filtering Process by Which Records Are Preselected for Public Consumption.* Ann Arbor: University of Michigan Institute for Social Research, 1969.

Horkheimer, Max, and Theodor W. Adorno. *The Dialectic of Enlightenment,* trans. John Cumming. New York: Continuum, 1972.

Horwitz, Robert Britt. *The Irony of Regulatory Reform: The Deregulation of American Telecommunications.* New York: Oxford UP, 1989.

Hoyt, William Graves. *Lowell and Mars.* Tucson: U of Arizona P, 1976.

Hundley, Heather. "The Naturalization of Beer in *Cheers.*" *Journal of Broadcasting and Electronic Media* 39 (1995): 350–59.

———. "Sex and Suds: The Discourse of Sex and Alcohol in *Cheers.*" Master's thesis, California State University, Sacramento, 1992.

Innis, Harold. *The Bias of Communication.* Toronto: U of Toronto P, 1951.

Ishii-Kuntz, Masako, Les B. Whitbeck, and Ronald L. Simmons. "AIDS and Perceived Change in Sexual Practice: An Analysis of a College Student Sample from California to Iowa." *Journal of Applied Social Psychology* 20 (1990): 1301–21.

Jackson, Carlton. *Hattie: The Life of Hattie McDaniel.* Lanham, MD: Madison Books, 1990.

Jackson, Kenneth T. *The Crabgrass Frontier: The Suburbanization of the United States.* New York: Oxford UP, 1985.

Jasanoff, Sheila. *The Fifth Branch: Science Advisers as Policymakers.* Cambridge: Harvard UP, 1990.

Jome, Hiram L. *Economics of the Radio Industry,* Chicago: A. W. Shaw, reprinted by the Arno Press, New York, 1971.

Kalmus, Herbert T. "Technicolor Adventures in Cinemaland." *SMPTE Journal* 100 (March 1991): 182–90.

Kammen, Michael. *Selvages and Biases: The Fabric of History in American Culture.* Ithaca, NY: Cornell UP, 1987.

Kellner, Douglas. "Cultural Studies, Multiculturalism, and Media Culture." In *Gender, Race, and Class in Media: A Text-Reader,* ed. G. Dines and J. M. Humez. Thousand Oaks, CA: Sage, 1995.

Killmeier, Matthew A. "Voices between the Tracks: Disk Jockeys, Radio, and Popular Music, 1955–60." *Journal of Communication Inquiry* 25 (2001): 353–74.

Kohs, David J. "Paint Your Wagon—Please! Colorization, Copyright, and the Search for Moral Rights." *Federal Communications Law Journal* 40 (1988): 1–38.

Lawton, Sherman P. *The Modern Broadcaster: The Station Book.* New York: Harper & Bros., 1961.

Lewis, Tom. *Divided Highways: Building the Interstate Highways, Transforming American Life.* New York: Viking, 1997.

Lipsitz, George. *Rainbow at Midnight: Labor and Culture in the 1940s.* Urbana: U of Illinois P, 1994.

Lochte, Robert. "Invention and Innovation of Early Radio Technology." *Journal of Radio Studies* 7 (2000): 93–115.

Lowi, Theodore J. "Four Systems of Policy, Politics, and Choice." *Public Administration Review* (Summer 1972): 298–310.

———. *The End of Liberalism: The Second Republic of the United States,* 2nd ed. New York: Norton, 1979.

Lowry, Dennis T., Gail Love, and Malcolm Kirby. "Sex on the Soap Operas: Patterns of Intimacy." *Journal of Communication* 31 (1981): 90–96.

Lowry, Dennis T., and David E. Towles. "Soap Opera Portrayals of Sex, Contraception, and Sexually Transmitted Diseases." *Journal of Communication* 39 (1989): 76–83.

Marchand, Roland. "Visions of Classlessness, Quests for Dominion: American Popular Culture, 1945–1960." In *Reshaping America: Society and Institutions, 1945–1960,* ed. Robert H. Brenner and Gary W. Reichard. Columbus: Ohio State UP, 1982.

Marx, Karl. "The General Formula for Capital." In *The Marx-Engels Reader,* 2nd ed., ed. Robert C. Tucker. New York: W. W. Norton, 1978.

Mattelart, Armand. *The Invention of Communication,* trans. Susan Emanuel. Minneapolis: U of Minnesota P, 1996.

Matteson, Donald W. *The Auto Radio: A Romantic Genealogy.* Jackson, MI: Thornridge, 1987.

Mayer, R. L., R. Word, and B. Young. "Colorization: The Arguments For." *Journal of Arts Management and Law* 17 (1987): 64–78.

McChesney, Robert W. "Media Made Sport: A History of Sports Coverage in the United States." In *Media, Sports, and Society,* ed. L. A. Wenner. Newbury Park, CA: Sage, 1989.

———. *Telecommunications, Mass Media, and Democracy: The Battle for the Control of U.S. Broadcasting, 1928–1935.* Oxford: Oxford UP, 1993.

McMahon, A. Michal. *The Making of a Profession: A Century of Electrical Engineering in America.* New York: Institute of Electrical and Electronics Engineers, 1984.

Meehan, Eileen. "Why We Don't Count: The Commodity Audience." In *Logics of Television: Essays in Cultural Criticism,* ed. Patricia Mellencamp. Bloomington: Indiana UP, 1990.

Millard, Andre. *America on Record: A History of Recorded Sound.* Cambridge: Cambridge UP, 1995.

Miller, Douglas T., and Marion Nowak. *The Fifties: The Way We Really Were.* Garden City, NY: Doubleday, 1977.

Munslow, Alun. *Deconstructing History.* London: Routledge, 1997.

Nelkin, Dorothy. *Selling Science: How the Press Covers Science and Technology.* New York: W. H. Freeman, 1995.

Newman, Z. *The Impact of Southern Football.* Montgomery, AL: Morros-Bell, 1969.

Nystrom, Christine L. "What Television Teaches about Sex." *Educational Leadership* 40 (1983): 20–24.

Pfeffer, Jeffrey, and Gerald R. Salancik. *The External Control of Organizations: A Resource Dependence Perspective.* New York: Harper and Row, 1978.

Piccirillo, M. S. "On the Authenticity of Televised Experience: A Critical Exploration of Parasocial Closure." *Critical Studies in Mass Communication* 3 (1986): 337–55.

Powe, Lucas A., Jr. *American Broadcasting and the First Amendment.* Berkeley: U of California P, 1987.

Powers, Ron. *Supertube: The Rise of Television Sports.* New York: Coward-McCann, 1984.

Riesman, David. "Listening to Popular Music." In *Mass Culture: The Popular Arts in America,* ed. Bernard Rosenberg and David Manning White. Glencoe, IL: Free Press, 1950.

Roberts, E. J. "Television and Sexual Learning in Childhood." In *Television and Behavior: Ten Years of Scientific Progress and Implications for the Eighties.* Vol. 2, *Technical Reviews,* ed. D. Pearl, L. Bouthilet, and J. Lazar. Rockville, MD: National Institute of Mental Health, 1982.

Rogers, W. W., R. D. Ward, L. R. Atkins, and W. Flynt. *Alabama: The History of a Deep South State.* Tuscaloosa: U of Alabama P, 1994.

Rosen, Philip T. *The Modern Stentors: Radio Broadcasting and the Federal Government, 1920–1934.* Westport, CT: Greenwood Press, 1980.

Rosene, J. M. "The History of Radio Broadcasting at Auburn University." Master's thesis, Auburn University, 1968.

Rothenbuhler, Eric, and Tom McCourt. "Radio Redefines Itself, 1947–1962." In *The Radio Reader: Essays in the Cultural History of Radio,* ed. Michele Hilmes and Jason Loviglio. London: Routledge, 2002.

Sapolsky, Barry S. "Sexual Acts and References on Prime-Time TV: A Two-Year Look." *Southern Speech Communication Journal* 47 (1982): 212–26.

Sapolsky, Barry S., and Joseph O. Tarbarlet. "Sex in Prime Time Television: 1978 Versus 1989." *Journal of Broadcasting and Electronic Media* 35 (1991): 505–16.

Schiffer, Michael Brian. *The Portable Radio in American Life.* Tucson: U of Arizona P, 1991.

Seifer, Marc. *Wizard: The Life and Times of Nikola Tesla: Biography of a Genius.* Secaucus, NJ: Carol, 1996.

Sheehan, William. *Planets and Perception: Telescopic Views and Interpretations, 1609–1909.* Tucson: U of Arizona P, 1988.

Sherman, Barry L., and Joseph R. Dominick. "Perceptions of Colorization." *Journalism Quarterly* 65 (1988): 976–80.

Silverman, Teresa L., Joyce N. Sprafkin, and Eli A. Rubinstein. "Physical Contact and Sexual Behavior on Prime-Time TV." *Journal of Communication* 29 (1979): 33–43.

Slotten, Hugh Richard. *Radio and Television Regulation: Broadcast Technology in the United States, 1920–1960.* Baltimore, MD: Johns Hopkins UP, 2000.

Smulyan, Susan. *Selling Radio: The Commercialization of American Broadcasting, 1920–1934.* Washington, DC: Smithsonian Institution Press, 1994.

Sprafkin, Joyce N., and Teresa L. Silverman. "Update: Physically Intimate and Sexual Behavior on Prime-Time Television, 1978–1979." *Journal of Communication* 31 (1981): 34–40.

Spigel, Lynn. *Make Room for TV: Television and the Family Ideal in Postwar America.* Chicago: U of Chicago P, 1990.

———. *Welcome to the Dreamhouse: Popular Media and Postwar Suburbs.* Durham, NC: Duke UP, 2001.

Sterling, Christopher, and John Kittross. *Stay Tuned: A History of American Broadcasting,* 3rd ed. Mahwah, NJ: Lawrence Erlbaum, 2002.

Summers, Harrison B., ed. *A Thirty-Year History of Programs Carried on National Radio Networks in the United States, 1926–1956.* New York: Arno Press, 1971.

Susman, Warren I. *Culture as History: The Transformation of American Society in the Twentieth Century.* New York: Pantheon, 1984.

Towers, W. M. "'Gee Whiz!' and 'Aw Nuts!': Radio and Newspaper Coverage of Baseball in the 1920s." Unpublished paper presented at the 62nd Annual Meeting of the Association for Education in Journalism (Houston, Texas, 1979) (ERIC Document Reproduction Service No. ED 179 957).

United States v. Zenith Radio Corporation. 12 F2nd 614 (1926).

U.S. Department of Health and Human Services. *Sexually Transmitted Disease Surveillance.* Atlanta, GA: Centers for Disease Control and Prevention, 1990.

Veeser, H. Aram, ed. *The New Historicism.* New York: Routledge, 1989.

———. *The New Historicism Reader.* New York: Routledge, 1994.

Wantuck, Michael Sissine. "Artistic Integrity, Public Policy, and Copyright: Colorization Reduced to Black and White." *Ohio State Law Journal* 50 (1989): 1013–33.

Ward, Brian. *Just My Soul Responding: Rhythm and Blues, Black Consciousness, and Race Relations.* Berkeley: U of California P, 1998.

Williams, Raymond. *Television: Technology and Cultural Form.* New York: Shocken, 1974.

———. *Marxism and Literature.* London: Oxford UP, 1977.

———. *Culture.* London: Fontana, 1981.

Notes on Contributors

Susan L. Brinson is a professor in the Department of Communication and Journalism at Auburn University. Her research interests focus on the history of the Federal Communications Commission and broadcast licensing. She is the author of *Personal and Public Interests: Frieda Hennock and the Federal Communications Commission* and *The Red Scare, Politics, and the Federal Communications Commission.*

Michael Brown is an associate professor with the Communication and Journalism Department at the University of Wyoming. His research focuses on media history, including radio and visual communication.

Samuel J. Brumbeloe lives in Auburn, Alabama, with his wife, Kelly. Sam is the webmaster and a radio producer for the Auburn Network, the multimedia right shoulder for Auburn University Athletics. Sam also is an instructor in the Department of Communication and Journalism at Auburn University.

Chad Dell is an associate professor in the Department of Communication at Monmouth University in West Long Branch, New Jersey. His work has been published in the *Journal of Broadcasting and Electronic Media*, the *New Jersey Journal of Communication,* and in the edited collection *Theorizing Fandom:*

Fans, Subculture, and Identity. His research interests include network programming strategies and historical broadcast audiences.

Douglas Ferguson graduated from The Ohio State University with both bachelor's and master's degrees in communication. He spent thirteen years as a programmer and manager of an NBC television affiliate in Ohio before getting his doctorate degree in mass communication at Bowling Green State University. After a dozen years teaching in Ohio, Dr. Ferguson went to South Carolina as the inaugural chair of the Department of Communication at the College of Charleston. He has cowritten three books on the television industry and numerous journal articles.

Michele Hilmes is professor of Media and Cultural Studies and director of the Wisconsin Center for Film and Theater Research at the University of Wisconsin–Madison. She is the author of several books on broadcasting history, including *Radio Voices: American Broadcasting, 1922–1952* and *Only Connect: A Cultural History of Broadcasting in the United States.* She is coeditor, with Jason Loviglio, of *The Radio Reader: Essays in the Cultural History of Broadcasting.*

Heather Hundley is an assistant professor at California State University, San Bernardino. Her research interests are focused on media, culture, sports, and feminism. She published a historical examination of the Lifetime Television Network, is currently completing a feminist critique of golf, and is coauthoring a paper on the subject of transliterature.

Matthew A. Killmeier is an assistant professor of Communication at Truman State University. His research interests include the cultural history of radio and popular music, media technology, and communication and social class.

Fritz Messere is chair of the Communication Studies Department at SUNY Oswego and professor of broadcasting and telecommunications. In addition to writing *Broadcasting, Cable, the Internet, and Beyond,* he is the coauthor of four books on the media. He has served as external assistant to FCC Commissioner Mimi Wayforth Dawson, as senior fellow of the Annenberg Washington Program in Communication Policy, and on the National Experts Panel on Telecommunications for the Rural Policy Research Institute.

His research interests include broadcast policy and regulation, new media, and broadcast history.

George Plasketes is a professor of Radio-Television-Film in the Department of Communication and Journalism at Auburn University. He has authored numerous scholarly articles, chapters, essays, and reviews. He also is the author of *Images of Elvis Presley in American Culture, 1977–1997: The Mystery Terrain* and coauthored *True Disbelievers: The Elvis Contagion.*

J. Emmett Winn is an associate professor of Communication and Journalism at Auburn University. His research focuses on film and television studies, with special interest in issues concerning race and class in the media. He serves on the editorial board of the *Journal of Communication* and has published scholarly articles in the *Journal of Broadcasting and Electronic Media, Critical Studies in Media Communication, Southern Communication Journal,* and *Kinema,* as well as other outlets.

Index